GAMES COLLEGES PLAY

Games Colleges Play

SCANDAL AND REFORM IN INTERCOLLEGIATE ATHLETICS

John R. Thelin

. . . .

THE JOHNS HOPKINS UNIVERSITY PRESS

Baltimore and London

IN MEMORY OF SOME "GOOD SPORTS"

Kenneth G. Beyer

William Clifford

Lawrence A. Cremin

Ralph J. Kennedy

Bill Reynolds

Eugene F. Riddle

Alfred Schenkman

© 1994 The Johns Hopkins University Press
Preface to the 1996 edition © 1996
All rights reserved
Printed in the United States of America on acid-free paper

Johns Hopkins Paperbacks edition, 1996
05 04 03 02 01 00 99 98 97 96   5 4 3 2 1

The Johns Hopkins University Press
2715 North Charles Street
Baltimore, Maryland 21218-4319
The Johns Hopkins Press Ltd., London

Library of Congress Cataloging-in-Publication Data
Thelin, John R., 1947–
    Games colleges play : scandal and reform in intercollegiate athletics / John R. Thelin.
        p.   cm.
    Includes bibliographical references and index.
    ISBN 0-8018-4716-8   ISBN 0-8018-5504-7 (pbk.)
    1. College sports—United States—Corrupt practices—History.   2. College sports—Unites States—Moral and ethical aspects.   3. College sports—United States—Organization and administration.   I. Title.
    GV351.T43   1994
796'.071'173—DC20   93-26950

A catalog record for this book is available from the British Library.

CONTENTS

• • • • • • • • • • • • • • • •

• • • • • • • • • • • • • • • • •

The hardcover edition of *Games Colleges Play* ended with cautious optimism about the 1991 Knight Foundation Commission's report calling for a new model whereby intercollegiate athletics would "keep faith with the student-athlete" ideal. The plan was for college and university presidents to give renewed attention to three interconnected dimensions: academic integrity, financial integrity, and program accountability through certification.

Following release of the 1991 report, the Knight Commission continued its work. The 1992 sequel to its original study proclaimed "A Solid Start" in the reform of intercollegiate athletics, and in 1993 the commission's final report heralded "A New Beginning for a New Century."[1] These last two reports are exciting and intriguing, but they are not wholly convincing. Those who are committed to substantive reform of intercollegiate athletics are now cast in the role of what may be termed "athletic agnostics": they *want* to believe in the feasibility of reform, yet they are not able to erase reasonable doubts about the prospects for success.

How to explain such troubled reservations? Reviewing the historical research that constituted the heart of *Games Colleges Play* includes tracking the life cycle of reform efforts in intercollegiate sports during the past century. What we find is that perennial confidence in blue-ribbon commission reports has often elicited a groundswell of immediate publicity and discussion. However, both the diversity and the inertia of American higher education, not to mention its mixed and complex purposes, tend to derail any attempts at implementing lasting policy changes. All too often significant reform effort has been illusory at worst and transient at best, inflated by a foundation's good intentions to seize the moment and to *appear* to be making consequential progress. Meanwhile, chronic abuses persist. Most troubling is that any attempt to instill strong academic standards and educational values into highly commercialized college sports teams runs the risk of antagonizing those who like the established programs. This was the case with the 1929 Carnegie Foundation Report—and is all too familiar in reform efforts of the 1990s. In sum, the historical legacy is that whereas changing the curriculum has been compared to "moving a graveyard," reforming college sports is like excavating a minefield.

Good intentions and wishful thinking rather than enduring accomplishments have characterized campaigns to restore integrity to college sports. For starters, there is a historical problem with the Knight Foundation Commission's aim to *restore* integrity, because it is not at all clear when intercollegiate athletics ever truly enjoyed such a condition. Second, the Knight Commission and those educational leaders who subscribe to its principles are hardly the only or even the dominant voice within the sprawling landscape of American higher education. Despite these reservations, the Knight Foundation Commission's argument and efforts are well made. Perhaps a fair resolution is to say that in 1996 it is simply too soon to tell whether the National Collegiate Athletic Association and its member institutions will implement the spirit and letter of the Knight Commission recommendations.

Since a primary focus in *Games Colleges Play* has been on the role of private foundations as participants in the nationwide concern over the condition and character of college sports, it is appropriate to introduce the paperback edition by alerting readers to an interesting development: The Andrew W. Mellon Foundation will be a new, conspicuous participant in the long-term analysis of college sports. In joining the ranks of such earlier players as the Carnegie Foundation for the Advancement of Teaching, the American Council on Education, and the Knight Foundation Commission, the Mellon Foundation will shift the emphasis away from discussion by a panel of university presidents and other distinguished influentials and toward fundamental and systematic research designed to test basic hypotheses about student-athletes.

The Mellon initiative owes much to the interest in college sports sustained by its president, William G. Bowen, an economist and former president of Princeton University. Following Bowen's lead, principal researcher James Shulman will try to avoid making facile generalizations about institutions and sports programs. Instead, the Mellon Foundation's focus will be on the role of intercollegiate athletics at academically selective institutions over the past half century. It will examine such topics as institutional investments, admissions, alumni, governance, and historical context.[2] One of the first fruits of this research agenda, a study of contemporary student-athletes at Princeton, Columbia, and Amherst by psychologists Nancy Cantor and Deborah Prentice, indicates that even student-athletes at strong academic institutions that do not offer athletic grants-in-aid find the demands of varsity sports to be inordinate when compared with other major student activities.[3] I should note that this fundamental research agenda is possible because the Knight Foundation established a base of policy discussion and gathered presidents and government officials, thereby setting the stage for more detailed analysis outside the spotlight of publicity associated with a blue-ribbon commission.

The Knight Foundation Commission's optimism about reform stemmed in large part from a Harris Poll showing that between 1989 and 1992 the proportion of Americans who believed that big-time intercollegiate sports were "out of control" had declined from 78 percent to 47 percent, which the commission took as evidence that there had been an impressive acceleration in the pace of reform. If the American public was ready for college sports reform, however, there was also deep-seated public resignation and acquiescence in the fact that the major teams in the televised revenue sports are far removed from any true educational activities. Indeed, at the big-time programs, there already are rumblings from varsity players who ask why they are not entitled to some share of the earnings, especially when their coaches can endorse shoes and athletic directors can balance budgets with bowl game receipts and television revenues. This quest for acknowledging the professionalism of Division I—an embarrassing issue raised by the players who no longer see themselves as student-athletes—will be the grit of sand in the eye of the NCAA credo. If reform does veer toward revenue sharing and overt professionalism, many of the disgruntled, underpaid college players may gain a Pyrrhic victory. Apart from the exceptional superstars who could command a high "salary," most college players will find that they have overestimated their market worth, which previously had entitled them to a grant-in-aid valued at about $25,000 per year.

Since 1992 there have been a number of troubling developments and episodes that have real as well as symbolic importance for the history of intercollegiate sports. Signs of financial stress include the discontinuation by UCLA of its varsity men's swimming program. At the collective level, the break-up of the historic Southwestern Conference was testimony to each institution's scramble for more lucrative associations in new conference alignments. The College Football Coaches Association has lobbied for a special tax exemption for member coaches—yet another sign of the increasing commercialism of big-time sports. In the same vein at the state level, the legislature in Alabama opted to exempt college coaches at public universities from the requirement that state employees disclose their outside earnings from endorsements.

A revealing illustration of the mixed signals in reform efforts came in 1993, when the United States Department of Education published its report to Congress, *Revenues and Expenditures in Intercollegiate Athletics: The Feasibility of Collecting National Data by Sport.*[4] The Department of Education's research staff conducted a thoughtful, exhaustive study of existing policies and practices which documented the confused finances and deficits of college sports programs and concluded that "the implications are troublesome. That is, if the educational budgets of colleges and universities are covering intercollegiate athletic program deficits, then the academic program suffers—and the academic program is the principal function of colleges and universities."

Unfortunately, the research findings were blocked from any possibility of being implemented as policy. Secretary of Education Lamar Alexander, in his 1991 Letter of Transmittal to Congress, seemed to defuse the report, writing, "I believe it is *not advisable* for Congress to require institutions to report information on revenues and expenditures for intercollegiate athletics and athletic departments." Alexander, the former president of the University of Tennessee and a member of the Knight Foundation's Commission on Intercollegiate Athletics, acknowledged that financial integrity in intercollegiate athletics was a serious concern at many institutions, but concluded that the federal data collection effort did not "serve an obvious purpose" and would be "inappropriate." The logic he used in explaining why it was inadvisable for the federal government to become involved in systematic data collection was peculiar and unconvincing: such an investment in federal dollars "did not serve an obvious purpose," he stated, mainly because college sports have little involvement with federal student aid dollars. Furthermore, collecting data on revenues and expenditures for intercollegiate athletics which were accurate and comparable would be difficult to achieve, probably requiring the addition of new data elements to the existing Integrated Postsecondary Education Data System (IPEDS). This begs the question: If such analysis and compilation is inappropriate, why has Congress over time held extensive hearings on abuses in college sports programs? Quite apart from the administration of federal student-aid programs, what happened to congressional concern about the "right to know" for students and their families?

Alexander's logic was most curious in that the reason he gave for *not* undertaking the project shows precisely why federal involvement is needed. Of course such collection is difficult—but the Secretary of Education's statements evade the issues and leave data collection to voluntary efforts, even though the NCAA and its member institutions have yet to show much initiative in publishing in-depth data on their own. If voluntary compliance with NCAA financial surveys has led to only about a 60 percent participation rate by member institutions, is there not some rationale for mandatory reporting? If it were made easy to collect data, would the task *then* be attractive for the U.S. Department of Education?

Finally, the Secretary of Education cited the Knight Commission's own report, noting that it did *not* call for the federal government to become involved. Did Congress want the data? Ironically, the one member of the Knight Commission who strongly dissented from the majority opinion was Congressman Thomas McMillen of Maryland. McMillen wrote, "I cannot agree that the federal government does not have a positive role to play in the reform process. The 1984 Supreme Court ruling that allowed universities to negotiate for broadcast rights exacerbated the chase for money in college sports. Until that ruling is overturned by Congress, and college presidents have the tools they need to redistribute the wealth more evenly, the pattern of abuse will continue. As the 1992 Harris survey demonstrates, a sizable percentage of Americans believe that federal legislation is necessary to control college sports."[5]

Given the Secretary of Education's strict constructionist argument, Congress will not have the requisite college data. Reform will be left to the private foundations and the voluntary initiatives of college and universities themselves. If the historical record is any guide, the residual implication is that coherent, large-scale, substantive reform will be difficult to achieve by such means simply because so many presidents and colleges embrace the existing arrangements.

In contrast to the Secretary of Education's reluctance, a heartening sign of active concern about excesses in college sports is that at many universities, a number of senior administrative officers are joining presidents in examining the workings of intercollegiate athletic departments. For example, vice presidents for business and finance are taking the initiative to study and intervene in the finances of intercollegiate athletics through such organizations as the National Association of College and University Business Officers (NACUBO), which in 1993 published a critical analysis of the organization, governance, and financing of college sports.[6]

There is some evidence that the Knight Commission's recommendation on institutional self-study and program review can be consequential when combined with regional accreditation. At some institutions, the Southern Association of Colleges and Schools and the National Collegiate Athletic Association's joint program certification initiative has already assisted university presidents and faculty in identifying and reprimanding university board members who have intruded into the administration of intercollegiate athletic programs. This is the model of cooperation, driven by educational mission, that will be imperative to meaningful sports reform.

This review of disparate recent developments leads to the observation that dramatic changes are taking place in intercollegiate athletics—but only part of this can be attributed to the reform commission reports or to anything resembling coherent educational policy drafted by academic leaders. A more accurate portrayal is that two potent external forces—economics and law—have converged in the mid-1990s to prompt rethinking of college sports by analyzing the budget.

For example, almost a quarter century after its passage, court rulings on Title IX show signs of forcing colleges to take seriously the mandate for gender equity in athletic programs. The most significant case has involved Brown University, which was sued by a group of women student-athletes, leading courts and colleges to wrestle with the standard of "proportionality" (i.e., the percentage of varsity sports resources allocated to women's programs at a given school should equal the percentage of women undergraduates). Yet Title IX and recent court cases have not provided clear guidelines for institutions, and regulation and enforcement remain uneven. Further, a number of athletic departments have inaccurately and unfairly blamed cutbacks in men's sports programs on the pressure to upgrade women's sports. In fact, studies by the U.S. Department of Education indicate that uncontrolled expenditures in men's revenue sports, not increases in women's sports, are the main reason for financial strain. The net result of these diverse developments is hesitation, marked by watchful waiting for the outcome of some intense high-stakes court cases. But for most institutions, it is a time of suspension or evasion in the matter of pursuing gender equity in college sports.

Even though the prospect of "proportionality" will prod athletic directors and university boards to review program budgets, an alarming finding is that few intercollegiate athletic programs have demonstrated the sustained ability to reduce expenses—except by the dubious practice of eliminating selected sports. Seeking additional revenues by enhancing programs or by petitioning for institutional subsidies continues as the accepted practice in the annual budget confrontation. The significant historical finding is that each year, even among Division I programs, the number and proportion of athletic departments running a deficit increase yearly. Even in the powerful College Football Association, about half the athletic programs show an annual deficit.

Nevertheless, there have been some remarkable shifts in the balance of finances, academics, and athletics. Northwestern and Wisconsin are prominent examples of athletic programs that have faced problems in generating both revenues and victories. Each has enjoyed football success in the Big Ten Conference, and each in the last three years has gone to the Rose Bowl, erasing an operating deficit. But these institutions' lesson and legacy are problematic: they may raise premature, even false hopes that programs can be self-supporting and that an institution can maintain high academic standards while fielding nationally recognized championship teams.

A more sobering and prevalent trend is characterized by developments at Vanderbilt and Tulane: in both cases, the institution has made a substantial financial commitment, which indicates that it is no longer likely that intercollegiate athletics can truly be "self-supporting."[7] There may be an unexpected windfall if intercollegiate athletics at Division I schools increasingly depend on the largess of institutional subsidies: namely, such regular financial support out of the university's general fund may allow academic administrators to reduce the autonomy and arrogance of athletic associations and booster clubs. If these quasi-independent groups can no longer deliver the resources, which was their raison d'être, it means that a president and vice president can force the varsity sports program to sit at the campuswide budget table without bypassing it. But such a structural change will require presidential and board initiative.

The attraction of upgrading sports programs to Division I continues to tempt ambitious university presidents and boards. It can take place at a young urban institution such as Indiana University–Purdue University at Indianapolis, where the prospect of a Division I basketball program looms large. Or, at Rutgers University, whose president, grown weary of losing football teams, dedicated expanded resources to recruiting top coaches and players in the hopes of having a winning Division IA program, even though that has never been a strong part of the campus heritage. Given such pulls and pressures, the question will not be "How much money can sports bring in?" Rather, it will be "How much can and should an institution dedicate to promoting winning teams?"

One source of historical continuity in American culture has been the procession of articles about abuses in college football and basketball, as cases involving recruiting violations and player misbehavior continue to proliferate. The tone of authors (and their readers' responses) suggests a gallows humor, as even such an unlikely periodical as New York's *Village Voice* features a seasonal report called "Illegal Procedures," which systematically documents the payoffs, rap sheets, and coaching scams of "College Football's Real-Life Top 20."[8] The prevalence and appeal of such staple articles indicate that the American public is no longer shocked by college sports scandals and good-naturedly expects the abuses to occur. College alumni and sports fans seemed to have acquired an immunity to exposés, not unlike the ninth generation of mosquitoes no longer hurt by DDT. Ironically, women's varsity teams from time to time show progress in acquiring some of the benefits traditionally reserved for men's basketball and football. An example is the sell-out crowds for the women's basketball NCAA Final Four, along with national television coverage, and even a marketing promotion in which Sears now lists itself as an "Official NCAA Corporate Sponsor" and sells "Legends of the Final Four" trading cards, featuring both men and women college basketball players and coaches. The pursuit of parity can readily lead to increased commercialization of college sports, with little if any attention paid to educational propriety.

Notes

1. Commission on Intercollegiate Athletics, *A Solid Start: A Report on Reform of Intercollegiate Athletics* (Charlotte, N.C.: Knight Foundation, Mar. 1992); *A New Beginning for a New Century: Intercollegiate Athletics in the United States* (Charlotte, N.C.: Knight Foundation, Mar. 1993).

2. James Shulman and William Bowen, "'Native Hue': Intercollegiate Athletics at Elite Colleges and Universities, 1955–1995" (prospectus draft; New York: Mellon Foundation, Apr. 1996).

3. Nancy E. Cantor and Deborah A. Prentice, "The Life of the Modern-Day Student-Athlete: Opportunities Won and Lost," paper presented at the Princeton Conference on Higher Education (Mar. 21, 1996).

4. *Revenues and Expenditures in Intercollegiate Athletics: The Feasibility of Collecting National Data by Sport,* A Report Submitted to Congress by Lamar Alexander, Secretary of Education (Washington, D.C.: U.S. Department of Education, Office of Educational Research and Development, 1993).

5. Rep. Thomas McMillen, quoted in Commission on Intercollegiate Athletics, *Keeping Faith with the Student-Athlete: A New Model for Intercollegiate Athletics* (Charlotte, N.C.: Knight Foundation, Mar. 1991), p. .

6. National Association of College and University Business Officers, *The Financial Management of Intercollegiate Athletics Programs* (Washington, D.C.: NACUBO, 1993).

7. Debra E. Blum, "Trying to Reconcile Academics and Athletics: Vanderbilt's Struggling Sports Program Seeks a New Sense of Direction," *Chronicle of Higher Education* (Apr. 26, 1996), pp. A51–A52.

8. Mike Rubin, "Illegal Procedures: The Rap Sheets, Payoffs, and Coaching Scams of College Football's Real-Life Top 20," *Village Voice,* Jan. 16, 1996, pp. 27–29.

In 1980, the themes of "shame" and "scandal" in college sports conspicuously connected *Newsweek, Time,* and *U.S. News and World Report* with *Sports Illustrated.* Magazine editors took turns uncovering good copy about abuses of intercollegiate athletic programs that involved recruiting student-athletes, tampering with academic transcripts, failing to comply with Title IX regulations, and manipulating illegal "slush funds."[1] Nationwide in the daily press, the excesses and commercialization of intercollegiate athletics moved from the sports page to the front page. Such newspapers as the *New York Times,* the *Washington Post,* and the *Los Angeles Times* devoted extended coverage and analysis to the policies and control of college sports.[2] At the same time, journal articles, task forces, and commission reports within the higher education community signaled concern about the "sports problem."[3] At another level, serious and highly regarded writers and scholars, including James Michener, Michael Novak, and Allen Guttmann, wrote books that brought their respective disciplines to bear on the place of sports in American education and society.[4]

This abundant attention from varied sources given to college sports over a two-year period formed a discernible pattern of exposé, alarm, investigation, and analysis, and concluded with proposals for reform. By 1983, it appeared that the topic had been exhausted and that readers' attention had waned. The surprising wrinkle was that the melodrama of revelation and reform started to repeat itself, ratcheted up a notch to a new level of indictments over corrupt practices and a new threshold of outrage followed by emphatic strategies for correction.

Throughout the remainder of the decade, the flow of articles on scandal and reform continued—and the ritualized pattern escalated to higher and higher levels of concern by Congress, state legislatures, governors, private foundations, and the United States Department of Education, and by such educational groups as the American Association of University Professors, the American Council on Education, the College Entrance Examination Board, and the American Association of Higher Education. One landmark in editorial concern was that in 1985 the weekly "industry" paper of college and university administrators and faculty, the *Chronicle of Higher Education*, added a section on athletics as a permanent major area of feature coverage in each issue. In a similar vein, such higher education journals as the American Association of University Professors' *Academe* and the American Council on Education's *Educational Record* devoted issues to the reform of college sports. Articles about abuses of athletics persisted as a weekly, if not daily, theme in newspapers. Within this bulk of press coverage were outstanding examples of institutional research, including one series whose authors were awarded a Pulitzer Prize for their investigative reporting on the administration of a university intercollegiate athletic department.[5] In sum, for the decade 1980 to 1990, the scandals and shame of big-time college sports endured as a conspicuous problem that would not go away.

The growing public concern about abuses in college sports coincided with the unprecedented popularity and appeal of college sports, as measured by attendance, advertising sponsorship, newspaper coverage, and television broadcasts of big-time intercollegiate football and basketball games. During this period of sustained scrutiny and reform, one conspicuous void was that athletic directors and coaches at major universities had relatively little to say about the character and conditions of the varsity programs under their charge. There was little indication that they initiated critical analysis within their own ranks or explained their practices, policies, or problems to interested audiences and campus constituencies. This syndrome often carried over into a selective memory, an institutional amnesia. For example, in 1991 when the athletic director at a large state university was asked about major abuses in its football program, which the National Collegiate Athletic Association had investigated two years earlier, the athletic director replied that "what happened in 1989 is old history. There is nothing more to talk about."[6]

But there is more to talk about, and it ought to be based on research that fuses the topic of college sports with important educational themes. Given the silence among intercollegiate athletic officials, my research initially focused on essential questions about the present-day economics, finances, and governance of intercollegiate athletic departments and their integration within academic planning and decision making at both campus and state levels.[7] Having acquired some reasonably sound information and analyses, I was left with this question: How did this contemporary issue of college sports scandals and subsequent reform efforts fare as a *historical* problem? I wondered whether college sports had descended to an unprecedented low point between 1980 and 1990, with little continuity and few examples from earlier decades and, if so, what policies and practices had characterized healthy, appropriate sports programs in earlier eras. Bringing attention to this historical dimension of intercollegiate athletics and academic policies carries out a mandate suggested by psychologist Alexander W. Astin: namely, that significant research on higher education issues and policies is best seen as "moving target research," subject to change.[8]

Thanks to a generous research grant from the Spencer Foundation, I was able to spend 1990 through 1992 studying historic relations between intercollegiate athletics and academic policies at numerous major American universities. My hypothesis was that the scandals and reforms of big-time college sports had acquired over time a distinctive pattern and heritage in American culture and higher education. However, this was a genuine hypothesis, not a conclusion, since the particulars of these patterns and their place in the history of higher education had not been adequately studied. In sum, a documented, overarching interpretation was not yet in sight and would not be until I was able to test my general hypothesis on the basis of original research that drew from primary sources in university archives and in the files of foundations, associations, and athletic conferences that reconstructed not only what the athletic director called the "old history" of 1989 but also the older history of college sports since 1929.

The sensational scandals reported in the press of the 1980s did not mean that college sports reform was an inherently scholarly or substantive topic. To the contrary, the danger was that exposés of these excesses might have generated a myopia of the present that attracted newspaper readers by exaggerating immediate events. Also, the peril of publicity was that preoccupation with contemporary scandals misread the character and operation of college sports by diverting analysis from some less conspicuous, though enduring, institutional issues. If the scandals and controversies of athletics were confined to athletic departments and sports pages, the import of college sports might be transient or superficial. Therefore, my emphasis has been on implications for academic policy and the whole of a university in American culture for more than a half century.

The history of college sports acquires increased significance when it is incorporated into American social history and the serious study of higher education. To do so calls for reliance on such works as Edwin Slosson's 1910 book, *Great American Universities;* Clark Kerr's 1963 Godkin Lectures, published as *The Uses of the University;* Burton R. Clark's notion of institutional saga presented in *The Distinctive College;* and Laurence Veysey's 1965 study of the rival conceptions of the higher learning, 1870 to 1910, *The Emergence of the American University.* These provided a historical context for the structural developments that characterized American universities over the past century. Their central theme is that by 1910 higher education writers and editors had identified the "Standard American University": a skeletal structure characterized by a capacity to accommodate numerous seemingly incongruous activities while avoiding destructive infighting within a campus. In terms of institutional history and organizational behavior, it was what Laurence Veysey called "the tendency to blend and reconcile." An administrative strategy and resolution that has characterized the American university during the twentieth century is that disparate activities are not necessarily expected to be integrated. Hence, the university structure accommodates the seemingly separate, even contradictory, activities of athletics and academics—with the ground rule being that each activity has a place so long as it manages to be self-supporting, big, or even excellent. This is a structural arrangement that allows substantial institutional choice in setting and changing priorities.

The connections drawn here between twentieth-century American culture and the American campus are shaped in large measure by Christopher Jencks and David Riesman's 1968 work, *The Academic Revolution,* and by David O. Levine's 1986 book, *The American College and the Culture of Aspiration,* an interpretation of higher education and American society from 1915 to 1940.[9] Grounding this study in such perspectives may provide a serious context, but does it result in interesting history? As historian Frederick Rudolph noted in his 1977 study of American undergraduate education: "There is no way to make a history of the American college and university curriculum read like an account of the winning of the West or the collapse of the Old South. Martin Duberman's study of the history of sexuality in America, three years in the offing, has something going for it that curricular history does not."[10]

Rudolph may be correct. However, his own earlier research on the rise of football in his 1962 classic, *The American College and University: A History*, suggests by example that it is in the extracurricular area of college sports that American higher education may find its dramatic saga that is crucial for connecting the American campus to American culture. Certainly this concept fits well with Daniel J. Boorstin's notion of the late nineteenth-century "booster college" as a part of community building in America and with historian Warren I. Sussman's analysis of culture heroes in the transformation of American society in the twentieth century.[11] And, along with the drama and excitement of college sports programs, there are underlying serious educational questions.

There is no shortage of secondary sources and books about the history of college sports. But these sources share in their scope and tone an imbalance toward celebration of great players, coaches, and teams. They convey a nostalgia characterized by a rich collection of memoirs that go into great detail about innovations in playing techniques and coaching strategies. Seldom do the college sports histories go beyond the playing field into either the office of the athletic director or the executive committees of such governing groups as conference commissioners or the National Collegiate Athletic Association.[12] In contrast, my study extends analysis beyond athletic departments to such campus groups as faculty senates, curricular committees, boards of trustees, and the offices of university presidents and provosts, and to such external settings as major foundations, courtrooms, and congressional subcommittees.

My study follows a groundswell of recent scholarship on intercollegiate sports as part of American higher education and society. From the disciplines of the social and behavioral sciences, this has included geographer John F. Rooney, Jr.'s, *The Recruiting Game*, a demographic analysis of regional trends in the development and distribution of college athletic talent; sociologist James Frey's 1982 anthology on the governance of intercollegiate athletics; Nand Hart-Nibbrig and Clement Cottingham's 1986 work dealing with the political economy of college sports; Donald Chu's social and philosophical treatment of the character of American higher education and intercollegiate sport; and Paul R. Lawrence's *Unsportsmanlike Conduct,* a study of the National Collegiate Athletic Association and the business of college football.[13] Historical studies that have been especially important are Ronald A. Smith's 1988 book, *Sports and Freedom,* an account of the rise of big-time college athletics; Patrick Bryant Miller's 1987 doctoral dissertation, "Athletes in Academe"; and John S. Watterson's 1988 article for *American Heritage,* "Inventing Modern Football."[14] Whereas these historical studies have dealt primarily with the place of college sports on the American campus during the late nineteenth and early twentieth centuries, *Games Colleges Play* picks up analysis after 1900, with particular attention to proposed reforms around 1929–30, and then extends the historical narrative close to our times. My original intent was to end discussion around 1980. But the events and reforms during the past decade suggested that to overlook the years 1981 to 1993 was a scholarly sin of omission. In other words, if this historical writing were to be pertinent to policy discussions, the imperative was to attempt to connect present and past.

ACKNOWLEDGMENTS

· · · · · · · · · · · · · · ·

The proposition that intercollegiate athletics is a significant part of the history of American society and higher education has intrigued me for over twenty years. To develop this research theme has called for patience and persuasion because several years ago I found that few scholars and editors shared my view. That is no longer so. Contrary to conventional depictions, I did not find scholarship to be a lonely activity, because this book has included a collective effort in which intellectual and financial support from many sources has generated scholarly excitement. I am pleased to acknowledge numerous groups and individuals who helped me as I wrote *Games Colleges Play*.

The Spencer Foundation has taken my work seriously and has been generous in awarding me a major grant during the years 1989 through 1992. This enabled me to conduct archival research to track down connections between academics and athletics policies. Marion M. Faldet, vice-president and secretary of the Spencer Foundation, worked with me during all stages of the grant, from application to publication. Program Associate Sunita Parikh took time to ask good questions that strengthened my grant proposal. President Patricia Albjerg Graham, through her own scholarship and leadership at the Spencer Foundation, showed that the history of education can be central to policy analysis and debates. My one regret is that I did not finish the book earlier, because I am indebted to the late Lawrence E. Cremin, who as president of the Spencer Foundation until his death on September 4, 1990, encouraged me to pursue this topic.

Frederick Rudolph, professor of history at Williams College, assisted me on this project in two ways. His obvious influence was his chapter "The Rise of Football" in his 1962 work, *The American College and University: A History*. Less obvious but crucial was his correspondence with me while I was writing *Games Colleges Play*. He candidly recalled the resistance he faced more than three decades ago when he advanced the unorthodox view that intercollegiate football was central to the history of American higher education. Without his pioneering work and recent encouragement, my own research would have floundered.

George Hanford, president emeritus of the College Entrance Examination Board and himself a participant observer in landmark struggles over intercollegiate athletics, sent me documents and commentary related to his 1974 studies on intercollegiate athletics for the American Council on Education. The late Alfred Schenkman of Cambridge, Massachusetts, combined confidence in my work with insistence that I deal with essential questions generated by athletics as a part of educational philosophy. Robert M. Rosenzweig, then president of the Association of American Universities, helped me gain access to university archives and official records.

Archives, indeed, have been the essential workshop for fresh scholarship by preserving primary sources, many of which had been overlooked by or closed to an earlier generation of researchers. My debt to archivists is immense because I relied heavily on documents from universities in California for information on institutional histories as well as the case study of the Pacific Coast Conference. Philip Bantin, university archivist at the University of California, Los Angeles, was most helpful in making university records and chancellors' files available. Acquiring access to archival materials was only the first step toward scholarly publication. Carli V. Rogers, copyright officer, Office of Intellectual Property Administration at UCLA, kindly arranged for me to gain permission for quotation and publication of archival materials. Also, I wish to thank the University of California Regents for giving me permission to quote from university records.

At the University of Southern California, University Archivist Paul Christopher and Archives Assistant Susan Hikida were knowledgeable guides through the excellent records and files about the University of Southern California, especially its role in the governance of the Pacific Coast Conference. Their expertise included taking initiative to steer me toward episodes and materials that I did not know about.

The University of Oregon was a fertile source for research on the case of the Pacific Coast Conference controversies. J. Fraser Cocks III, curator of Special Collections, and Keith Richards, university archivist, enabled me to consult the complete files of the now defunct Pacific Coast Conference. During my research trip to Eugene, Oregon, they also took time to introduce me to Orlando Hollis, dean and professor emeritus of law at the University of Oregon. Since Dean Hollis had been a long-time leader of faculty athletic representatives in the Pacific Coast Conference, his interview sessions with me constituted invaluable oral history and institutional memory. In Corvallis, Colene Voll and Mervin Mecklenburg of the Oregon State University archives arranged for me to obtain microfilm copies of Pacific Coast Conference records.

During the summers 1989 through 1992 I reviewed materials associated with the history of the University of Kentucky. Thanks to Frank Stanger, Jr., assistant archivist, I was able to study carefully this institution that was so important in the history of intercollegiate athletics.

Many historical themes I studied transcended the records of an individual campus. Jill Bogard, librarian at the American Council on Education offices in Washington, D.C., assisted me in reviewing various drafts and documents associated with preparation of the 1952 Presidents' Report of the American Council on Education. The Knight Foundation Commission on the Future of Intercollegiate Athletics paid attention to the studies Lawrence Wiseman and I had done on the economics of intercollegiate athletics. I wish to thank Knight Foundation president Creed Black and Commission staff director Christopher Morris for having invited Professor Wiseman and myself to make a presentation at the Foundation's hearings in Washington, D.C., in June 1990. The Commission's report gave my own historical research important contemporary perspective on perennial issues that academic leaders face nationally with athletics policies.

Thomas G. Dyer has been a mentor and colleague throughout this project. His own 1985 book, the bicentennial history of the University of Georgia, stands as a model of how institutional histories of colleges and universities ought to be written. His attention to developments in intercollegiate athletics at the University of Georgia showed how these themes can be significant parts of state and regional history.

Hugh Hawkins, professor of history and American studies at Amherst College, gave me good advice and insights at the early stages of my study. George Keller of the University of Pennsylvania and editor of the journal *Planning in Higher Education* has given me critical commentary along with an excellent forum to develop my arguments that connect the historical context of college sports to present and future conditions. Professor Ellen Condliffe Lagemann of Columbia University Teachers College took time at a History of Education Society Conference held in New York City to brief me on the role of the Carnegie Foundation for the Advancement of Teaching as a major force in formulating American educational policies in the twentieth century. William Reese, editor of *History of Education Quarterly* and professor at Indiana University, has critiqued and endorsed my research interests throughout this project. Morgan Odell of the Association of Independent California Colleges and Universities gave me rich accounts of higher education and college sports in California. Jack Schuster, professor of education and public policy at Claremont Graduate School, carefully read and commented on the entire manuscript. Rick Platt literally provided running commentary on the complexities of amateur athletics and college sports as we both combined lifelong running and writing in our friendship and careers. I wish to thank Bruce Mallette, associate director of Institutional Research at North Carolina State University, the editors of the New Directions in Institutional Research series, and Jossey-Bass Publishers for kind permission to draw from materials I wrote for a chapter in their New Directions in Institutional Research monograph series.

The College of William and Mary has been an interesting place for me to teach, write, and talk about intercollegiate athletics as part of higher education. President Timothy J. Sullivan, who served as chair of the governor of Virginia's Task Force on Intercollegiate Athletics, has followed and been supportive of my extended research on college sports as part of higher education policy. William and Mary has contributed to my research perspective by giving me opportunity to supplement my primary affiliation with the Higher Education Doctoral Program with appointment as a member of the program faculties of American Studies and Public Policy Studies. I wish to thank the School of Education, especially my colleagues and students in the Higher Education Program, for their interest in my project. John Callahan, a graduate student in the higher education program and himself a former college student-athlete, allowed me to cite his work on Governor Huey Long and Louisiana State University. Lawrence L. Wiseman, professor and chair of biology at William and Mary, has been my friend and coauthor on a book and numerous articles dealing with the economics and policies of intercollegiate athletics. His insights gained as a researcher and as chair of William and Mary's athletic policy advisory committee define for me what the proper balance of academics and athletics for American higher education ought to be.

Kay Domine, university archivist, assisted me in locating key documents dealing with the William and Mary sports story; she also helped put me in touch with archivists at other institutions. My project gained from the expertise of William and Mary's Office of Grants and Research. Professor David Kranbuehl, in his role as associate provost for research, was supportive of my project. Cheryl Pope, director of Grants Fiscal Administration, and Anne Womack, director of Sponsored Program Grants and Research Administration, advised me in drafting the original project budget and helped me throughout the three-year grant period. Ray Betzner, director of Public Information, and Dean Olson, university editor, gave superb coverage and counsel as I was doing research. James Heller, librarian at William and Mary's Marshall Wythe School of Law, helped me track down court records on cases involving intercollegiate athletics.

Reliance on official records and commission reports hardly tells the whole story of college sports as part of American life. Professor Barbara K. Townsend of Memphis State University, my coauthor on a 1988 study of college fiction as historical sources, contributed perceptive analysis of images of student-athletes in novels from the period 1920 to 1950.

Research for this book has allowed me to be in touch with a sister institution, the University of Virginia. Jeanne Pardee, university archives assistant, thoughtfully found for me a copy of an important document on the faculty role in college sports, the University of Virginia's 1951 "Gooch Report." Jay Lemons, special assistant to the president, stimulated analysis through conversations and his own writings. And President John T. Casteen III continued his interest as scholar and administrator by talking with me about college sports issues. His perspective erases any notion that intercollegiate athletics are peripheral to the life of a university president.

Sharon Thelin-Blackburn was a patient listener, reader, and editor throughout the project. The readings on the culture and institutions of the South that she brought to my attention, combined with her commentary, pleasantly prompted me to rethink my simplistic assumptions about regional history. Her editorial skill, including special attention to my transitions, once again helped to salvage my prose.

This study benefited from the research assistance several people have contributed. Allen Brooks Chamberlain worked on materials dealing with the Carnegie Foundation for the Advancement of Teaching reports, circa 1929 to 1931. Valise Shields provided clerical support. Graduate assistants Todd Cockrell, Robbie Cordle, and Louis Eaffalla helped me with citations and bibliographies. Robert Seal was most helpful in editing and reviewing the final drafts of the manuscript. At the Johns Hopkins University Press, Carol Ehrlich provided skilled copy editing.

No historical analysis of intercollegiate athletics would be complete without attending to the distinctive legacy of the Big Ten conference—a perspective I am now able to acquire at Indiana University. I am grateful to Dean Donald Warren, Chancellor Kenneth Gros Louis, President Thomas Ehrlich, and my faculty colleagues for giving me that opportunity. I am also grateful to the Indiana University Office of Research and the University Graduate School, whose support was helpful in the editing of the project.

Faculty customarily invoke the slogan Publish or Perish to bemoan the problems associated with writing. My experience differs, for it is the pleasure of publication that has characterized this book. I owe great thanks to Editor Jacqueline Wehmueller of the Johns Hopkins University Press for having encouraged me to develop the topic of the history of intercollegiate athletics.

GAMES COLLEGES PLAY

. . . .

American Higher Education's "Peculiar Institution"

Intercollegiate athletics are American higher education's "peculiar institution." Their presence is pervasive, yet their proper balance with academics remains puzzling. A visit to a typical large American university indicates the remarkable prominence of varsity sports: a football stadium seating sixty thousand, a basketball arena for fifteen thousand, an indoor football practice complex, and perhaps a dormitory complex or training center reserved for varsity athletes are all facilities virtually unknown at universities in other countries yet taken for granted in the United States. A glance at a university budget shows that annual operation of a large varsity sports program costs about the same as running a professional school in engineering, law, or even medicine.[1] It is standard practice for a head football or basketball coach to be paid at least as much as an academic dean. Today at some American universities, the varsity football coach draws a base salary that exceeds that of the president—an arrangement that, although unusual, is not deemed inappropriate by some boards of trustees.

For all this prominence, the place of intercollegiate athletics in the priorities of the university remains unclear. In contrast to the publicity generated by winning teams, a detailed budget for an intercollegiate athletics program remains one of the most inaccessible documents. Even though sports information directors readily provide press guides with detailed statistics on basketball players' field goal percentages or teams' victories from past and present, athletic directors claim they do not have sufficient staff to compile the annual graduation rates of student-athletes.[2] A check of institutional accreditation self-studies, mission statements, and annual reports suggests that an American university seldom discusses intercollegiate athletics as part of its primary purposes of teaching, research, and service. The irony of this silence is that, for many universities, big-time athletics stand out as a central activity, a program likely to be protected and promoted.

This blurred identity also characterizes the place of college sports in institutional governance. Athletic directors often report directly to university presidents, which indicates an access to leadership and decision making that far exceeds the privileges of an academic dean. At some universities, a head coach (usually of football or men's basketball) may also serve as athletic director, creating a strange reporting arrangement conducive to self-dealing and relatively unchecked concentration of administrative power within a department. Foundations, associations, and fund-raising groups incorporated for the special purpose of supporting a university's sports program often become fiefdoms that gain leverage from their affiliation with the campus and use of the name and logo of the university, but with only limited accountability to the host institution. These special sports foundations and associations typically have their own board of directors, staff, and payroll and often marginal requirements for reporting to the university's administration or board. Meanwhile, in formal reports about institutional mission and structure, universities usually bury intercollegiate athletics among extracurricular activities or auxiliary enterprises, masking their actual importance.

How do we explain such peculiar arrangements? What is the place of intercollegiate athletics in terms of the governance and organization of the American university? How do colleges and universities characterize intercollegiate athletics in relation to educational purposes? How does the funding of intercollegiate athletics compare with financial arrangements for other institutional departments and activities? And, to each of these queries, we need to add an important historical dimension: How, over time, have intercollegiate athletics come to occupy their distinctive, peculiar place within the American campus?

University officials historically have shown a tendency to avoid reconciling their commitment to and investment in intercollegiate athletics with the educational mission of the institution. There is a slippery quality that characterizes the justifications that university presidents and athletic directors invoke when they are asked to explain the connection between college sports and higher education. At one time, college sports are described as an educational activity, often praised for their power to "build character"; at another time, intercollegiate athletics are conveniently endorsed for having contributed to institutional publicity and prestige, or they are depicted as helpful to university fund raising, with benefits supposedly accruing to the entire institution. On closer inspection, these separate, shifting claims constitute a liturgy, not substantiated conclusions. The rationales are not wholly convincing because they are untested claims and, if taken together, are often inconsistent, even conflicting.

A corollary is that although avoiding scrutiny of college sports as part of higher education may allow campus presidents, deans, and trustees to avoid hard questions over the short run, it is a reprieve that ultimately weakens the institution. It has potential to dilute the administrative credibility of a university president and diverts resources and attention from educational priorities. I have no wish to dictate a single formula for the proper balance of academics and athletics. American higher education is sufficiently diverse to allow for variation and institutional self-determination. Nor is raising these questions to be mistaken for an abolitionist tract. To think of the American campus *without* intercollegiate athletics would be difficult, even undesirable. Rather, my concern is that within American higher education, most institutions have been reluctant to study and accurately state what their own policies, practices, and priorities involving intercollegiate athletics are—while at the same time they have resisted public review, external scrutiny, or oversight.[3]

Why bother? One could invoke Mark Twain's dictum that it is "all right to break laws so long as you obey customs." In other words, the tradition of accommodating intercollegiate sports as an exception to standard policies and procedures within academe is all right because it "works" and the university allegedly has benefited from this custom. This raises two linked questions: What specifically *does* a university gain from intercollegiate athletics? What price does it pay for the exceptional practices that surround intercollegiate athletics? These are best seen as largely historical questions to be answered by looking at how intercollegiate sports have operated and interacted with the campus as a whole.

Though university presidents and board members may evade essential questions about varsity sports, other groups do not.[4] In 1991, for example, a subcommittee in the House of Representatives recommended that colleges and universities be required to disclose student-athletes' graduation rates as well as detailed, systematic information on how college athletics programs are financed.[5] The proposed legislation has been resisted both by higher education lobbying groups and by the National Collegiate Athletic Association (NCAA). At the same time, the Internal Revenue Service has questioned the practice of granting tax exemptions for ticket receipts and broadcasts of postseason college football bowl games, and has extended this concern to bowl games and regular season games that rely on corporate endorsements. And the Federal Trade Commission is trying to show that the College Football Association's television contract violates antitrust laws.[6] This signals a new wrinkle in higher education public policy because historically the federal government has avoided intrusion into college affairs. Whether or not such legislation and regulation come to pass, the activity itself signifies that some groups outside colleges are questioning the customary rationale for accommodating big-time college sports as an *educational* activity. Given this external interest and an American tradition of voluntary self-regulation, ought not colleges examine their own intercollegiate athletic programs as part of comprehensive self-study? To trigger extended historical analysis of intercollegiate athletics as an important part of higher education and American culture, the following episodes provide context for exploring the peculiar balancing act of athletics and academics.

The College Hero:
The Symbol of Which Age and Which Value?

On January 29, 1991, newspapers across the United States gave front-page coverage to the death of Harold "Red" Grange, All-American halfback at the University of Illinois from 1923 to 1925. Grange was remembered as the "idol of his age and a legend to later generations," as "the most famous, most publicized single player in the history of football." One nationally syndicated columnist wrote, "The news that Red Grange has died at 87 marks the end of a company that made a decade roar," arguing that Grange symbolized innocence and amateurism in American sports.[7]

Grange captured the popular imagination as the college student-athlete who was the consummate All-American: the self-made hard-working hero. For example, sportswriters reminded readers time and time again that Grange had not received an athletic scholarship when he enrolled at the University of Illinois, that he had earned money to pay his college bills by working summers delivering ice in Wheaton, Illinois. He was a diligent student who took courses in trigonometry, history, and economics as part of his business major. He was modest about his sports triumphs and was well-regarded by his teammates.

His accomplishments were impressive, and his honors as an All-American and most valuable player in the Big Ten Conference were well earned. At the same time, Grange's own example symbolized the start of another era that substantially changed the American conception of the collegiate student-athlete. His heroism helped consolidate intercollegiate sports as a highly commercialized activity characterized by publicity and promotion. If Grange stood for dedicated amateurism, he also helped to transform college football into mass entertainment. For example, the football game in which he acquired national fame on October 18, 1924, when he scored six touchdowns against the University of Michigan, marked the dedication of the University of Illinois's new stadium that seated over sixty-six thousand—testimony to the place of spectator sports on the American campus.

Although Grange's accomplishments and modesty were genuine, his popularity as a national hero was a product of mass media and the press. Sportswriters, not teammates or classmates, created and projected his legendary image. As Gerald Eskanazi recalled, "He was a perfect football figure for the age of hyperbole in American sports." New York sportswriter Grantland Rice dubbed him the "Galloping Ghost" and glorified his self-generated ascent as the hard-working "Wheaton Ice Man." Grange's embellished reputation was projected by the national press coverage of daily newspapers, and also by the relatively new medium of radio broadcasts. Writer Damon Runyon, whose beat usually dealt with the racetracks, gambling, and sporting life of New York City, looked to the Midwest for subject matter and wrote that Red Grange "is three or four men rolled into one. He is Jack Dempsey, Babe Ruth, Al Jolson, Paavo Nurmi, and Man o' War." After reading such articles, Grange's own coach at the University of Illinois wryly observed, "Often an All-American is made by a long run, a weak defense, and a poet in the press box."[8]

The result was that Red Grange was the model of the college athletic hero as a celebrity for whom publicity was followed by profession-alism. When Grange finished his last college game of the 1925 season, he immediately signed a contract with the Chicago Bears, an important event because he was the crucial player whose college fame could bring out fans to the financially struggling new professional football league's games. So, although Red Grange had not received an athletic scholar-ship when he enrolled at the University of Illinois, he was the first great college player to receive a large salary as a professional; in his first four months in the professional league, he earned $100,000. He set the precedent for a college athlete to leave college without a degree, in favor of immediate wealth. Commercialization worked two ways: Grange earned a high salary, and teams earned large revenues from ticket sales as crowds of over sixty thousand packed into the Polo Grounds in New York City and the newly constructed Soldiers Field in Chicago. Thanks to Grange's example, college and professional football henceforth would compete for athletic talent, coaches, paying audi-ences, advertising sponsors, and press coverage. And, for Red Grange, commercial celebration extended into nonathletic promotions; he later starred in a movie serial, *The Galloping Ghost*. When he retired from playing, he was a sports broadcaster. Each and every phase of his profes-sional career had been predicated on his initial success as a varsity college athlete.

Here were the elements of publicity and heroism that have made sports, including college teams and players, central in twentieth-century American life. Grange did not create the highly popular and commercial character of college sports, but he did legitimize and ele-vate them. He was an example of a college hero turned culture hero, celebrated beyond the campus due to the publicity of national media.

Grange's transformation of the American collegiate ideal of the student-athlete stands in contrast to the story of the greatest collegiate hero of the pre–World War I generation: Hobey Baker of Princeton. It represents a regional shift of All-American status from an embellished Ivy League ideal to the populist virtues attributed to the Big Ten state universities of the Midwest. For example, Hobey Baker—an All-American in football and hockey—did not receive an athletic scholar-ship, shunned newspaper publicity, and rejected all offers of profes-sional contracts. Whereas Hobey Baker was an alumnus of a prestigious East Coast private boarding school, Red Grange graduated from a public high school in the Midwest. Furthermore, Baker's adherence to a strict code of amateur sportsmanship prompted him to refuse to play in any games that included professional players on the opposing team. After having finished college, he shifted his heroic feats from the playing field to military service. In World War I, he was the foremost American flying ace. Baker was killed in a fluke accident as he made a ritual last flight before leaving his fellow pilots in France. His death at an early age increased his legendary stature as a hero.[9]

The collegiate ideal that Red Grange personified contrasted not only with the student-athlete ideal of an earlier generation but also with other variations of heroic college student achievement from Grange's own college era. About a week after Grange's obituary, the *Washington Post* published an interesting letter to the editor:

> Last week marked the passing of two great men of the University of Illinois, one a popular athlete, the other a great scientist. While the news of football player Harold "Red" Grange's death rightly appeared on *The Post*'s front page [January 29], physicist John Bardeen's obituary [January 31] was consigned to the Metro section. True, the former was a household name, while the latter was a man who spoke in a whisper and shunned the public eye, but John Bardeen did as much to change our everyday lives as Albert Einstein or Thomas Edison.
>
> John Bardeen was the only person ever to win two Nobel Prizes in the same field. Perhaps his greatest achievement was to solve one of the mysteries of modern physics by developing a microscopic theory of superconductivity. As a co-inventor of the transistor, he helped to revolutionize the electronics industry. Look around. Practically every electronic device you see depends on the transistor: the computer, TV, radio, even the car. For these contributions, Mr. Bardeen should be noted as one of the most influential scientists of the 20th century.
>
> The *Post* often bemoans the state of science literacy in this country. Part of the solution is to award as much honor to our great scientists as to our great athletes.[10]

A fact of life for American universities in the twentieth century is that inordinate publicity has accrued to the extracurricular activities of intercollegiate athletics. The simultaneous accommodation of Red Grange the football player and John Bardeen the scientist illustrates well the example of what editor Edwin Slosson observed in his 1910 book, *Great American Universities,* and historian Laurence Veysey reaffirmed in his 1965 study, *The Emergence of the American University:*

the university umbrella has accommodated disparate activities without integrating them. This coexistence has meant that one hallmark of the American university in the twentieth century has been its ability (and decision) to emphasize and excel in both Big Science and Big Athletics. It is important to note in the letter about physicist Bardeen that the author does not recommend that intercollegiate athletics be eliminated or even removed from front page press coverage; indeed, the writer accepts the popular interest and merely asks for balanced coverage of great achievements in athletics and academics.

The notion of excellence in disparate parts of the university is intriguing, and perhaps this strategy has served many American universities reasonably well. Indeed, a persistent claim is that the visibility of successful athletic teams can assist a university in its less conspicuous educational programs. The danger is that we accept this contention without careful historical analysis.

One reason to be cautious in accepting claims about the benefits of large-scale intercollegiate athletics is a long record of scandals. It is not enough to deplore the proliferation of college sports controversies. The connection between institutional governance and intercollegiate athletics can be understood only by considering two historical questions: How have our colleges and universities gotten into these compromising situations? and, Are these "problems" associated with college sports by accident or by design? Finally, historical research on this understudied dimension of higher education policy can bring attention to the uncomfortable question, How and why have big-time college sports been able to resist substantive reform despite the recurrent attention of academic leaders, higher education associations, and educational foundations?

Perhaps the answer is that the temptation to overemphasize college sports is not exceptional but is, rather, part of both higher education's institutional heritage and our national culture from which few colleges and universities have been immune. The flurry of publicity over college sports scandals is a legacy of varsity sports and American boosterism in which campus glory has come to be connected with (or tolerated as part of) alumni, regional, and state pride. It is a situation that even colleges and universities with strong academic reputations have not been able altogether to avoid. An intriguing hypothesis is that the excesses of commercialized intercollegiate athletic programs may well be the norm, not the exception, for the character and operation of the twentieth-century American university.

To understand the coexistence of academics and athletics within the American campus calls for consideration of the historic perspective of university presidents. For example, a quarter-century ago the University of California's Clark Kerr gave the legendary advice to fellow university presidents that they would do well to avoid entanglements in policy matters of intercollegiate athletics. The conventional wisdom in the presidential primer was that football for the alumni, along with parking for the faculty and social life for undergraduates, was an entrenched domain of campus life where administrative reform was risky business. A university president might rationalize this accommodation because, after all, winning teams allegedly brought national publicity and loyalty among alumni and students, provided funding for the entire athletic department, and perhaps even stimulated donors to contribute to the university's educational programs.[11] A successful large-scale intercollegiate sports program was sometimes seen as an instrument of total institutional enhancement.

This presidential strategy of avoidance and accommodation, however, ultimately exacted a price. Today, the scandals of big-time college sports stand as a sustained, conspicuous issue in American higher education that is noteworthy on two counts: first, the inordinate negative publicity can cancel the favorable visibility of large-scale sports; second, a revisionist interpretation suggests genuine uncertainty about the traditional belief that a campus accrues numerous spin-off benefits from a college sports program—and the belief that the gains still offset the liabilities. Certainly this reasonable doubt surfaces in the finances of intercollegiate athletics. A 1990 report by the College Football Association indicates that at least 40 percent of the intercollegiate athletic departments at sixty-three universities with big-time football programs now run an annual deficit. And there is evidence that Clark Kerr's avoidance ploy for university presidents provides little guarantee of administrative security, let alone success. Several presidents and chancellors have been fired in the aftermath of intercollegiate athletic scandals at their respective institutions. A residual feature of university governance is the charge that higher education leaders have not been able to contain or reform abuses in intercollegiate athletics.

The Ritual of Reform among Campus, Commission, and Culture

This book emphasizes national episodes involving national associations and foundations that transcended the particulars of a single campus. To reform college sports in the United States is to encounter a paradox: on the one hand, we have a long tradition of campus autonomy and institutional self-determination, which suggests that a college president and a board are the appropriate leaders to make certain that a sports program is on course. On the other hand, abuses in college sports tend to defy solutions by a single institution because they are, by nature, an interinstitutional venture. Only when like-minded institutions act in concert, whether in conferences or in associations, is essential reform likely to take place. Therefore, to study the attempts to reform intercollegiate athletics directs research beyond the campus to levels of transinstitutional policy.

To speak of "academic policy" in the United States is misleading because we have no central ministry of higher education. At both the state and the federal levels, higher education has been a remarkably decentralized arrangement characterized by institutional autonomy, voluntary association, and relatively little government regulation. It is no accident, then, that this study is grounded in some interesting reports of national scope that came from private foundations and associations. These reports constitute a loose de facto public policy; although not government documents, they do point toward discussion of national accountability, mutual concerns, collective solutions, and practices for the commonwealth. As historian Ellen Condliffe Lagemann emphasized in her study of the Carnegie Foundation for the Advancement of Teaching, the major foundations have represented "private power for the public good" in twentieth-century America.[12] Specifically, the four national reports that provide the major points of departure for discussion by academic leaders about the condition and character of intercollegiate athletics are Howard Savage's *American College Athletics*, published in 1929 under the sponsorship of the Carnegie Foundation for the Advancement of Teaching; the 1952 report of the Special Committee on Athletic Policy of the American Council on Education; George Hanford's 1974 report to the American Council on Education on the need for a national study of intercollegiate athletics; and the March 1991 report of the Knight Foundation Commission on Intercollegiate Athletics, *Keeping Faith with the Student-Athlete,* which proposed a new model for college sports.[13]

Although the report of a major foundation or a higher education association provides a broad view and a national context for problems between academics and athletics that have percolated up from the various colleges and universities, it does not follow that a report or recommendations from a blue ribbon panel or a national commission leads to reform. The reforms put into place have only an incidental connection with the original intent of the report's authors and advocates. Therefore, analysis of intercollegiate athletics reform ultimately must include some tracking of diffusion from a national report to the level of athletic conferences and individual colleges and universities.

Setting policy and making recommendations have not necessarily been congruent with enforcement of college sports reform measures. Nor does a survey of developments within the National Collegiate Athletic Association suffice as a lens by which to view the history of athletic policies as part of educational missions. The institutional case studies presented in subsequent chapters are not a comprehensive survey of controversies involving academic leaders and athletic departments. They compose, instead, a selective history of some significant episodes that had implications for many institutions and that suggest some sampling according to institutional categories and regions, so as to suggest the size and diversity of American higher education. A good illustration of the ironies of a national reform effort is provided by my beginning with a significant case at the start of the historical period with which this book is concerned: the varied responses fostered by Howard J. Savage's 1929 report, *American College Athletics.*

Using the landmark national reports as key documents, my aim is to connect the history of college sports to American social history and to the study of higher education. The title of this book refers literally to the games colleges play: namely, varsity football, basketball, and other sports. But colleges and universities also play games of evasion and self-deception.

Central to this work is the premise that a university's athletic policy is ultimately important for defining its educational philosophy. A theme for higher education in the twentieth century is that American colleges and universities have had difficulty achieving (and maintaining) a proper balance of academics and athletics. Intercollegiate athletics have been a perennial source of opportunity and temptation as the American campus has worked and reworked its relations with American culture. Undergirding this historic dynamic between school and society is the thesis that academic leaders, not just athletic officials, have often been central players. The ambiguities, dilemmas, and compromises that have characterized the policies and practices of intercollegiate athletics constitute as important a legacy in American higher education as the games colleges play.

• • • • • • • • • • • • • • • •

CHAPTER ONE

The Reform Canon

The 1929 Carnegie Foundation Report

Any substantive discussion about the reform of intercollegiate athletics in American higher education starts with and eventually returns to *American College Athletics*, the 1929 report that Howard J. Savage prepared for the Carnegie Foundation for the Advancement of Teaching (CFAT).[1] Despite its auspicious official designation as "Bulletin Number Twenty-three," this volatile report attracted widespread public attention. It became the canon that set the standard for reform proposals and policy analyses about the place of intercollegiate sports in American colleges and universities. Wedged among a series of Carnegie Foundation reports dealing with such topics as pension plans for Colorado schools, problems in dental education, and local provisions for higher education in Saskatchewan, *American College Athletics* was distinctive among educational studies in its power to generate immediate controversy. When the report was released on October 24, 1929, it received front page coverage in major newspapers across the United States. Headlines in the *New York Times*, for example, proclaimed, "College Sports Tainted by Bounties, Carnegie Fund Finds in Wide Study," followed by the elaboration that "one in seven athletes" was "subsidized," and that New York University, Fordham, Columbia, Harvard, and Princeton were accused of abuses involving "slush funds" and "recruiting."

Publicity kindled by the report contrasted with the secrecy that characterized its drafting. Based on a study of over 130 college and university sports programs, its subject matter was sufficiently sensitive that Henry S. Pritchett, president of the Carnegie Foundation, departed from customary foundation practice when he deliberately decided not to distribute galley proof of the forthcoming report to college presidents—or even to members of the Carnegie Foundation board. In the preceding quarter-century, the only Carnegie Foundation report that rivaled the Savage study's controversy was Abraham Flexner's famous 1910 "Bulletin Number Four," a study of medical education in the United States and Canada.[2]

American College Athletics was a detailed report whose 347 pages of documented examples were marbled with quotable passages. That the report was frequently cited was little assurance that it was carefully read.[3] The president of the Carnegie Foundation for the Advancement of Teaching noted in his preface that he justified including a condensation of the report to increase the likelihood that the report's insights would reach diverse audiences. He explained:

> The college president or teacher interested in the place of organized sports in American colleges and the effects of these upon the intellectual life of his college will desire to go carefully into the details as set forth in the chapters of this report. On the other hand, experience shows that few busy men find the time to read a detailed report. It is also realized to-day, in all fields of public affairs, that the facts must be presented in a form available to the intelligent layman as well as to the professional student.[4]

Later generations of analysts have often revived selected passages from the report as a prelude to discussing conditions of college sports in their own times. Since *American College Athletics* was elevated to symbolic stature, the volume was usually invoked more as a liturgy and less as a closely argued, documented text. Furthermore, it is not clear how closely resurrectionists have read the original report or understood the circumstances that led to its preparation. As primary author Howard Savage recalled in his own 1953 memoirs: "Although Bulletin Number Twenty-three has survived its usefulness, it will not stay decently dead. Roughly four college generations after it appeared, the National Collegiate Athletic Association undertook to compel observance of some of its principles."[5] Given the report's immediate publicity and enduring symbolic influence, it warrants being placed in historical perspective.

Context for the Canon, 1900 to 1929

"Bulletin Number Twenty-three" was not the first sign of national concern over problems of intercollegiate sports. In the early 1900s, numerous articles by college presidents in such national magazines as *McClure's, Harper's, Century,* and the *Saturday Evening Post* brought public attention to injuries and abuses taking place in college football games. College football was a brutal sport that, according to legend, led famous heavyweight boxing champion John L. Sullivan to exclaim, "There's murder in that game!" Public statements of outrage from high places were central elements in the organizational saga of the National Collegiate Athletic Association (NCAA). The most famous episode is traced to United States president Theodore Roosevelt, whose concern over football violence was provoked by a news photograph of a battered, bloodied Swarthmore varsity football player leaving the field. This prompted Roosevelt, himself a former college athlete and advocate of the "strenuous life," to summon to the White House football representatives of the so-called Big Three, Harvard, Princeton, and Yale, as well as spokesmen from other major universities, on October 9, 1905. Roosevelt's charge was that they consider either reform or abolition of college football. One consequence of Roosevelt's White House summons was a December 1905 meeting of delegates from thirteen eastern colleges to form the Intercollegiate Athletic Association of the United States (IAAUS), a group that by 1910 had been renamed the National Collegiate Athletic Association (NCAA).[6] At the regional level, by World War I several conferences, including the Western Intercollegiate Conference (whose popular name was the Big Ten), the Southern Conference, and the Pacific Coast Conference, were operating.

After the initial rush of publicity, these heroic founding events in the reform of college sports waned in their ability to establish enduring gains. The first constraint was that the reform organizations dealt almost exclusively with conduct and rules on the playing field, with some secondary attention to player eligibility. "Reform" meant reducing brutality, prohibiting dangerous tactics, setting specifications for size of playing fields, improving uniforms and equipment, and measures to make the game physically safe. Within the ranks of coaches and athletic directors, much debate was devoted to standardizing the *style* of play, characterized by long negotiations over restrictions on blocking, passing, and kicking. It had little to do with the administrative control or the structural and financial place of college sports within American universities. Nor did it concern itself with integrating intercollegiate sports into the curriculum. Second, the national scope of the National Collegiate Athletic Association was exaggerated, since the most powerful East Coast universities were marginal or reluctant members. This left the organization susceptible to regional schisms and snobbery.

All this was consistent with the limits of previous efforts to reform college football. Conferences formed by college presidents and athletic directors historically had been silent on policies associated with the governance, finances, and academic regulations of intercollegiate athletics. The usual provision of voluntary college associations was that conference delegates were prohibited from intervening in matters of institutional structure and control. Indicative of the traditional limits of structural reform was the 1898 Brown University Conference called by faculty representatives, a well-intentioned event that was derailed first by Yale's refusal to send a delegate, and second by feuding and the departure of faculty representatives from Pennsylvania and Columbia. The impression that athletic programs were exempted from the jurisdiction of academic policies is reinforced in historian Ronald Smith's *Sports and Freedom: The Rise of Big-Time College Athletics*. The few times that faculty boards discussed academic standards they were declared out of bounds by some fellow delegates. Institutional autonomy was the norm among the college football establishment.[7]

The College Football Establishment Prior to the Report

One irony of reform efforts prior to the 1929 Carnegie Foundation Report was that the Big Three—Yale, Harvard, and Princeton—did constitute an informal athletic establishment that might have provided the machinery for policy reform. This pathway to reform was not followed, however, because the establishment guarded its territory jealously and avoided integration of academics and athletics. A related deterrent was intense rivalry, even distrust and contempt, among the most influential institutions. Sportswriters and college football fans referred to Harvard, Yale, and Princeton as the Big Three in the quest for national football championships. Despite this linkage in the public imagery, the three institutions did not constitute a league or voluntary association. One surprising historical finding is that during this era there was no Ivy

League. To the contrary, intercollegiate relations among these historic institutions were so hostile that in the decade prior to 1900 Harvard and Yale refused to play each other in 1895 and 1896. In the 1890s, the "big game" at the end of the season was Yale versus Princeton! Elsewhere, such universities as Cornell and Pennsylvania made their own claims to national championships, feats that in turn led to arrogant avoidance by one or more members of the Big Three. As late as the mid-1920s, there were few encouraging signs that Harvard, Yale, and Princeton displayed any commitment to cooperation or to nationwide voluntary association, even though theirs were the athletic programs most eligible to be leaders.[8]

Among the prestigious Big Three, Yale was the real and symbolic force in American collegiate athletics. No nationwide reform organization could expect to succeed without Yale's support. It was the best-known and most popular embodiment of college life because "Yale's Democracy" was depicted by journalists as a distinctive educational philosophy, a "dynamo" of undergraduate activity that emphasized the harnessing of individual ambition to group accomplishment. It was a model enhanced by Yale's approach to (and success in) an energetic extracurriculum in which varsity sports, especially football, were central. And, since Yale literally was the "cradle of coaches," its former players spread its distinctive football gospel to scores of colleges throughout the United States. Yale's presence in American popular culture was conspicuous, as sports page coverage of its winning teams combined with the mass circulation of the fictional "Frank Merriwell at Yale" juvenile stories to capture the American imagination in shaping the "collegiate ideal" and the glorification of the "student-athlete" as culture hero. The dime novel Merriwell stories, for example, had an average weekly sales of over two million copies during the years 1890 to 1915.[9]

If Frank Merriwell embodied the fictional heroism of Yale, then the real-life personification was to be found in Yale's Walter Camp, celebrated as the "Father of American Football." A star player as an undergraduate at Yale, his reputation soared for decades as Yale's football coach, athletic director, and spokesman. For years the announcement of the "All-American" football team was known as "Walter Camp's All-American team." Camp also was editor of the annual college football guide for forty-two years. Excerpts from his 1925 eulogy indicate Camp's traditional image as an American sportsman:

Walter Camp pre-eminently was a philanthropist in American sport. His was the genius to play his country's games surpassingly well; to improve and to increase their technique; to surround them with customs and features that added intensely to their attraction; to accompany them with a code of chivalry and nobleness that coincidentally trained players and spectators in American manhood at its best. . . . No collegian ever devoted greater zeal to his alma mater than Walter Camp to Yale; and yet in his loyalty he was scrupulously fair to Yale's athletic adversaries.[10]

A good sampling of this collegiate ideal associated with Yale was the secular sermon Camp wrote for American boys in the introduction to the popular 1893 work, *Walter Camp's Book of College Sports:* "Be each, pray God, a gentleman! It is an easy word, and a pleasant one. I don't doubt but that you all pronounce it trippingly enough, and have each one his own high ideal of what a gentleman should be. Do you live up to it?" According to Camp, a gentleman competing against a gentleman always played to win; a gentleman did not make his living from his athletic prowess, and gained only glory and satisfaction from his victories. Gentlemen were neither physical nor mental cowards. Camp's sermon concluded: "Now, my young college friend, it is your turn. Remember it is upon you that the younger brother looks for example, and whatever you do in your four years' course, you will see magnified by the boys who come after you. Support your class and your college in every way compatible with your position."[11]

Camp did not always practice what he preached when it came to his own conduct as an athletics administrator. In the language of fictional Frank Merriwell of Yale, a growing body of historical research indicates that Camp as an administrator was at times a cad and a bully, and hardly was regarded as a "good sport" by his fellow coaches. Although Camp was traditionally depicted as a champion of fair play, close inspection reveals self-congratulation and promotion, and some indication that he was not beyond compiling dubious statistics that supported his views. Patrick Miller's 1987 study, *Athletes in Academe: College Sports and American Culture, 1850–1920*, presents research on Camp's professional activities that make him enigmatic as well as influential.[12] Although he was a prolific writer and speaker about amateurism and the college athlete as student and gentleman, Camp was at times an opportunist who made a career and fortune as a "professional amateur" via endorsements, book royalties, syndicated columns, and newsreels. His compilations of the annual All-American teams were partisan, slow to acknowledge football talent outside historic northeastern universities.

At the campus level, a profile of the varsity athletic program at Yale around 1905 to 1910 reconstructed from student memoirs suggests an equally critical view of Camp's values and practices. Yale was important because it was both the most powerful football team in the United States for decades and also had the strongest financial and administrative organization. The Yale Athletic Association, abbreviated YAA, was misleading. A more accurate name would have been the "Yale Football Association," as Camp served as both football coach and athletic director. One story circulating among Yale student-athletes and alumni was that Camp was hoarding gate receipts for construction of a large new football stadium, which meant that varsity teams in such minor sports as swimming and wrestling received little or no allocation for travel expenses or even for a coach. Sports other than football often had to rely on direct gifts and contributions from benefactors and volunteer coaches. As Robert Caro observed,

> Every attempt to upgrade such sports at Yale had run head on into the frenzy over football—it was the era when gridiron heroes like Ted Coy and Tad Jones were campus gods, when the winner of the Big Three title was national champion, when every victory was celebrated with bonfires and torchlight parades down Chapel Street—and into the personal opposition of Camp, who, in addition to being first among the Eli football pantheon, had the more practical advantage of being treasurer of the Athletic Union.[13]

Apparently by 1909 Camp had been "squirreling away the annual surplus of the Union with such enthusiasm that it had already reached $120,000, and he was not about to turn any of it over to the sports he derided." Robert Moses, later a famous figure in New York politics, was a Yale undergraduate and member of the swimming team and an advocate of systematic funding for minor sports. He recalled about Walter Camp: "What you have to understand is what a colossal influence he had; he dominated all of athletics there; his word was absolutely law."[14] The upshot was that Camp continually refused to distribute any of the football receipts surplus to the minor sports. Tales about dedication of funds for a monumental stadium turned out to be well founded, as Camp's dream came true in 1914: the magnificent new Yale Bowl attracted a crowd of over seventy thousand for its inaugural game.

Hence, within Yale's athletic program, run by students and alumni, there were issues of control quite apart from the faculty and president. Undergraduate Robert Moses sought to break Camp's hegemony by creating the Yale Minor Sports Association—an effort that at first bemused, then angered, Camp. To thwart the renegade student movement headed by Moses, Camp called in chips owed him by campus administrators; the dean of the college tried unsuccessfully to dissuade Moses from his new endeavor. So, although football continued its primacy, cooperation among Yale's diverse sports had been shattered.

Had these practices been confined to a single campus, Walter Camp's influence might have been minimal. Yet the striking finding is that these issues percolated beyond Yale to the national sphere. For example, although Walter Camp was most famous as the "Father of American Football," he also came to be known among coaches and athletic directors as the "czar of college football"—not a flattering title, given his advocacy of "Yale's Democracy." As adviser to Yale's president Arthur Twining Hadley and secretary of the national football rules committee, Camp made certain that Yale resisted cooperation with other institutions on reform of college sports.[15] Yale (or, specifically, the Yale football program represented by Camp) had too much to lose to embrace cooperation or systematic reform. Yale, for example, refused to join the original group in 1905 that responded to President Roosevelt's dictum; later, it rejected an invitation to founding meetings of what would, in 1910, become the NCAA and by its own choice was not a charter member of the association. Only in 1915, a decade after the initial gathering of Eastern colleges, did Yale join the NCAA.

In attempting to understand the nature of the college sports enterprise of the 1920s, I was first tempted to apply a corporate or business model, as if there were rational, standardized procedures. True, coaching and training had adopted some industrial practices. Camp himself borrowed the mass production techniques he learned as a manager at the New Haven Clockworks to shape his coaching drills at Yale. Elsewhere, in 1915 the University of Pittsburgh brought quantitative data and publicity to the college game by having players wear numerals on their jerseys. And coaches emulated industrial efficiency strategies as they increasingly devoted attention to record keeping and statistical compilations of player performance.[16]

On balance, analogies to industry misread the character of power in college sports. A better image than the industrial model is to see athletic departments and coaches in terms of a medieval metaphor: they bring to mind dukes and barons whose territories were only loosely controlled by university boards and presidents. At a university where there was a successful and charismatic football coach and an enthusiastic alumni group, the president was not even king in his own campus castle. If presidents resisted external examination of campus athletic programs by conferences and national associations, it usually was for one of two reasons: either the university president was an advocate of big-time college sports; or, at the other extreme, he was embarrassed to reveal his lack of control over the campus sports enterprise.

To speak of "intercollegiate sports" is misleading in that football dominated attention and resources in this period. Athletic directors and coaches showed little inclination toward a comprehensive, broad-based varsity program. Basketball had yet to gain a following as a spectator sport. With selected exceptions (e.g., crew, baseball, and hockey at some campuses), all sports were at best a distant second to football. This issue surfaced throughout the next half-century in that justification for a big-time football program was couched in the rhetoric that it in turn supported a comprehensive varsity program—a claim not supported by the historical record.

The inertia of the football establishment resulted in a paradox of reform. It meant that even though the 1929 Carnegie Foundation's "Bulletin Number Twenty-three" was a belated compilation of excesses in college sports, it was in the vanguard of reform initiatives. According to historian Ronald A. Smith, the reform impulse was slow and weak because the young NCAA was a "ruling body lacking power and prestige."[17]

Equally perplexing were the marginal results elicited by reform measures. On paper, creation of the NCAA was remarkable. Its statement of principles was on the mark. But, lacking the support of the historic eastern universities and dependent on voluntary membership and compliance, the NCAA tended to be not only weak but at times also counterproductive: it helped to perpetuate the vices it purported to eliminate because its formal statement could send the false message that things were under scrutiny and control.[18] Creation of the NCAA code was a hollow victory because, although technically the reform campaign had been won, the terms of the treaty could not be enforced. The fact that between 1916 and 1926 the NCAA repeatedly requested help from the Carnegie Foundation for the Advancement of Teaching to conduct its comprehensive study reinforces the notion of the NCAA's weakness and underscores the influence attributed to the Carnegie Foundation.

Prelude to Publication of the Report

Historically, even local and regional arrangements such as athletic conferences exerted little control over member institutions. Hence, one pioneering contribution of Howard Savage's *American College Athletics* was that it was an encyclopedic survey of conditions concerning governance and finance of college sports, providing data that were sufficiently compelling to break the silence about the commercialization of college sports. In the argot of the day, it injected into a respected public forum what was called "plain talk" and systematic data about a pervasive topic that had been avoided for several years.

Publication of the 1929 study came about only after several years of pilot studies and negotiation. The Carnegie Foundation for the Advancement of Teaching had been concerned about abuses in the control of college sports prior to 1920. However, it was only in November 1921 that the CFAT executive committee placed the topic on the agenda of the CFAT's board—which led to little because the board recommended that the topic be referred back to the executive committee and "kept under advisement . . . with the possibility of action in the future." A year later, when the trustees again considered the topic, it was deferred because "it was too hot a topic for concerted handling *ex tempore*."[19] One other crucial event that fostered national reform was the death in 1925 of Walter Camp, the person who heretofore had stalled any national organization that threatened to intrude on the powerful Yale football program.

Henry Pritchett, former president of Massachusetts Institute of Technology and president of the Carnegie Foundation for the Advancement of Teaching for over two decades, had a persistent interest in the college sports issue as part of the larger scheme of raising academic standards in American secondary and higher education. In his tenure at the Carnegie Foundation, he had been dedicated to the gospel of social efficiency, the proposition that American education could best be improved by raising standards, encouraging strong institutions to cooperate, and persuading weak institutions to wither. It had meant using voluntary associations, shared responsibility for pension plans, agreements on adherence to admissions requirements, thresholds for minimum numbers of enrolled students, and secularization of the college curricula to foster simultaneously higher standards and uniformity. His vision included support for creation of the Educational Testing Service and reliance on the Scholastic Aptitude Test to make college admissions decisions increasingly systematic. Perhaps the best measure of his influence on the articulation between secondary and higher education was widespread adoption of the so-called Carnegie Units to designate bona fide academic courses on high school transcripts for consideration by college admissions officers. For Pritchett, the waste of commercialized college sports was antithetical to a sound plan for higher education.[20] Intercollegiate athletics were not his central interest, but they were a persistent nuisance that could not be ignored or even quarantined because they were debilitating to the entire intellectual atmosphere of the American campus.

Eventually this led Pritchett to encourage some cautious Carnegie Foundation inquiries into the problem of college sports. Pritchett, for example, received permission from the foundation's executive committee to provide up to one thousand dollars for a study of college sports in the South conducted by the Association of Colleges and Secondary Schools of the Southern States. After the Carnegie Foundation had provided this modest funding to an outside group, its executive committee in May 1923 again asserted that the foundation did not wish to study the topic.

Over the next few years, the Carnegie Foundation received numerous requests from college groups to investigate the excesses of intercollegiate sports. In 1925 the foundation allowed staff member Howard Savage to write a preliminary study, called the "Twenty College Report," which introduced a theme that Savage would emphasize again in his 1929 report: namely, that responsibility for the condition of an institution's athletics program was "at the door of the college president." This study, however, received scant attention in the formal work of the Carnegie Foundation. Meanwhile, Savage was sent to England for several weeks to investigate the characteristics of college sports at

British universities. At first glance, emulation of the Oxford-Cambridge model of college sports appeared intriguing to U.S. colleges. However, although a number of major American universities had experimented with rugby as an alternative to football several years earlier, this was a naive, short-lived experiment that evaded the central issue: that American college sports programs' expenses, crowds, and public appeal had long departed from the Oxford-Cambridge model of genuine amateur sports by and for students. Until this was acknowledged, questions of standards, policies, and reasonable control would remain unaddressed.

The Carnegie Foundation finally became involved in a study of national scope on January 8, 1926, when its executive committee accepted the NCAA's invitation to "make an investigation of the whole question of intercollegiate athletics and its relation to modern education." The primary investigator was Howard J. Savage, who was 33 when he wrote *American College Athletics*. An alumnus of Tufts University, he received his master's and Ph.D. degrees in English from Harvard. From 1915 to 1923, he taught at Bryn Mawr, with an interruption for army service in World War I. In 1923 he joined the staff of the Carnegie Foundation, with assignment to the projects on intercollegiate athletics. For years after publication of "Bulletin Number Twenty-three" he was in demand as a speaker on the character of intercollegiate sports. In 1931, after having completed several studies on other educational topics, he was named secretary of the Carnegie Foundation for the Advancement of Teaching, an influential staff position he would hold for over two decades.

Anatomy of the Analysis: Features of the Savage Report

The aim of Savage's three-year study was to "ascertain the significant facts concerning college athletics in the United States and Canada, to analyze these facts in relation to American college and university life," and "to present a summary of American college athletics, their merits and their defects, together with such suggestions looking to their improvement."[21] Savage's research team made some deliberate decisions about focus and methodology: first, they decided not to rate or rank institutions according to their respective successes in enforcing amateur rules and "making athletics a part of the curriculum and encouraging mass participation, under faculty direction and control with good administrative methods, and make training the mind of primary importance while athletics were secondary" (p. 5). Second, they opted not to send questionnaires to institutions, relying instead on site visits; interviews with students, faculty, alumni, administrators; and review of campus documents. The report focused on problems facing college sports, which the authors justified on the grounds that "if abuses seem to be overemphasized it is because the developments during the last two decades of American college athletics have been very great and the ideals to be served very high" (p. 12).

Savage and his coauthors devoted chapters to the topics of administrative control of college athletics, the place of the professional coach, recruiting and subsidizing athletes, the place of the press, the values in college athletics, and the growth of professionalism in college athletics. Surprisingly, their scrutiny of financial records led them to give favorable reviews to most institutions. Their inquiry probably overlooked the activities of unofficial groups whose records were outside university files.

The report's conclusion emphasized probing the causes of the defects in college athletics, which were identified as "commercialism, and a negligent attitude toward the educational opportunity for which the college exists" (p. 306). Savage and his coauthors recognized the limits of reform and observed that these problems could be abated, but not "absolutely eliminated" from college sports. *American College Athletics* was a manifesto against commercialism: the authors emphasized that the financial and public aspects had united to make college sports "not so much activities of undergraduate life as joint cooperative enterprises involving presidents, trustees, faculties, alumni, and townsmen, and the vast publics of radio and the press; they are undertaken less for the diversion of the schoolboy or the undergraduate than for the amusement of others." The pervasiveness of such conditions muted any claims that big-time college sports had "educational value" and led to the conclusion that "naturally, then, the desire for power and influence is the source of most controversies over athletic administration and control" (p. 79). Intercollegiate athletics were associated with the "pageantry of college life," not its academic or intellectual side. And, "as matters now stand, their fundamental purpose is financial and commercial" (p. 82). One indication of these nonacademic values, which had come to characterize college sports, was the ascent of the hired coach, who was highly paid, dependent on victories, distant from the faculty, and opportunistic.

Who, according to the Savage Report, bore responsibilities for these abuses? Trustees received little mention, since their function was "delegation of responsibilities." Another surprising point was that Savage did not see "faculty control" as a panacea because it was often "pseudo-control," existing only in name. Further, faculty control removed authority from students and left programs susceptible to deference to a professional athletic administration (p. 309).

Sections dealing with the "hygiene of college sports" were tedious. Lengthy discussion of the impact of athletic participation on academic performance was equivocal: Henry Pritchett, in his preface to the report, brushed aside any pretense that the data had much utility:

> Extensive statistics have been gathered as to the comparison between the college performance of those taking part in inter-college contests with that of students who take no part in athletics. Some of these tabulations are given in this report. They mean little. When the intellectual life of a body of college students is on a low plane, the difference between the formal credits of men in training for intercollege contests and those of the ordinary student who is not in training, may be inappreciable. But it requires no tabulation of statistics to prove that the young athlete who gives himself for months, body and soul, to training under a professional coach for a gruelling contest, staged to focus the attention of thousands of people, and upon which many thousands of dollars will be staked, will find no time or energy for any serious intellectual effort. The compromises that have to be made to keep such a student in the college and to pass them through to a degree give an air of insincerity to the whole university-college regime.[22]

The report's authors and the president of the Carnegie Foundation agreed that the heart of the problem facing college sports was commercialization: an interlocking network that included expanded press coverage, public interest, alumni involvement, and recruiting abuses. The victim was the student-athlete in particular, the diminishing of educational and intellectual values in general. Also, students (including non-athletes) were the losers because they had been denied their rightful involvement in sports. As Savage elaborated: "Commercialism in college athletics must be diminished and college sport must rise to a point where it is esteemed primarily and sincerely for the opportunities it affords to mature youth under responsibility, to exercise at once the body and the mind, and to foster habits both of bodily health and of those high qualities of character which, until they are revealed in action, we accept on faith."[23]

Savage devoted a substantial chapter to scolding newspapers and radio for fostering commercialism. He documented that press coverage of college sports had been increasing and that many newspapers depended heavily on the sports page (hence, college sports) for subscriptions and sales. Once again, however, he pointed out that college officials had to take much blame for the situation because colleges themselves had adopted the widespread practice of establishing a publicity bureau designed to "keep the college in the news." The result was that the commercial and profit interests of the press, the college, and the community intersected. Savage called on publishers and editors of newspapers to adopt an enlightened policy for "leading public opinion to esteem the true value of the amateur status for American higher education" and deplored the proliferation of All-Star teams and All-American selections, which led to creation of the "pre-professional athlete."[24]

The report's discussion of the "mercenary student" noted that recruitment activities left behind few documents that could be traced. Despite this absence of a substantial paper trail, the researchers were able to compile an appendix that featured an array of recruitment correspondence. What about the plight of the financially poor high school student for whom an athletic scholarship was a means to a college education? The report showed little concern for athletic scholarships as a means of providing educational opportunity, since Savage felt that athletic scholarships hurt far more than they helped because they sullied the academic priorities of the entire institution.

The Savage Report accomplished two important things: it exposed college sports' resistance to systematic investigation, and it triggered refutations and denials by college and university presidents. In 1926 there were no systematic data on the control and finances of college sports, so that to speak of "standard operating procedures" or a "model" of governance was difficult because there were no sources to document any claims. Practices were diverse and unregulated. Over three-fourths of the colleges studied were found to have violated codes and principles of amateurism, suggesting that commercialization of college sports had gained acquiescence, if not legitimacy.

The Ritual of Rhetoric: Differential Responses in the Press

Publication of the report brought a predictable pattern of mixed responses. At first, there was a rush to support or to deny the report. *American College Athletics* continued to generate controversy, as major newspapers over the next year carried related stories at least once per week. Coverage included four editorials in the *New York Times* in 1930, and flurries of accusations and rebuttals between various college representatives and the Carnegie Foundation report's authors. One ritual was for a college official to endorse the Carnegie study in principle, with the specific disclaimer that its charges did not describe the athletic program at his own campus. Protestations included charges that Howard Savage and the Carnegie research team had been misleading in their investigation and exaggerated in their description of the extent of bad practices. In sorting out the enduring features of the report, a difficult task from the perspective of the 1990s is to discern patterns of alignment; that is, offenders cited in 1929 may now be stalwart examples of academic-athletic propriety. For example, the Savage study reported substantial abuses at what we now call "Ivy League" colleges—Columbia, Brown, Pennsylvania, Dartmouth, Harvard, and Princeton.

The reform ritual of denial and denunciation followed by reconsideration was illustrated by Brown University's successive responses to "Bulletin Number Twenty-three." Brown initially dismissed the report: the chair of its Athletic Council said the report was "in part false and in toto so misleading as to make it difficult to believe that the authors could present it as the result of a bona fide survey or that the Carnegie Foundation could allow its name to be attached to it." However, after having conducted its own internal investigation of athletic policies, university administrators retracted their harsh stance and made a public announcement that Brown "does not deny any of the specific charges contained in the Carnegie bulletin." Brown's administration sought to make amends with the conciliatory statement that "although the athletic council believes that certain allegations concerning Brown University are unwarranted, it is willing to forgo its own differences in the thought that the status of intercollegiate athletics will be improved by the publication of the bulletin."[25] Sorting through the charges and countercharges in the six months following release of "Bulletin Number Twenty-three," the verdict was that Howard Savage's research was carefully documented and tended to understate the uncontrolled athletic recruiting funds at Brown and other universities.

Although the sampling for the study included large and small institutions, the Carnegie team alerted readers to a "curse of bigness," in which problems and flagrant abuses were concentrated in a handful of "big time programs." Athletic programs at Catholic colleges, including Notre Dame, received special critical analysis in the report. One also sees signs of the emergence of the powerful programs in the state universities of the Midwest. The commissioner of the Big Ten conference was critical of the report; speaking to a reporter on October 24, he said:

> I have not had an opportunity to read the report, but judging from the excerpts I don't believe the Carnegie investigators have given a fair picture of the Big Ten condition. We have nothing to be ashamed of. I think that I am better informed of Big Ten athletic conditions than any investigator for the Carnegie Foundation. And I honestly believe that the Western Intercollegiate Conference universities are cleaner in regard to proselytizing and subsidizing athletes than are any other ten universities anyone may name. When the Carnegie report relies upon the facts uncovered by an agent in a twenty-four-hour visit to a university, it seems to me that it is evident that the report cannot be always fair to the institution.[26]

Ironically, the Big Ten had recently become the Big Nine because one of its members, the University of Iowa, had been expelled for major violations of conference codes. This expulsion sent mixed messages on reform: it showed that the conference was vigilant but contained the acerbic reminder that major infractions were taking place.

The Big Ten commissioner's complaint about the Carnegie Foundation research was reinforced by faculty representatives who felt Howard Savage had been more a prosecutor than an investigator in looking at conference members' athletic programs. The day the report was released, the University of Michigan football coach denied charges that he relied on an "intensely organized" system to recruit and subsidize athletes. The faculty representative from the University of Michigan was not pleased with the report; he told the *New York Times* that the Bulletin was "wild, almost vicious" and claimed that the investigator had unauthorized possession of university documents. Michigan's faculty representative considered Savage's report to refer to the Big Ten with a "sort of veiled half sneer," indicative of an East Coast bias.[27]

Howard Savage refused to retract the report's claims that were contested by the various colleges, asserting, "Up to the present hour we have not been apprised of any inaccuracy in the study as printed, and no one who has charged us with inaccuracy after doing us the honor to read it, has substantiated his statements."[28] When pressed by reporters about allegations that his staff had taken letters from university files without permission, Savage displayed detailed correspondence that refuted these charges.

Elsewhere, several institutions either had no comment or denied the report's findings. For example, the graduate sports manager at Washington and Jefferson College in Pennsylvania said, "There is not a word of truth in the report."[29] Stanford and Syracuse denied giving financial aid exclusively to athletes. Officials at the University of Pennsylvania were both "shocked and silent." Student editors and coaches at Yale felt the report was unreasonable in its criticisms of recruitment at Princeton and Harvard. Student editors at Columbia applauded the general motivation for the Carnegie report but thought it was unfair in its depiction of practices at their institution.

Savage continued to display documents to counter allegations that the report's research was suspect. In his 1953 memoirs, he emphasized that no critic had been able to refute the conditions described in the report. On balance, his findings were upheld and the report was accepted in principle. The National Collegiate Athletic Association endorsed "Bulletin Number Twenty-three" at its annual conference on January 20, 1930, and urged "all college officials to be guided by the document in curbing the evils of sports." One perceptive review of the report was by C. W. Mendell, former chair of the Board of Athletic Control at Yale. Writing in the *Saturday Review of Literature*, Mendell lauded its general aim and scope, with an aside that it was unfortunate that its roster of violations did not adequately distinguish between minor and major offending institutions. He concluded:

Perhaps the best way to look at the report as a whole is to accept it as a challenge. For good or evil, and most of us are convinced for good, athletics are with us to stay. The present survey leaves the colleges with no excuse for ignorance as to the nature, growth, advantages, and misfortunes of college sports. It makes its points clearly and specifically. It goes so far as to suggest that perhaps a source of weakness in athletics is the weakness in intellectual appeal in the rest of college life. . . . Any college that is alive to its responsibilities must respond to the facts with a renewed determination to make its athletic procedures as well as the rest of its program serve to the highest possible degree the ideals of education which are the sanction for its very existence.[30]

Internal Disagreement on the Mechanics of Reform

More interesting than the posturing denials in the newspapers by outraged college officials were the differences within the Carnegie Foundation for the Advancement of Teaching. President Pritchett disagreed in part with the report drafted by Howard Savage. To Pritchett, the culprit in the "football frenzy" was the professional coach, whereas Savage and the other investigators emphasized that the ineffectual university president was the key figure and noted that "many university or college presidents have left the shaping of athletic policies to conferences, committees, or specialists in physical education, who represent not so much the welfare of the institution and its undergraduates as special interests of one sort or another, all of which apparently feel that material prosperity, their own prestige, or professional standing must be served before other ends can be considered."

A few pages later Savage continued, "First, then, university presidents must be considered by virtue of their responsibilities and functions as coordinators of general policy. . . . The athletic situation in most American colleges and universities has been met by a compromise that involves the yielding of the less vocal interests. Often, however, the shaping of policy has depended upon satisfying as many special claims as possible without due regard to the best interests of the undergraduates, and especially to the diversification of those interests."[31]

Even though Pritchett found the professional coach to be the main source of problems, he agreed with Savage and the research staff that correcting problems was the responsibility of the president in concert with the faculty. How this was to take place was not clear.

The report was optimistic about a shift in student and public attitudes, noting, "Fortunately, many indications point to a growing feeling . . . that athletics are far from the most important feature of college days."[32] What remains confusing is precisely how critics of highly commercialized college football expected this vague feeling to be implemented. The Savage study stands as an interesting case related to the larger question of how educational reform is intended to take place in American public life and institutions. In other words, what is the role of the commissioned report? Mendell's insightful review of "Bulletin Number Twenty-three" reminded readers that commissioned investigative reports were a "favorite amusement of the American public," yet "with singular regularity they turn out to be unsatisfactory to the very public that clamors for them."[33] Savage's own concluding comments in *American College Athletics* were a peculiar blend of insight and naiveté.

A recurring theme was that amending formal structures for control of college sports was of little use; enforcement of existing codes and arrangements, especially the spirit of such codes, was time better spent than drafting new structures. Savage wrote, "He who believes that clean and sportsmanlike games, chivalrous rivalry, and magnanimous competition are to be attained through mere administrative provisions and procedure is indeed naive."[34] Report authors were quite correct that no structural or formal change guaranteed reform, since both Pritchett and Savage wanted the university president to take responsibility for making decisions, purging abuses, and transferring (or restoring) programs to undergraduates. Pritchett was adamant about "what ought to be done":

> The paid coach, the gate receipts, the special training tables, the costly sweaters and extensive journeys in special Pullman cars, the recruiting from the high school, the demoralizing publicity showered on the players, the devotion of an undue proportion of time to training, the devices for putting a desirable athlete, but a weak scholar, across the hurdles of the examination—these ought to stop and the intercollege and intramural sports be brought back to a stage in which they can be enjoyed by large numbers of students and where they do not involve an expenditure of time and money wholly at variance with any ideal of honest study.[35]

Policy Reform and the Problem of Nostalgia

Howard Savage and the Carnegie Foundation research staff succumbed to the pitfalls of nostalgia in their recommendation that college sports ought be returned to their rightful place as a program run by and for students. "Student control" was no assurance of proper balance because, as historian Laurence Veysey noted about American undergraduate life between 1870 and 1910, there was a wide gulf between faculty and students.[36] At many colleges, student-controlled athletic associations of the early 1900s were autonomous entities, with football fundraising controlled by students—and sometimes students were in concert with alumni. As Henry Seidel Canby recalled about Yale and sister institutions at the turn of the century in his memoir, *Alma Mater: The Gothic Age of the American College:*

> And there were the Strong Silent Men I had read about in the newspapers, the football and crew heroes, calming the crowded field by the full-breasted dignity of the white letters on their blue sweaters. And there were the other slighter figures in tiny top coats with upturned collars, who seemed to exercise an equal authority. These, I was told, were the Big Men, the managers, the powers behind college life, more important, because brainier, than the athletes. These were the real masters of this new [campus] state.[37]

The student culture of the American college of the 1890s was organized, with athletic teams and clubs that were beyond control by university presidents, deans, and faculty. In some cases, alumni continued their participation in the extracurricular life. Student and alumni coalitions, for example, initiated the practice of hiring professional trainers and paid coaches. In the early 1900s, presidents and deans attempted to corral and co-opt these organizations, with limited success.

The impotence of the NCAA raises a crucial point for responding to Savage's 1929 call for a restoration of student control of athletics. Savage argued that the abuses of the period 1905 to 1929 represented an erosion of a once admirable intercollegiate athletic arrangement, implying that somehow things had gone awry. Smith's, Miller's, and Watterson's respective historical researches indicate a different view of the college sports heritage: it had not fallen into disrepute in the 1920s, because from the start it had been characterized by commercialism and cheating.[38] How could a state that had never existed be restored? In looking back at the commercialism of college sports in the 1890s, it is often inaccurate to say that the practices were illegal. Rather, they were unregulated, because there were no rules to break.

The Health of College Athletics: Lessons from the Medical Model?

Pritchett's commentaries did not speak explicitly to the matter of *how* the report's proposed changes in organizational behavior were to diffuse from the foundation report to the campus. The best estimate is that the Savage report might work the same wholesale reform on college sports as Flexner's Carnegie Foundation for the Advancement of Teaching report supposedly had done with the elimination of academically and financially marginal medical schools. Comparing the two reports is intriguing, since, as noted earlier, Flexner's 1910 study of medical education and Savage's 1929 analysis of college athletics were by far the most controversial studies commissioned by the Carnegie Foundation. One other reason comparison is logical is that, in both cases, administrators at many institutions under scrutiny (whether athletic programs or medical schools) believed the rumor that the Carnegie Foundation was considering substantially endowing programs. These expectations were unfulfilled because in both medical education and college sports, the foundation's role was to study, not to subsidize.

According to the approach exemplified by the Flexner report on medical schools, institutional reform was predicated on the belief that exposing dubious practices would lead indicted organizations to shut down. The problem with this strategy was that there was little confirmation of a cause-effect relation between research and reform. The "success" often attributed to Flexner's study in closing shoddy medical schools was both exceptional and exaggerated. The legacy of Flexner's Carnegie Foundation study as a model reform instrument wanes in the light of historical analysis, which shows that problems of licensing, rising costs, and expenses of new equipment, meant that economic conditions, rather than the Flexner reform report, purged the medical education ranks.[39]

Was there a comparable purge of "bad" football programs at colleges and universities? One does find after 1905 some move to drop football programs. Stanford, California, and Columbia opted for rugby for a few years; elsewhere, there were scattered examples of colleges abolishing football. But this was a premature obituary for football programs, because most colleges that had dropped the sport eventually resumed it; and reinstatement still left unresolved questions of control, although progress was made in the conduct of the game and in safety provisions on the field. Furthermore, the decision to abolish football was usually not based on economic grounds. To the contrary, even in the mid-1920s, many presidents of small, struggling colleges embraced varsity football as a good investment by which to produce income from gate receipts and to catapult their campus into national prominence. The costs could be kept down by avoiding construction of one's own stadium; in fact, the best strategy for a rising new college football team was to play popular teams whose games were covered by major newspapers, at a large stadium. The result was that a football season resembled a barnstorming tour, with student-athletes spending days, often weeks, away from campus. Nowhere was this formula better illustrated than at little Centre College of Kentucky, whose Praying Colonels team gained a national following when they played a series of games against Harvard. Even defeat brought favorable publicity; and, when the Centre team defeated the prominent Harvard team, its football fame skyrocketed and became part of the heroic history of the college.[40] Hence, a frequent consideration by college presidents in the 1920s was, If it worked for Centre College, why not for our campus?

The example of Centre College and dozens of other small institutions attempting to emulate the established programs of Yale, Notre Dame, and the University of Southern California underscored another factor that limited the applicability of the Flexner Report to the Savage Report: the "bad" programs in medical education and intercollegiate athletics often were of opposite character. The scourge of medical education typically was the small, financially impoverished, freestanding medical school that lacked faculty and facilities and was susceptible to any venture or compelled to admit any paying student in order to survive. In contrast, the problem child of intercollegiate athletics was the large, prosperous athletic program that brought in and spent inordinate money and whose achievements enabled the program to go beyond academic control. In sum, reform of medical schools called for focus on its numerous weak institutions, whereas reform of college sports demanded that the large, successful athletic departments be brought to heel.

Then there was the question of a program's institutional affiliation.

The problem of small, weak medical schools in the early 1900s could often be remedied by bringing the freestanding medical schools into the university structure. University affiliation promoted academic oversight to ensure that admissions, instruction, and certification were in line with the university's other degree-granting programs. Unfortunately, this strategy had limited applicability to policing athletic programs. Regulating college sports was harder than shoring up medical departments, since varsity programs already were part of the university. The unresolved problem was that varsity athletic departments were affixed to the institution but not integrated into the curriculum.

The model of medical education reform was incongruent with college sports reform for another essential reason. Medical schools were central to the educational mission, whereas athletic programs were (and would continue to be) extracurricular. Hence, a "good" medical school was characterized by high admissions standards, faculty scholarship, adequate laboratories and equipment, and student academic achievement, along with ample size and resources. In contrast, a "sound" athletic program, as defined by Howard Savage or Henry Pritchett, was not the same as a "successful" program, as envisioned by a coach or an athletic director. For the professional coaches and athletic directors in college sports, a program would ultimately be judged by nonacademic indicators: winning teams, fan support, ticket sales, and gate receipts.

Another difference in reform strategies was that varsity sports, unlike medical schools, were at heart a cooperative activity in that college teams played against one another. They were, by definition, *intercollegiate,* unless one wanted sports to be limited to an intramural event. The implication was that individual initiative by isolated college presidents and boards was an unlikely route for effective nationwide college sports reform. Collective solutions would ultimately be necessary, yet each college or university was quite free to strike its own deal with other institutions. There was no counterpart to medical education's licensing requirements that would declare an institution's athletics program to be deficient or ineligible to operate. What is not clear is the extent to which Pritchett and the Carnegie Foundation research staff envisioned the National Collegiate Athletic Association as an appropriate, effective organization for reform and regulation.

Given Pritchett's fondness for raising standards via voluntary associations, a curious omission in the Carnegie Foundation study of college sports is the lack of discussion about regional accreditation as a reform vehicle. Accreditation was in line with Pritchett's gospel of social efficiency and educational improvement. Regional accreditation associations avoided government intrusion, left initiative and control to colleges, emphasized academic standards, and promoted sound administration. Here was a logical organization by which to connect athletics to the educational priorities of an institution. By 1930 the absence of any such connection meant that reform would be carried out by individual institutions and their selective, voluntary membership in such athletic bodies as the NCAA and athletic conferences. There was no compelling historical evidence that a return to student control or a reliance on the external economy would reform intercollegiate athletics, at least in the manner that either Henry Pritchett or Howard Savage had in mind. Answers to questions about the influence of Savage's *American College Athletics* would be found not by looking backward for legacies from a nostalgic depiction of undergraduate life or from lessons provided by reforms in medicine and professional schools. The contours of institutional and policy reform in American intercollegiate sports would be found by looking forward to the unexpected consequences that followed from disparate responses to the Savage Report between 1930 and 1946.

· · · · · · · · · · · · · · ·

CHAPTER TWO

Responses to Reform, 1930 to 1946

Did intercollegiate athletics undergo reform after 1929? What was the impact of Howard Savage's Carnegie Foundation report, *American College Athletics*, in changing the attitudes, structures, and policies that characterized varsity sports? In the two years following publication of "Bulletin Number Twenty-three," several constituencies sought prompt answers to these questions. Foremost was the Carnegie Foundation for the Advancement of Teaching, which was understandably concerned about the consequences of the report it had sponsored, leading it to commission a follow-up study. Another prominent source of inquiry was the Associated Press, whose extensive survey of college and university presidents and athletic officials was published in a series of newspaper articles in 1931. In the same year, the U.S. Office of Education released its findings on the finances and operation of college sports at land-grant institutions. Taken together, these were the first returns on the report card for college sports reform.

The rush to judgment soon after publication of *American College Athletics* was symptomatic of an eagerness for results that often blurred the lines between analysis and advocacy. Attempts to reconcile the respective findings from these disparate studies generated more heat than light since their data were often incomplete or in conflict. The net contribution of the evaluations by the Carnegie Foundation, the Associated Press, and the Office of Education was to raise troubling questions about the connections between research and reform, rather than to provide definitive answers about the changing character of college sports. Ironically, the one clear finding that emerged from the varied responses to the 1929 study was that there was no consensus among higher education leaders about the direction intercollegiate athletics policies were taking—or ought to take—over the next decade.

The Deflation of College Football

The Carnegie Foundation for the Advancement of Teaching commissioned Howard Savage to analyze his own 1929 study. His follow-up report was published in June 1931 as "Bulletin Number Twenty-six," *Current Developments in American College Sport*.[1] Although it received less publicity than Savage's "Bulletin Number Twenty-three," it managed to sustain debate in the press and among college presidents, coaches, and athletic directors. Its major finding was to report a trend away from commercialism in intercollegiate athletics. The study was optimistic about the growth of intramural sports and physical education programs within colleges. It also provided a forum for reinforcement of themes that had been introduced in 1929. The new president of the Carnegie Foundation, Henry Suzzallo, successor to Henry Pritchett, wrote in April 1931 that "final responsibility for the effective administration of American college sport belongs not to the alumnus, the downtown business man, or the newspaper writer, but to university or college officers." Suzzallo offered his "somewhat" reassuring conclusion that Savage's follow-up study pointed to both immediate and future improvement. At the same time the new president of the Carnegie Foundation warned that "administrative confusion" about the proper control of college sports programs still represented a "serious impairment of the product of our secondary and higher education."[2]

Savage and his research team were confident that they had documented what they called the "changing character of college sports." Their claim was that a "renewed emphasis is being placed upon the amateur status" and that there was an "appreciation of the spirit" of sports for sports' own sake that was "stirring numbers of American undergraduates."[3] Implicit in their conclusion was that college sports represented a zero-sum proposition: that is, an increased interest in student participation in recreational activities meant a decline in commercialized varsity athletics programs. Savage repeated his 1929 theme that colleges should "give the game back to the boys," noting that "concerning the changing relation of undergraduates to college sport, little remains to be said. The increasing popularity of intramural athletics speaks for itself."[4] The corollary was the bold announcement that "the deflation of American football has begun." Savage noted, "In many respects it is an unpleasant process. Yet the poverty that results from a decline in football gate receipts will lighten parts of the task of those who administer college athletics. The return to a more sincere appreciation of the values of sport and sportsmanship is under way. The road, at times, seems long, but the American college will not weary in well-doing."[5]

For impartial readers, the problem was to distinguish wishful thinking from actual achievements because the Carnegie Foundation's decision to have Howard Savage and his research team evaluate their own original report was susceptible to the self-fulfilling prophecy. In support of their optimistic conclusion, the report authors cited examples from alumni associations and athletic conferences that indicated signs of hope for an essential change in attitude and expectations. There also were selected data on the finances of college sports that lent credibility to the observation that college sports were losing both spectator appeal and undergraduate support. This in turn was reinforced by examples of increased involvement of presidents at influential universities in collective discussions about the future of college sports.

Some noteworthy external events supported this latter observation. For example, in 1931 Charles W. Kennedy, president of Princeton, was elected president of the National Collegiate Athletic Association. Further evidence of cooperation among influential academic institutions was that when Kennedy accepted the NCAA leadership, he gained as an ally James R. Angell, president of Yale, who pledged support and unity. Both gave major addresses to the 1931 NCAA convention, emphasizing commitment to strong varsity sports programs while seeking to reduce the influence of fans, spectators, and other external audiences.[6] In addition to the promising evidence and the public commitment of the presidents of Yale and Princeton to be leaders in the NCAA, Howard Savage's reform campaign received added momentum from both old and new academic reformers in higher education. The former included the veteran of Carnegie Foundation studies: Abraham Flexner. The latter was represented by Robert Maynard Hutchins, the newly inaugurated, outspoken president of the University of Chicago.

Flexner on Football

The fact that Flexner had taken time to read Savage's 1929 report, *American College Athletics*, established continuity in the Carnegie Foundation's efforts to raise American educational standards over three decades. It reaffirmed Flexner's close ties with Henry Pritchett (Flexner would later be Pritchett's biographer). It showed that comparing Flexner's 1910 study of medical education with Savage's 1929 analysis of American college athletics as a model of reform strategy was not a spurious association.[7] The two reports were spiritually and intellectually connected parts of a sustained reform effort. Flexner's 1930 book, *Universities: American, English, German*, was his grand attempt to provide a comprehensive, critical analysis of American higher education, an expanded version of the microscope and scalpel he had earlier applied to medical schools in the United States and Canada. And it included specific attention to the abuses of intercollegiate athletics.

If Flexner's report worked for substantial change in medical education in 1910, why not try the same formula for the entire American university two decades later? This time Flexner and Savage reversed roles. Whereas in 1910 Flexner's study set the standard, in 1930 the veteran reformer deferred to the younger Carnegie Foundation analyst's work. Flexner began his critique of intercollegiate athletics by citing Savage's report:

> They are all mad on the subject of competitive and intercollegiate athletics—too timid to tell their respective alumni that excessive interest in intercollegiate athletics is proof of the cultural mediocrity of the college graduate, and a source of continuous demoralization to successive college classes, not a few members of which are forced to simulate an interest they do not feel. The colleges cannot except very slowly improve the secondary schools, for their own graduates—not usually the most vigorous, scholarly, or ambitious—become high school teachers; they cannot rapidly improve the quality of their own faculties, for that depends on education, salaries, and social prestige—all slow and difficult to change; but they could, given the courage and intelligence, frankly tell the world that their problem is infinitely complicated by giving loose rein to the athletic orgy in order to amuse and placate a populace, largely consisting of their own graduates. There is not a college or university in America which has the courage to place athletics

where every one perfectly well knows they belong. On the contrary, as we shall see, proportionately more money is spent on college athletics than on any legitimate college activity. The football coach is better known to the student body and the general public than the president; and, professors are, on the average, less highly remunerated. Does the college or university have to endure this? Of course not. But it does more than endure: it "advertises."[8]

Flexner's central exhibit was the football program at the University of Chicago: at two of the most prominent crossings in Chicago, huge painted signboards fifteen feet high and fifty feet long proclaimed, "The University of Chicago Announces Its Football Schedule for 1928," which included games against the University of South Carolina, Ripon College, the University of Wyoming, Lake Forest College, and such nationally ranked teams as Purdue and the universities of Iowa, Minnesota, Pennsylvania, and Wisconsin. These advertisements were exhibited for two and a half months and cost the university five hundred dollars a month each. According to Flexner, the disappointing dilemma was, "Does the university tolerate an unavoidable evil or exploit a demoralizing appetite?"[9] In retrospect, Flexner's 1930 discussion and Savage's 1929 report were markedly harmonious, although each followed a separate logical path. Whereas Savage used intercollegiate athletics as the starting point to reach the conclusion that the American campus was intellectually diluted, Flexner's starting point was what he considered a weak educational core of the institution; this fundamental weakness led him to focus on athletics as part of the larger problem of educational incoherence and anti-intellectualism.

A year after Flexner had cited the University of Chicago's football billboards and powerful athletic program as the epitome of overemphasis, there was evidence that the views of Flexner and Savage were starting to take hold. Nowhere was this more evident than in the example of the new, young president of the University of Chicago, Robert Maynard Hutchins. Not only did Hutchins agree with Flexner, Savage, and Pritchett about the dangers of overemphasizing college sports for the mission of the university, he moved decisively to change the character of undergraduate education at his own campus, as shown in his 1931 manifesto about what he thought college was *not*:

College is *not* a great athletic association and social club, in which provision is made, merely incidentally, for intellectual activity on the part of the physically and socially unfit. College *is* an association of scholars in which provision is made for the development of traits and powers which must be cultivated, in addition to those which are purely intellectual, if one is to become a well-balanced and useful member of any community.[10]

During his tenure as president of the University of Chicago, Hutchins turned rhetoric into reality. The single greatest transformation of an institution's varsity athletic policy in the aftermath of the critical reports by Savage and Flexner was the change in the football program at the University of Chicago, a charter member of the Big Ten and often a powerhouse well after World War I. Its founding president, William Rainey Harper, recognized the magnetism of winning teams as part of civic and institutional publicity. Several University of Chicago star players had been named to the All-American team. It claimed the first recipient of the Heisman Trophy, which honors the outstanding college football player in the nation, as well as a rich tradition of famous coaches, including Amos Alonzo Stagg and Clark Shaughnessy. Despite this heritage, the program underwent persistent deemphasis throughout the 1930s, with varsity football being dropped in 1939—an event that fulfilled Henry Pritchett's claim that college sports reform would come of age if and when a major university would set such a precedent.[11]

Hutchins's support for the abolition of varsity football at the University of Chicago was an extreme extension of the purification process that Pritchett and Flexner advocated for creating the "real" American university. As Pritchett had emphasized in his prelude to the 1929 Carnegie Foundation report by Howard Savage, "We cannot serve every cause—scholarship, science, business, salesmanship, organized athletics—through the university. The need to-day is to re-examine our educational regime with the determination to attain in greater measure the simplicity, sincerity, and thoroughness that is the life blood of a true university in any country at any age."[12]

Did Reforms Take Place?

The reform initiative personified by Savage, Flexner, Pritchett, and Hutchins commanded national attention, but it was hardly the whole story. By early 1931 there were signs that the Carnegie study, publicly acclaimed in principle in 1929 and 1930, did not evoke wholesale changes. The *New York Times* reported that college athletic officials were "widely split in their reaction to the inquiry of the Associated Press: 'What, if any, changes have been manifest since the publication a year ago of the Carnegie Report on subsidizing and recruiting?' . . . A substantial majority, perhaps two out of every three to whom the inquiry was addressed, side-stepped the issue by giving a flat negative reply."

According to the same article, opinions varied. The athletic director at the University of Maryland said he believed that the Carnegie Report "gave an impetus to recruiting." At the other extreme, the athletic director at the University of Nebraska said that the report forced a "much more rigid check-up of athletic subsidizing and recruiting." Problems were brought into the open; however, "the remedies, it seems, are as varied as the conditions themselves, but there has unquestionably developed a widespread attempt by prominent leaders in every section to eradicate alleged evils."[13]

In fact, this last "unquestionable" claim was no longer uncontested. Indicative of the inconclusive data and varied opinions about the 1929 report's impact was an article that called the Carnegie report "fruitless." For example, officials representing the major Southern football programs, including the universities of South Carolina, Tennessee, Kentucky, and Alabama Polytechnic (later to become Auburn University), reported their opinion that the Carnegie report "had no effect whatsoever." Athletic directors, faculty advisers, and publicity directors at southern colleges and universities "are overwhelmingly of the belief that the publication of Carnegie Bulletin No. 23 has had little if any effect in their territory." The director of athletics at Vanderbilt said, "I do not see any evidence of any changes generally." Dean S. V. Sanford, of the University of Georgia, stood apart from his southern university colleagues by praising the Carnegie report, stating, "It has been accepted as a real asset." Even this endorsement was vague about exactly which reforms were to be implemented.

The attitudinal survey that hinted at dissolution of support for the Savage study reflected regional differences, especially when the Carnegie Foundation report was depicted as a product of the East Coast establishment. Factions also included differences within institutions, as presidents were not always in accord with athletic directors. After having allowed the initial reform campaign to pass, institutions started to assert their disagreement. How could there be consensus on reforms when there was no agreement on what editorial writers had called the "evils of athletics recruiting and subsidies"? In contrast to the widespread public endorsements of the principles of the Savage Report in 1929, by 1931 some athletic directors and coaches denied the existence of a college sports "problem."

As part of the commentary gathered in the Associated Press survey, officials representing the southern universities were asked, "Do you think college football is over-emphasized?" The answer, according to the Associated Press, was unanimous: "a ringing, 'No!'" The Vanderbilt athletic director elaborated, "I do not think football is over-emphasized so far as students and players are concerned, although it apparently is in the minds of a certain element of the public." His statement was puzzling because he also told the Associated Press that there was a strong need for "sharp action to curb subsidizing and recruiting." According to the athletic director at the University of Maryland, "There is no such thing as over-emphasis in college football in the sense that the word is generally used. However, there are some things in college football that might well be rectified." Elsewhere, one prominent coach from the Midwest disagreed with the Carnegie Foundation's charges that college football was "over-commercialized." In his opinion, the problem was that it was "not commercialized enough," because college officials had not fully tapped the revenue-producing potential of spectator sports.[14]

Around the same time that Savage and Flexner were citing data to indicate optimism about declining commercialism, other sources reported troubling news. Most important was the U.S. Office of Education's study of college sports programs at sixty-nine land-grant universities. According to the summary released on New Year's Day 1931, the major characteristic of intercollegiate athletics at these institutions was a "great emphasis on winning."

Most of the state universities used an "athletic board" arrangement for college sports—some combination of alumni, students, and administrators. The biggest surprise of the land-grant study was its criticism of *student* control of athletic programs. Contrary to Howard Savage's 1929 idyllic recommendation, the federal study noted that the worst abuses in commercialization occurred where students controlled the program, especially at four major public universities on the West Coast. Again, contrary to Savage's depiction, the report observed that "students tend to overemphasize athletics. Student migrations to great out-of-town games cause the most worry to the administration." The land-grant institution study's recommendation for structural and governance reform was to locate control with academic officers, a "passing of control from students to administration," to stem the rising enthusiasm for football. It recommended that programs in health and recreation not be tied to intercollegiate athletics but be funded as any other educational department.

The study commanded attention because it analyzed established football programs at large state universities in the Midwest and West. Specifically, it included the universities of Illinois, California, Ohio State, Cornell, Minnesota, Purdue, Maryland, and Texas A&M, as well as Utah Agricultural College. Among the highest totals in gate receipts from football per campus were $500,000, with some at $400,000 and $350,000, amounts that made college football a "big business." According to the report, "Eleven schools admitted recruiting seniors from high schools for freshman football squads but all protested ignorance of subsidizing of players. Each denied existence of loan funds for athletes only. Practically all reported coaches' salaries higher than professors'."[15] The alleged deflation of football heralded by Howard Savage's report on current developments in college sports apparently had yet to reach the land-grant universities.

Economic Indicators and the Finances of College Sports Programs

For Howard Savage and the Carnegie Foundation research team, bad news about the economic condition of college sports programs was good news for reform. Declining attendance and reduced gate receipts were harsh yet necessary medicine to purge the abuses of the highly commercialized college football programs. And, congruent with Savage's 1931 follow-up study, most data indicated that intercollegiate athletic programs were starting to show signs of financial strain. For example, reports from forty-nine colleges indicated a total football attendance of about 3.6 million in 1929, followed by a decline to about 3.3 million in 1930. For the same institutions, football gate receipts went from just over $9 million in 1929 to about $8.4 million a year later.

Identifying a large athletic budget in the 1930s is an inexact exercise. Across the nation, eight universities showed annual football revenues over $500,000. Most big-time football programs brought in at least $100,000 in gate receipts. The best estimate was that the seemingly robust athletic budgets at the large universities were enjoying a temporary reprieve from problems encountered by most institutions. Shortly after release of the U.S. Office of Education's study of land-grant institutions, fresh data pointed to signs of a serious nationwide economic shake-out in college sports. According to a survey conducted by the Associated Press in 1931, college football was "facing a crisis" precipitated by the collision of "over-emphasis and reduced income." The finding was that "college athletics in general and football in particular, still suffering somewhat from the growing pains of super-salesmanship and ballyhoo have been abruptly brought face to face with somewhat critical conditions for 1931."[16] Along with mention of the evils (and expenses) of recruiting and subsidizing student-athletes, the Associated Press reported that college officials were considering such cost-saving measures as reducing schedules, eliminating spring football practice, and abolishing varsity training tables. Some colleges reported that they had drastically cut budgets for recruiting potential student-athletes.[17]

The policy implications of the economic condition of college football in 1930 became more complex when the data were disaggregated by region and institutional type. Financial problems appeared to have been most severe for college athletic programs in the East and South. At Harvard, for example, football revenues of about $700,000 were among the highest in the nation; but these were offset by athletic department expenditures of more than $1,000,000. Yale's receipts for football were even higher than Harvard's, due in large part to the extraordinary seating capacity of the Yale Bowl. Both Harvard and Yale were exceptional in that they sponsored a large number of varsity sports, most of which generated little revenue.

In contrast to the athletic department deficits at the eastern universities, the major football schools on the West Coast were enjoying a "prosperous year" and expressed no intent to cut back their athletic programs. The graduate manager at the University of Washington said, "The tendency at Washington and I believe at all other schools in the Pacific Northwest is to expand rather than curtail." Plans included stadium expansion in the cities of Portland and Seattle, where attendance for intercollegiate football had included sellout crowds at several games. In California, gate receipts declined slightly for Stanford and the University of California, but they claimed relatively high revenues of $499,822 and $615,000, respectively. In Los Angeles, the University of Southern California reported increased revenues for the 1930 season, exceeding $500,000 in football gate receipts. Although intercollegiate football programs in the Rocky Mountain region could not match the Pacific Coast programs, they showed gains in attendance and revenues.[18]

Two years later, the economic shake-out for athletic departments continued. Officials at Harvard discussed the idea of reducing the football schedule from eight games to seven by 1932, and even considered reduction to a six-game schedule by 1933. Princeton had already limited its varsity football season to seven games.[19] This was a puzzling strategy that seemed counterproductive. If the aim was to balance the athletic budget, it meant that the football program would be losing two games from which to generate revenues, without reducing such fixed costs as coaching staff salaries.

At most colleges, however, cutting back on varsity football programs was usually a last resort. During the Great Depression, the first and typical adjustment for an athletic director was to protect football at the expense of other sports so that the so-called minor teams and nonrevenue sports were the first to be canceled. For example, in January 1933 Cornell and Syracuse responded to revenue shortfalls by canceling most of their winter and spring sports. In a similar vein, the University of Wisconsin suspended its varsity crew program.[20]

The deflation of football was likely to take place at small private colleges where athletic departments encountered financial problems after 1929. Ernest H. Wilkins, president of Oberlin College in Ohio, undertook a survey of revenues and expenses for football at small colleges and found that only two of twenty-two respondents showed a surplus for football (one for $79, the other for $1,492). Annual football program deficits ranged from $268 to $5,530, while expenses for a small college football program ranged from $3,829 to $18,050. Once again, there was reasonable doubt that Howard Savage's belief that financial decline would foster reforms was working, because despite these financial losses, it was not evident that small colleges were reducing or eliminating varsity football. Wilkins, for example, concluded his study with these wry observations: "Football is made possible for colleges of this group and for others which they typify, by the use of funds given or paid for educational purposes"; and, "Realization that this is the case should lead those responsible for college budgets to ask themselves more carefully than ever whether the intercollegiate football program is justified as an 'educational' expense."[21] Apparently, the answer for many colleges was that even a financial shortfall need not jeopardize institutional commitment to varsity football.

How can the economic data be incorporated into Pritchett's vision of the Carnegie Foundation for the Advancement of Teaching as a force for raising educational standards in the United States? Counting on the Great Depression to place a financial strain on college sports programs was a perverse solution of sorts in that it forced an institution to make hard choices. This sudden reversal of fortune meant that in some ways intercollegiate athletics did appear to be following the model for educational improvement espoused by Pritchett several decades earlier when the Carnegie Foundation sponsored a number of measures designed to move American higher education away from a preponderance of small, academically weak, financially starved colleges. In other words, college sports programs of 1930 (not unlike colleges in 1910) were increasingly standardized, governed by rules and procedures, and forced to confront a harsh economic environment. "Minor" sports that were "weak" (i.e., did not generate revenue) tended to be eliminated. The survival of football at major universities suggested that the economic depression was in accord with Pritchett's strategy because it did promote excellence on a large scale.[22]

The problem is that Pritchett probably assumed that such developments within the university structure would be in concert with standards dictated by academics. He neglected to acknowledge the concept of parallel tracks within a campus. Most important, Pritchett probably underestimated the organization and insularity of a new breed of athletic directors and coaches whose priority was to protect their own intercollegiate sports programs, not the curriculum. A college's athletic program often was a self-contained unit in which realignments were distinct from academic priorities. The paradox of Henry Pritchett's preference for survival of large, strong institutions was that it was a dysfunctional approach to eliminating the excesses of college sports. When applied to intercollegiate athletics, it meant that the very programs Pritchett wanted to curb—large, commercialized football programs—were strongest and most likely to survive. It also illustrated an essential difference of opinion within American higher education. Whereas Pritchett, Flexner, and Hutchins saw intercollegiate athletics as a peripheral activity, many other college presidents and trustees did not.

The reformers were out of touch with many colleges and universities. A good illustration is provided by Abraham Flexner, who early in the 1900s was most impressed with the Johns Hopkins University as a model institution. Hopkins was one of the few universities in the United States that paid little attention to undergraduate life, including intercollegiate sports. Flexner's penchant for institutions outside the mainstream continued throughout his career. In 1937 he was named the first director of the Institute for Advanced Study, housed in Princeton, New Jersey. Finally, Flexner had found his ideal American campus, which concentrated on scholarship without the distractions of undergraduates who were not committed to serious study and which lacked extracurricular activities and intercollegiate athletics. Since the Institute for Advanced Study was unique, it was an inappropriate and unlikely model for colleges to emulate: not only did it lack undergraduate students, but it offered no courses and conferred no degrees. It was not a realistic option for college and university presidents whose institutions were obligated to serve large, diverse constituencies by offering a range of programs and services. For the mainstream of American higher education, including presidents and boards, as well as students, alumni, and external publics, varsity sports were often as valued as academics—or were even of paramount importance within the life of the institution.

When Howard Savage found in 1931 that the athletic programs of "four out of five colleges have been forced to economize or curtail activities," the implication was that this signaled substantive reform.[23] In some exceptional cases, this may have been so. But Savage's model for reform failed to acknowledge other contingencies that followed from the data on declines in revenues and attendance. In sum, Howard Savage and the Carnegie Foundation research team misread the implications of the economic data for institutional behavior and policy change. They put too much stock in immediate economic problems as being one and the same as college officials' concerns about the ethics of subsidies, recruiting, and commercialism associated with college sports. In fact, the athletic department budget shortfalls meant that questions of propriety could be at least temporarily avoided. Also, the Carnegie Foundation researchers underestimated the enduring appeal that college football held for the American public. As Foster Rhea Dulles observed in his classic 1940 essay, "Drawing the Big Crowds":

> In many ways the outstanding spectator sport of the 1920's and 1930's was intercollegiate football. It had a far larger following than the relatively select crowds that had originally supported it, the short fall season representing for countless sports enthusiasts the climax of the year. The millions who every Saturday afternoon made their way to the games were supplemented by many more millions who hovered over their radios in comfortable steam-heated living rooms to follow them play by play, and then spent Sunday mornings devouring long accounts in the sports section of how it all had happened. Football reigned supreme from the opening of early-season practice to the Tournament of Roses. "It is at present a religion," a contributor to *Harper's* stated in 1928—"sometimes it seems to be almost our national religion."[24]

A modest decline in football attendance for two years during a severe national depression did not necessarily mean that the public had lost interest in college sports. It could equally well indicate a temporary disruption because consumers had less discretionary income. They would resume buying college football tickets in the future when times were more prosperous. When Savage analyzed his follow-up data in 1931, he did not know whether the American public had shifted its sports interest elsewhere. Again, Foster Rhea Dulles's analysis provided insight that tempered the contention that a decline in attendance meant public disenchantment with commercialized college football:

> But the general public, and also the greater part of the nation's college alumni, only asked for more victories. Their attitude toward the criticism voiced by the professorial fraternity was aptly expressed in an editorial in *Liberty*. This popular magazine found the protesting faculty members jealous. "The problem is not the elimination or restriction of football," *Liberty* warned, "but how long it will be before red-blooded colleges demand the elimination or the restriction of those afflicted with this inferiority complex."[25]

Furthermore, reforming the essence of university athletics could not rely only on the external circumstances of "lean times" as a convenient stimulus. The test was also to confront the issues of recruiting and subsidization in "normal" or flush economic times. The depressed economic situation was not necessarily the source of an ethical solution because it left unanswered the question of how college sports programs would look and behave once the national and institutional economies rebounded. So, although Howard Savage believed that the economic problems confronting college sports programs in the early 1930s were signs of ethical qualms about the propriety of big-time athletics, in many cases they may well have been nothing more than straightforward manifestations of financial constraints.

Then there was the unexpected complexity of organizational behavior. It was true that lean times in the national economy and in a campus's finances forced a college or university to prune programs and reexamine priorities. More often than not, the pruning took place in academics, not athletics. Howard Savage tended to be tied to the conventional wisdom that when a college or university had diminishing resources, it first cut peripheral programs and activities not central to a university's educational mission. From the perspective of Pritchett and Flexner, this, of course, would mean that intercollegiate athletics were expendable. This rationale, although plausible, was simplistic because in the 1930s historians, sociologists, and economists were charting a more interesting, complex pattern of behavior as they discovered that people and organizations often responded to economic upheaval by salvaging the "frills" and abandoning staples. This is precisely what George Orwell found in his studies of poverty in England in his 1937 book, *The Road to Wigan Pier:* the unemployed working-class family preferred to savor the daily cup of tea with cookies and sweets rather than to buy vegetables.[26] For the American public, watching college football games or Hollywood movies provided a great diversion from the Great Depression. To understand the dynamics of college sports in the 1930s called for new interpretations of consumer behavior.

Perhaps the same principle George Orwell found in grocery shopping by unemployed families applied to budgeting at American colleges and universities, where faculty salaries often were "sweated" to protect varsity football. A good example was Southern Methodist University, in Dallas, where an ambitious athletic department built a large football stadium in the late 1920s. In 1931, when the university was hard pressed to meet mortgage payments, the board's solution was to finance the new stadium by garnisheeing faculty wages.[27]

The economics of higher education were only one part of the puzzle to explain, let alone to reform, developments in college sports. Direct attention needed to be paid to the structure and control of intercollegiate athletics in the years following publication of Savage's *American College Athletics*.

Conferences and Signs of Cooperation and Consolidation

Reliance on the external economy to reduce college sports expenditures was unwise because there was no assurance that program budgets would stay low once the economy rebounded. If reforms in the commercialization of college athletics were to endure, the need was for structural changes among institutions. Cooperation and consolidation to strengthen intercollegiate athletic conferences were signs that colleges themselves initiated reform.

The conference was the crucial collective unit for instilling standards in college sports. A league of eight to ten institutions was more important for shaping academic eligibility requirements and recruiting limits than was membership in a national association. The developments that characterized the growing strength of intercollegiate athletic conferences after 1929 included adopting restrictions on athletic scholarships, standardizing schedules to limit the numbers of games and practices, mutual agreements on recruiting practices, inclusion of university faculty representatives in conference discussions and governance, regulating player eligibility, and professionalizing athletic administration. Foremost among these changes was the emergence of the paid conference commissioner to oversee enforcement of conference regulations. Commissioners often had a background in military service or law enforcement, leading sportswriters to call them "conference czars."

The influential conference to which most colleges and universities looked for advice as a vigilant, organized group was the Big Ten. Known as the "Giants of the Midwest," its members were the universities of Chicago, Minnesota, Wisconsin, Iowa, Illinois, Michigan, and Indiana, along with Purdue, Northwestern, and Ohio State. Formed in 1895, the midwestern universities' alliance initially was snubbed by the historic eastern colleges. The conference's history through the 1920s was checkered with serious violations, first at one institution, then at another. In 1923, the Big Ten created a committee to curb alumni in recruiting and paying student-athletes. This turned out to be no threat to uncontrolled alumni boosters. But the conference countered by giving increased regulatory power to the conference staff in tandem with faculty athletic representatives.

Ironically, this was the same conference that Howard Savage had subjected to criticism in his 1929 report. The Big Ten was the first conference to have a paid conference commissioner. Its codes on faculty control, student eligibility, and athletic scholarships were emulated by many conferences and eventually by the National Collegiate Athletic Association. And the Big Ten showed resolution to enforce its regulations when in 1929 it expelled the University of Iowa for violating recruiting codes. According to Big Ten chroniclers, Iowa's "infractions of an athletic nature" meant that the athletic department and its associated alumni groups were operating outside the university administration's control. Among the violations were that "athletes were given a share of commissions on sale of yearbooks," along with "utilization of a businessmen's slush fund to subsidize teams, refund of tuition fees, and failure to certify athletes as bona fide students."[28]

Whether Henry Pritchett liked it or not, the Big Ten embodied his American institutional efficiency model applied to intercollegiate athletics. Its members were large universities whose athletic programs were well financed; its staff was professionalized and relied on expertise from both its coaches and its athletic directors; its teams were powerful and conference standards promoted competitive achievement. Most of all, it was highly organized. Universities who belonged to the conference took sports seriously so that at best its teams were both accomplished and regulated. It stood for an interesting ideal of athletic excellence combined with compliance to the rules that its members themselves had set. In the 1930s, the Big Ten was truly All-American. From time to time, the conference flexed its muscles in confrontations with member institutions. In 1936, the conference threatened to expel the University of Wisconsin because the university's Board of Regents attempted to fire the football coach and the athletic director. The Big Ten asserted its principle that the faculty representatives, not the university regents, had ultimate power in college athletic programs.

Another emerging group was the Pacific Coast Conference, which followed the Big Ten example by establishing a league office and hiring a professional commissioner. Like the Big Ten, its members were large universities with strong football programs who stood for enforcement rather than deemphasis. The best illustration of this vigilance came in

1933 when the conference commissioner, Edward Atherton, drafted the so-called Atherton Code of student-athlete conduct. Atherton was a former FBI agent who made good on his pledge to scrutinize how Pacific Coast Conference universities conducted their varsity sports programs. Between 1939 and 1940, after a few years of apparent inactivity, the commissioner distributed sections of his monumental report on violations of conference regulations. The Atherton Report was thousands of pages in length, a clinically detailed account of abuses large and small that served notice to athletic directors and coaches that the conference staff and its faculty advisers took their charge seriously.[29]

Elsewhere, colleges and universities formed associations to regulate the subsidizing and recruiting of student-athletes. For example, in 1931 a group of large southern universities declared that they were going to ban recruiting, a move hailed as a "victory for a united declaration for 'unquestioned amateurism' in sports."[30] Two years later, some of these institutions formed a rump group within the large, loose Southern Conference and created a new Southeastern Conference, whose intent was to provide a workable alliance with tighter controls and higher academic standards than they felt were possible within the sprawling Southern Conference.[31]

The Big Ten, the Pacific Coast Conference, and the Southeastern Conference exemplified the heights of the conference-building movement as a regional phenomenon that took place outside the established East Coast universities. Meanwhile, the conspicuous void was the continued inability of the influential historic institutions to cooperate and form a voluntary conference. During the period 1930 to 1946, the large, historic East Coast universities, bogged down by quarrels and jealousies, failed once again to create an enduring Ivy League.

In the 1920s, there were some signs of cooperation among the Big Three: Harvard, Yale, and Princeton. In 1920, the dean of Princeton had issued an "Appeal to the Friends of Harvard, Yale, and Princeton" to prevent a "too exalted notion of the importance of athletics in college life." Yet this was a limited gesture, confined to three institutions who were determined to avoid any formal collectivity. Even this gesture broke down when by 1926 animosity between Harvard and Princeton was so great that the two institutions severed all athletic ties with each other. As the chairman of Princeton's Board of Athletic Control wrote to Harvard's director of athletics, "We have been forced to the conviction that it is at present impossible to expect in athletic competition with Harvard that spirit of good-will between two undergraduate bodies of the two universities which should characterize college sports."[32]

The feud continued for several years. Even though the *New York Times* announced in 1931 that colleges nationwide looked to the historic Big Three for leadership, cooperation failed. By 1934, however, Harvard and Princeton started to make amends, thanks to mediation by Yale representatives. Meanwhile, the opportunity for a collective response to the Carnegie Foundation reports had passed. In December 1936, the undergraduate newspaper editors at Columbia, Pennsylvania, Dartmouth, Cornell, Harvard, Yale, and Princeton published an editorial that stated emphatically, "The Time Is Now," and called for "enlightened cooperation" among college presidents to create an "Ivy League in fact not just in the mind of sportswriters."[33] The joint student editorial was a landmark event in that it suggested a split between undergraduate opinion and the athletic priorities of administration and alumni.

Presidents and athletic directors at the seven historic eastern universities were reluctant to accept the student invitation for two reasons: first, no institution wanted to jeopardize its autonomy in academic and athletic policy; second, there was the sensitive matter that the construct of an Ivy League glossed over academic and athletic differences among the proposed seven members. This was in part a polite way for the Big Three to imply that the University of Pennsylvania had markedly lower academic standards and that it certainly emphasized varsity football at a level beyond what Harvard, Yale, and Princeton now found appropriate. It did not mean that these universities had diluted their football programs. Harvard, for example, was not averse to traveling long distances for intersectional games. In the 1930s, it sometimes played midwestern universities, including the University of Chicago and the nationally ranked University of Michigan. Yale traveled to Athens, Georgia, to play in the inaugural game at the University of Georgia's new stadium. Although the historic eastern colleges no longer dominated national championships as they had prior to World War I, they still fielded highly competitive teams in football and a large number of other varsity sports.

Negotiations among the potential Ivy League group proceeded slowly. In 1939, the presidents of Harvard, Yale, and Princeton signed a formal pact that established mutual policies on academic eligibility for athletes, financial aid provisions, and limits on recruitment. In November 1945, the presidents of Brown, Columbia, Cornell, Dartmouth, Harvard, Pennsylvania, Princeton, and Yale signed an agreement intended to avoid an overemphasis on football. It stated that the "players themselves shall be truly representative of the student body and not composed of a group of specially recruited and trained athletes." But this was a limited alliance. It included no conference commissioner or office, no round-robin schedule, no conference, no obligation that institutions play one another. And the presidents were careful to avoid any use of the term "Ivy League."[34]

Reversing the Reforms, 1933 to 1946

If analysis of reform had ended by 1933, one could possibly agree with Savage's optimism about the self-regulation of intercollegiate athletics. On closer inspection, subsequent developments within the major conferences between 1933 and 1946 dampened expectations about reforms intended to move college sports toward amateurism. And, in some cases, reforms initiated within conferences were reduced, derailed, or reversed.

Conferences had power to reinstate as well as suspend institutional members. For example, the Big Ten allowed the University of Iowa to return in good standing. Did this mean that Iowa had mended its ways? Even the historians of the Big Ten Conference conceded that it was not clear whether Iowa was reinstated because the university had corrected abuses or, in part, because Iowa alumni had undertaken independent study of other conference members and had "come up with charges against all nine other Big Ten schools that sounded uncomfortably like the charges used to suspend Iowa from the league."[35]

Equally discouraging were signs that conference members were having second thoughts about their commitments of 1929–30 to curb commercialization and overemphasis. In 1933, Big Ten representatives debated within their own ranks whether the conference would allow each university to establish dining hall training tables for varsity athletes, a practice heretofore prohibited by the conference. A minority voice was the Illinois athletic director, who objected because the training table and its free food was a step toward paying players.[36]

By 1938, training tables were acceptable, according to Big Ten regulations, demonstrating the power of the conference to promote practices as well as limit them. "Amateurism" and "acceptable practices" had no fixed standards and were entirely relative, subject to the vote of conference members. The legacy was not a conference prohibition against training tables but rather legitimization of them by the conference so that training tables would become the norm. This imitation and awareness of a rival's resources resembled a military arms race, characterized by stockpiling of talent and facilities. No conference member believed it could afford not to emulate the practices of its traditional opponents. So, the conference, intended as a mechanism for reform, ended up not merely allowing but promoting the kinds of practices that reformers once thought it would prohibit and police.

Regulations changed in other areas. In 1939, the Big Ten allowed a system of athletic scholarships, a decision that formally blessed the very practice that the Carnegie Foundation for the Advancement of Teaching had warned against a decade earlier. If the Big Ten was influential in building reform codes, it also was instrumental in raising the ante and expenses of standard practices. The irony of reform was the logical progression that recruiting constraints found to be unenforceable were poor policy; hence, standards were to be changed.[37]

Analysis of actions by Southeastern Conference officials between 1935 and 1945 suggests a comparable pattern of altering, even reversing, the reforms of the early 1930s. Again and again, when a conference restriction was deemed unenforceable, the resolution was to leave the problem to the individual university for oversight. This was the logic that prevailed in 1938 when the Southeastern Conference voted to allow athletic scholarships.[38] Whereas in 1931 a group of southern universities pledged unconditional amateurism, a decade later they had stepped away from such claims. Once again a conference approved measures moving away from the earlier reforms when, in February 1941, the Southeastern Conference voted to allow unrestricted recruiting of athletes. W. D. Funkhouser, of the University of Kentucky and conference secretary, explained, "We think this is a free country. A coach should be allowed to get his talent wherever he can. But he must abide by Conference rules against improper inducements."[39] The code no longer prohibited inducements, but now outlawed "improper" inducements. Conferences paid attention to practices elsewhere. In 1944, the Big Six Conference followed the Southeastern Conference's example by lifting its ban on proselytizing prospective student-athletes.[40]

Finally, establishing conferences as regulatory bodies did not necessarily reduce infractions. It meant that violations were cited and institutions were penalized. Whether that was an effective deterrent was unclear. Data from the Pacific Coast Conference's Atherton Report and the listing of violations from the Big Ten Conference indicated that violations were widespread between 1930 and 1946. Furthermore, the pattern of changes in regulations in major conferences drifted persistently toward allowing athletic scholarships, subsidies, and recruitment. For the college athletic establishment, relativism was the eventual response to reform. Coaches and athletic directors repeatedly complained that conference regulations that limited recruiting and subsidies were unfair because they were unenforceable. The corollary was that unenforceable regulations were brought into line with institutional practices. The message to coaches and athletic officials at universities that belonged to conferences was, Why jeopardize your athletic program by taking needless risks of breaking rules? A better strategy for associations of like-minded institutions was simply to change conference rules. The result was a paradox of reform: by 1945, conferences had codified and legitimized many of the practices that they were formed to curb in 1930.

The National Collegiate Athletic Association

From 1930 to 1946, the National Collegiate Athletic Association made only modest gestures toward regulating college sports. In the 1920s, the NCAA had been discounted as a weak organization, but this changed as the years passed and the NCAA acquired influence as the "voice of college sports" with national presence as an advocate and organizer. The NCAA was not really in the business of enforcing regulations to ensure that student-athletes were amateurs. According to Paul Lawrence's 1987 study, *Unsportsmanlike Conduct*, in the 1930s the NCAA started to exhibit the behavior of what economists call a *cartel*, that is, an organization preoccupied with control of markets and competition.

Although this characterization is intriguing, it seems a more apt description of the NCAA in later decades. From 1930 to 1946, its role as a lobbyist was most distinctive. For example, in 1934 its attempt to draft and implement a code on recruiting and subsidizing athletes did not reach fruition. In contrast, the NCAA showed great initiative and effectiveness in other kinds of activities: deterring any legislative or governmental intervention; operating national championship events; looking out for the legal and financial interests of big-time college sports. When the NCAA did show an inclination toward regulating its members, collective financial arrangements were usually at stake. Academic regulation of recruitment, subsidies, and admissions would remain in the hands of individual institutions and their conferences.[41]

The finances of radio broadcasts, for example, were a source of concern for the NCAA in the mid-1930s. The immediate alert centered less on the purity of the game and more on the potential for loss of attendance and gate receipts. Eventually, the NCAA mediated satisfactory agreements among colleges, sponsors, and radio stations.[42] The windfall from the radio question was the discovery by the NCAA and individual colleges and universities that this broadcast medium did not really pose a threat in terms of keeping paying spectators away from college football games. To the contrary, radio broadcasts enhanced the popularity of the college game. What had been feared as an intrusion turned out by 1940 to be an unexpected source of publicity and income as intercollegiate athletics became increasingly commercialized.

Postseason bowl games exhibited a comparable pattern. Initially the NCAA viewed these with caution, even alarm; however, by sponsoring and endorsing approved events, the NCAA extended its financial and institutional influence, all of which increased rather than reduced the commercial character of large-scale intercollegiate athletics.

Economic Developments after 1933

Economic data collected after 1933 also countered the claim that significant reform was in motion. Reformers' great expectations that attendance at college football games would decline were short-lived. Starting in 1933, annual attendance and gate receipts increased and each year set new records.[43] The South had been identified as a region especially hard hit by declining spectator interest between 1929 and 1931. This trend was arrested by revitalized attendance at regular college games, with additional energy from the creation of new postseason bowl games, as commercialism and popular interest in college sports soared in the late 1930s. Between 1933 and 1937, four cities in the South sponsored major new postseason events to supplement such older games as California's Rose Bowl. The new games were the Orange Bowl in Miami (originally called the Palm Festival), the Sugar Bowl in New Orleans, the Sun Bowl in El Paso, and the Cotton Bowl in Dallas. Bowl mania even spread to Havana, Cuba, which hosted a 1937 game between Auburn and Villanova in the first (and last) Bacardi Bowl.[44] Postseason bowl games placed intercollegiate athletics beyond campus control, since the events were the product of civic groups, newspaper publishers, and local businessmen. It also meant that the college football season stretched over six months, from August to January. Eventually, some bowl games worked out contractual relations with conferences; for example, the Pacific Coast Conference had a standing agreement that its champion would play in the New Year's Day Rose Bowl game, and the winner of the Southwest Conference played in the Cotton Bowl.

Prior to 1930, discussion of intercollegiate revenues and attendance dealt almost exclusively with football games. During the period 1930 to 1946, there was a new development that Howard Savage and the reform advocates had not foreseen: the popular attraction of other college sports. Basketball, for example, gained persistently as a spectator sport. Championship games held at such major arenas as Madison Square Garden in New York City drew paying crowds of over twelve thousand. Intercollegiate tournaments attracted over twenty thousand. What had started as an era of curtailment turned into a period of unprecedented growth and expansion for big-time college sports.

American Fiction and the Stereotype of the College Athlete

In his 1931 follow-up study, *Current Developments in American College Sport* ("Bulletin Number Twenty-six"), Howard Savage contended that American undergraduates were tiring of the resources and attention devoted to commercialized and professionalized college sports. One estimate of a popular view of college sports that supported this claim came from American fiction of that era. Around the time that the Carnegie Foundation studies of college sports were attracting attention, the stereotypic "dumb jock" had already been established as a familiar character in novels and short stories about college life. A good example comes from James Thurber's "University Days." Published in 1933 as a short story in the *New Yorker*, Thurber's entertaining memoir about undergraduate experiences at Ohio State University included his portrait of "Bolenciecwcz," a star tackle on the university's nationally celebrated football team:

> In order to be eligible to play it was necessary for him to keep up in his studies, a very difficult matter, for while he was not dumber than an ox he was not any smarter. Most of his professors were lenient and helped him along. None gave him more hints, in answering questions, or asked him simpler ones than the economics professor, a thin, timid man named Bassum. One day when we were on the subject of transportation and distribution, it came Bolenciecwcz's turn to answer a question. "Name one means of transportation," the professor said to him. No light came into the big tackle's eyes. "Just any means of transportation," said the professor. Bolenciecwcz sat staring at him. "That is," pursued the professor, "any medium, agency, or method of going from one place to another." Bolenciecwcz had the look of a man who is being led into a trap. "You may choose amongst steam, horse-drawn, or electrically propelled vehicles," said the instructor. "I might suggest the one which we commonly take in making long journeys across land."[45]

According to Thurber, "There was a profound silence in which everybody stirred uneasily, including Bolenciecwcz and Mr. Bassum." To break the stalemate, the instructor sent a look of appeal around the room: "All of us, of course, shared Mr. Bassum's desire that Bolenciecwcz should stay abreast of the class in economics, for the Illinois game, one of the hardest and most important of the season, was only a week off." After futile attempts to prompt the star tackle, the instructor asked, "'Name a means of transportation. What did you *ride* here on?'" When Bolenciecwcz answered, "'Train,'" there was a great collective sigh of relief throughout the lecture hall: the instructor was satisfied, the oral examination was completed, and students and alumni were pleased that the student-athlete was academically eligible for the big game.

A key point illustrated by Thurber's account is that for both faculty and students, allowances for varsity athletes were for the most part accepted—and often supported—as a customary part of campus life. Eligibility rules, even when adopted, were hurdles to be overcome. Most faculty were not hostile to intercollegiate athletics and often were acquiescent or supportive. It was an indulgence and acceptance that cut across regions and kinds of institutions. For example, at Yale, one famous professor who was also well known for his lenient grading of varsity football players, was asked, "Which gives you the greater kick, a perfect recitation in the classroom or a 50-yard run for a touchdown?" The professor replied, "Well, I can't get too excited over a perfect recitation."[46]

What were the changing images of the student-athlete? On the one hand, establishment of such awards as the Heisman Trophy in the 1930s signaled earnest effort to honor character and achievement. However, such awards and honors were not bestowed by students on fellow students. Nor did faculty or college administrators have much involvement in such public rituals. Annual awards for character and contribution were usually determined by external groups such as sportswriters or the Downtown Athletic Club. A better estimate of student and alumni views once again comes from American fiction, which suggests several trends.[47] First, gone from fiction about college life was glorification of the student-athlete; few serious authors reconciled the two dimensions. Second, college football continued to be depicted as an elevator of American social mobility; that is, the athletic scholarship was a vehicle for going to college, with only incidental guarantee of intellectual development or academic achievement. At the turn of the century, it was the Irish student-athlete who was depicted by writers as the hard-working, self-made American; by the 1920s and 1930s, the cast had shifted, exemplified by Thurber's depiction of the Polish immigrant son. Another variation on the changing composition of the varsity athlete comes from Max Shulman's early 1940s profile of the Scandinavian immigrant, the farm boy who plays football at the state university. In Shulman's 1943 novel, *Barefoot Boy with Cheek*, the character of Eino Efflukkinnenn at the University of Minnesota illustrates the mixture of the "Big Man on Campus" and the "dumb athlete": "Four years ago he was an unknown boy roaming around the North Woods precariously keeping body and soul together by stealing bait from bear traps. Then a Minnesota football scout saw him, lassoed him, put shoes on him, taught him to sign his name and brought him to the university to play football. And last year Eino was an All-American! All-American!"[48]

The same theme surfaces in *My Days of Anger*, James Farrell's 1943 autobiographical novel, which describes the captain of the University of Chicago football team of the mid-1920s: "He's taking a geology course. They pass rocks round for the students to examine, and Mike doesn't know what to make of the rocks. So he tosses them out of the window. The Geology Department has lost all its stones and is in a dither. Dr. Shafton is reorganizing a field expedition for geology students to hunt for his rocks on campus."[49]

As noted in "Fiction to Fact," an analysis of college novels, "The paradox is that athletes are portrayed as highly visible, influential campus figures yet are simultaneously ridiculed as 'dumb jocks' in a peculiar mixture of admiration and derision by fellow students, perhaps indicative of conflicting values and tensions within the American campus culture. Those most admired on campus are often those least equipped for classroom success. Their popularity is consistent with the picture and proportion of successful college life depicted in the novels: three-fourths extracurricular and one-fourth academic."[50] The indication from the fiction of the period was that neither the American public nor college undergraduates were fooled by the special treatment and provisions made to recruit and retain the highly commercialized college athlete. Was Howard Savage accurate in his claim that "almost every current indication is to the effect that the undergraduate is tiring of 'big time' athletics"? If there was resentment, it was often silent, as acquiescence was the norm. Howard Savage was unlikely to find undergraduates during the 1930s to be a source of organized discontent against the excesses of varsity football.

Pritchett's Pessimism

Perhaps the most perceptive analyst of the situation in the 1930s was Henry S. Pritchett. After he retired as president of the Carnegie Foundation for the Advancement of Teaching, he continued to monitor developments and to participate in public discussions about college sports. Whereas Savage and his fellow researchers cited developments that they believed marked a decline in commercialization, Pritchett seemed less sanguine and more realistic. In 1931 he went so far as to describe the limits of reform, concluding with a satirical proposal that colleges enamored of big-time sports would do well to sponsor horse racing instead of football.[51]

Pritchett's article was grudging acknowledgment, contrary to the optimism of Howard Savage and the Carnegie Foundation research staff, that the commercialism and spectator emphasis of college sports had not declined but were actually escalating. After Pritchett retired as president of the Carnegie Foundation, he continued to investigate college sports' excesses. In 1934, his articles were especially critical of the intercollegiate football programs at Notre Dame and the University of Southern California. He challenged officials at those institutions to show "how far the profits of their football teams are used in supporting their intellectual activities."[52] His public charges led the acting president of Notre Dame to reply that Pritchett was tied to a "false assumption that highly publicized football is inimical to the intellectual interests of the university." He went on to say that although Notre Dame did not issue a public financial statement, information would be available to "any investigator with the proper credentials." Furthermore, "only" 20 percent of Notre Dame's four-million-dollar income earned by its "material plant" during the last twelve years had been devoted to "athletic purposes."[53]

Pritchett's response to the chaos of intercollegiate athletics was consistent with the agenda he brought to his tenure at the Carnegie Foundation after having been president of MIT. As historian Ellen Condliffe Lagemann noted, he was the embodiment of Veblen's Captain of Erudition, believing that through standards and standardization one could improve American education; organization along "more modern, national, scientific, and bureaucratic lines" was central to improvement. Commercialism, to Pritchett, was no less than an "evil." Given his principles, no wonder the conditions of American college sports and, by extension, the prototypical American campus, literally did not meet his standards.[54]

The "Line of Demarcation" among College Sports Programs

Howard Savage concluded his study with the observation that "happily," a number of college officials were tending to matters: "Let only the chosen ideal be followed with sincerity and clear vision, and in the course of years our college sport will largely take care of itself." His confidence in natural adjustment and institutional self-correction was a premature celebration of reform. One limitation on the report's power to reform was its lack of connection with any organizational mechanism, leaving a cleavage within the ranks of intercollegiate athletics programs. An editorial on June 15, 1931 in the *New York Times* concluded that the "line of demarcation between colleges and universities whose athletics are conducted upon a basis of good sportsmanship . . . and those . . . where they are not is sharpening year-by-year."[55]

The biggest single triumph for reform was the University of Chicago's decision to drop varsity football in 1939; its deserted football stadium overgrown with weeds provided a graphic symbol of changing institutional priorities. Here was more than imagery to depict a decline in college football; here also was a demonstration of the shift from big athletics to big science. For although the stadium's exterior was in disrepair, its locker rooms beneath the stands were quietly converted to house the secret laboratory for the federally funded Manhattan Project, devoted to research and development of the atomic bomb.[56]

If Hutchins's priorities at the University of Chicago were intended to lead by example, this significant event had limited influence. Hutchins had few followers among college and university presidents. When Chicago chose to drop football altogether, it forfeited an opportunity to show by example that a football program could be compatible with educational standards. Few college or university presidents were prepared to accept the ultimatum either to reform or to abolish large-scale intercollegiate sports. The typical response at many universities after 1940 was to pursue both big science and big football simultaneously.

World War II caused some disruptions in college sports programs. Travel schedules were curbed, and fewer games were played. Threat of invasion on the Pacific Coast led to relocation of the Rose Bowl game from Pasadena, California, to Durham, North Carolina. At the same time, college sports exhibited resiliency during the war years as teams scheduled games against skilled squads fielded by neighboring military bases. If the military draft reduced the pool of men eligible for varsity sports, this was offset by a special dispensation that allowed freshmen to compete on college squads. And, between 1941 and 1946, markets for radio broadcasts of college sports expanded. The legacy from World War II was not reduction but continuity and growth in intercollegiate sports.[57]

This was a chapter in institutional history that started in 1930 with gloomy forecasts and declining receipts for college football and ended in 1945 with a news release that colleges and universities had spent in a single year an unprecedented twenty-five million dollars for construction of new athletic facilities.[58] In sum, between 1930 and 1946 the dominant organizational culture of the American campus, in concert with the popular appeal of college sports, neutralized the intense reform campaigns of the Carnegie Foundation reports. This reversal raises the question of how some colleges and universities went about enhancing their commitment to big-time intercollegiate athletics during a period that was supposed to be devoted to reform.

CHAPTER THREE

Regional Pride and Institutional Prestige

College Sports and the "Booster" Campus

The nationwide debates about intercollegiate athletics gain coherence when placed in the context of the changing character of American higher education during the 1930s. Disagreements with the reform reports were symptomatic of some fundamental demographic and institutional shifts between 1930 and 1940: namely, maturation of the large state university, expansion of public secondary education as a feeder to colleges and universities, and relative gains in size and influence of higher education in regions outside the Northeast.[1]

Taking Stock of the American University circa 1940

By today's standards, the striking features of American universities around 1940 were their modest size, the minor presence of externally sponsored research, and the limited number of graduate and doctoral programs. However, when compared to their counterparts of 1910, they exhibited remarkable growth and complexity. Prior to World War I, for example, the largest institutional enrollment was about six thousand students, at Columbia and Harvard. The five largest state universities each enrolled about forty-five hundred students, mostly undergraduates. By 1937, there were signs of a redistribution of higher education resources across regions, indicating that public universities of the Midwest and West had come of age. Many had tripled their enrollment over three decades. For example, Ohio State University enrolled fifteen thousand six hundred; Minnesota, fifteen thousand; and the University of California experienced about a fivefold increase after 1910 and enrolled twenty-five thousand students. Apart from the largest institutions, a more typical size for a state university ranged from about three thousand to seven thousand students.[2]

Despite severe dislocations in the national economy, enrollments in American colleges and universities increased during the 1930s as a result of population growth and a commitment to improved access to higher education. Whereas in 1910 between 5 and 10 percent of eighteen-year-olds enrolled in college, by 1940 15 to 20 percent did, indicating a gradual move toward mass higher education. In 1937, American colleges and universities enrolled 1.25 million undergraduates and conferred 150,000 bachelor's degrees, about a fivefold increase since 1917.[3]

The statistics charting growth were intertwined with the social fact that the American campus was an object of popular adulation. This is expressed in the photojournalism of the decade—"campus life" persisted as a staple feature. Public fascination was such that *Life* magazine devoted an entire issue to the Class of 1937, whose increased numbers represented "the world's first great experiment in mass higher education, an experiment which could only happen in America and has only happened here in the 20th century."[4] This enthusiasm led historian David Levine to place the American campus at the core of "the culture of aspiration" between World Wars I and II.[5] The center of higher education had moved geographically from the Atlantic seaboard to the Midwest; spiritually it had moved increasingly close to the heart of the American public.

One key to higher education's popularity in the United States was the notion of the "booster college." Historian Daniel J. Boorstin introduced this term in his essay "Culture with Many Capitals," referring to the civic pride and college building of the Midwest and West in the nineteenth century.[6] Often a new town used real estate promotion, discounted railroad fares, and promises of a college to attract newcomers. Founding settlers made donations to build a local college—usually private, church related, and small. The combination of noble aspiration and mild pretension was personified in the proliferation of college towns that were called Athens and Oxford, whether in Ohio, Georgia, or Mississippi. In addition to official city names, it meant that a college town and cultural center such as Lexington, Kentucky, was one of many places to call itself "the Athens of the West."[7] They extended the traditional American belief that a "real" community could perhaps lack plumbing, elementary education, running water, gas lines, or electricity—but it had to have a college.

By the 1930s, the college-community legacy had acquired a new twist: in place of small college pride, the large state university blossomed as the prototype of the American campus. What we call today a "comprehensive university," characterized by a proliferation of professional schools and selected graduate programs alongside an undergraduate arts and sciences core, became the higher education equivalent of the Ford Model T. The 1930s was a decade without dramatic curricular changes; and, despite some pockets of intellectual commitment or radical politics, student life represented a conservative collegiate culture. When *Life* magazine showcased the American campus in its June 1937 issue, it cited the University of Missouri as representative of American higher education. According to the article, illustrated by Alfred Eisenstadt's photographs, "Big Missouri," with an enrollment of six thousand students, was typical of state university education: "Like most land grant schools it stresses such training as Agriculture and Military Science." Undergraduate interest focused on those major fields most likely to connect to entry-level jobs: business administration, accounting, engineering, ROTC, and teaching.[8] And it had the "Mizzou Tigers" varsity football team that drew large crowds.

A corollary of twentieth-century campus "boosterism" was that the state university came increasingly to be seen by ambitious governors, state legislators, and mayors as a conscious instrument of aspiration. And intercollegiate athletics joined agricultural extension services as a means by which the state university could extend real and symbolic affiliation to all citizens of the state or region.

From Academics to Athletics

The June 1937 college issue of *Life* recognized the role of intercollegiate athletics in higher education's popular and regional transformation in a story titled, "Sports Records Move West." The University of Southern California, for example, had two students on the varsity track team who held the world record in the pole vault, a concentration of talent that "left Eastern collegians clinging to a steadily dwindling share of athletic supremacy." Such examples led the *Life* editors to observe:

In the past two decades, athletic reputation has largely moved West and South. A host of high-school athletes, graduating into the elaborate sports arenas of the State universities, have rudely trampled the belief of an older generation that Harvard, Yale, Princeton, Cornell and Pennsylvania symbolized greatness at football, crew and track. Today Minnesota dominates the $30,000,000 football business that draws 20,000,000 people into stadiums each autumn. Today Washington rules the rivers and its graduates coach the Eastern crews. For the past decade a handful of Stanford and University of Southern California track men have monotonously beaten the East whenever their teams chanced to meet. In specialized sports, the University of California is tops in tennis; and Michigan, having wrested swimming supremacy from Yale, now vies with Yale in golf.[9]

Other regional shifts in athletic talent were in such sports as wrestling, where teams from universities in Oklahoma and Iowa dominated national tournaments. Even Harvard and Yale's "invincible" record in polo was jeopardized as players from the University of Missouri and the University of Oklahoma claimed to have good riding skills, but were at a disadvantage because they were "forced to compete on $150 government-owned R.O.T.C. horses." The *Life* magazine editorial contained a measure of good-natured exaggeration, since the historic Eastern universities still remained nationally strong in all sports; they simply did not dominate national championships and All-American selections as they had in the pre-1925 era of Walter Camp. Here was a nationwide leavening of intercollegiate athletic talent, not a wholesale transfer from one region to another. It was no exaggeration to say that intercollegiate sports had magnetic appeal in the South and West with which no other organization could compete for popular support. Football was called a "regional religion" for the South.[10] Further, the absence of major league baseball teams or professional football franchises in the South and Far West expanded the void for spectator sports, which colleges in these regions were well suited to fill.

To understand why the reform campaigns of the Carnegie Foundation and the critical exposés of an Abraham Flexner fell on deaf ears among so many college and university presidents and trustees, one must invert analysis, turning away from the national policy reports and toward the grass roots of a campus. It was in institutional growth as part of state aspiration, especially in underserved regions of the country, where one found the strongest appeal of intercollegiate athletics as a central feature of the booster campus well into the 1940s.

To explore the populist booster campus theme, it is useful to consider institutional profiles of four institutions and their respective athletic programs, circa 1929 to 1946: Louisiana State University, the University of Georgia, the University of Southern California, and Notre Dame University. The sample includes several regions (Pacific Coast, Midwest, and South), both private and public institutions (Louisiana State University and the University of Georgia were publicly endowed, whereas the University of Southern California and Notre Dame were privately endowed). Each case develops variations on the themes of the importance of religious, ethnic, and regional affiliation in American culture and institutions. Above all, these cases created the models of funding, coaching, and recruiting that characterized big-time college sports after 1930.

Louisiana State University

Did an inherent conflict exist between college sports and educational improvement? Could athletics and academics be partners in institutional development? A dramatic challenge to the priorities of the Carnegie Foundation reformers came from the example of Louisiana State University between 1928 and 1940. Ironically, this university's development was itself the product of reform—a style of reform associated with a populist governor, not the top-down reform of experts who were part of the national establishment personified by Henry Pritchett, Abraham Flexner, and Howard Savage. The American state university literally was re-formed by a different public figure: Huey P. Long, governor of Louisiana from 1928 to 1932, then United States senator until his assassination in September 1935.[11]

Transforming the small, provincial, academically undistinguished state college into an expanded people's university was central to Huey Long's gubernatorial campaign. Not altogether unlike Senator Robert La Follette and University of Wisconsin president Charles Van Hise, who devised the Progressives' "Wisconsin Plan," Huey Long saw the state university as a source of opportunity for students and as the engine for providing Louisiana with trained, educated professionals in health, education, engineering, law, and business.[12] His statewide program included public works such as road and bridge improvements, hospital construction, and a policy of free textbooks in schools.

When Huey Long ran for governor, he became known as The Kingfish because of his campaign slogan, "Every man a king!" After being relatively quiet about higher education in his first year as governor, in 1929–30 one of his central planks of state government was to make a university education "available to every poor boy and girl in the state." Between 1929 and 1935, enrollment at Louisiana State University increased from eighteen hundred students to forty-three hundred, with another nine hundred enrolled in programs offered by the new medical school Long helped to build in 1931. He worked to make the state university accessible by lowering tuition and expanding financial aid. As the chancellor of Louisiana State University recalled in 1990:

> What happened is history. Within three years in the early 1930s, LSU's state appropriation jumped from about $1 million to $3 million. In the height of the depression, while most of the rest of the nation was cutting support of its colleges and universities, Louisiana was taking giant strides. As an example, better than half of the buildings on the LSU campus today were constructed during this period.[13]

Professional schools and "useful arts" abounded. In addition to building a new medical school, Huey Long pumped resources into a new School of Music. Once again not unlike the examples of the University of Wisconsin and Ohio State University, the flagship state university was in the state capital. His program was viewed in part as a slap at the prestigious, private Tulane University in New Orleans (possibly, according to political lore, because Tulane once had denied applicant Long admission).

The state university was the prime mover in Long's plan for state government. Governor Long identified the Louisiana State University varsity football team as the linchpin of his master plan both for higher education and for building statewide pride. When elected governor, Long declared, "LSU can't have a losing team, because that will mean I am associated with a loser."

To make good, Huey Long added athletic scholarships and created the new position of athletic director. He also picked the football coach, attended the team's practices, and took special interest in the marching band. The band had been a small, undistinguished military band until

Long transformed it into the jewel of the football game halftime show as well as a performing group at other public events. Their parades often included Huey Long marching with a baton as honorary drum major. It came to be known as the "Golden Band from Tigerland" and was expanded to 250 members. To lead this group, Long personally hired Castro Carazo, a popular, successful band director from New Orleans. Long posed with cheerleaders, participated in football activities, and collaborated with Carazo to write "Tiger Rag," the fight song for the LSU team. They also teamed to write "Darling of LSU," "Touchdown for LSU," and Long's political theme song, "Every Man a King."[14]

When LSU was scheduled to play Vanderbilt in Nashville in 1934, Long coerced the Illinois Central Railroad into reducing its train fares from nineteen dollars to six dollars so that thousands of LSU students and the LSU ROTC corps could attend the game. Long himself donated four thousand dollars to defray the six-dollar ticket cost for needy students. At another time, when the Barnum and Bailey Circus shows in New Orleans threatened to draw attention away from an LSU football game, Long invoked an obscure statute on animal quarantines to persuade the circus to reschedule its shows.

Long's commitment paid off. After three years and two coaches, the LSU football team, a latecomer to top-level competition, shifted from a local schedule to playing games against the best teams in the South. From 1933 through 1937, Louisiana State University was selected for the postseason Sugar Bowl game three times, defeated archrival Tulane three times against one defeat and a tie, and showed a record of thirty-two victories, four defeats, and six ties. To consolidate its commitment to big-time football, Louisiana State University was a founding member of the Southeastern Conference in 1933.[15]

With Long as governor or senator, the football program was not without its tensions. One famous football coach, wary of the meddling that had plagued his predecessors, included a clause in his contract that prohibited Governor Long from entering the team locker room. Long initially respected the agreement, in deference to the coach's success. Eventually Long disregarded the restriction at a crucial game on the grounds that the LSU team was losing at halftime, a condition that constituted a state emergency and required his gubernatorial attention.

Athletics led to architecture. The campus was underdeveloped, having moved to a new site outside Baton Rouge in 1925. With Long as governor, the first major architectural project was to expand the football stadium, since Long had approved an addition of over twenty thousand seats, which increased seating to forty-six thousand. Afterward, the entire campus became the object of the governor's pride: linked stylistically to the Italianate design of the state capitol in Baton Rouge, the adjacent university was a showplace of both landscape and architecture. According to Ruth Laney, "From 1930–35, Long diverted $9 million to construction at LSU. In one remarkable year (1931–32), he enabled the University to erect the Music and Dramatic Arts building, the fine arts building, girls' dormitories, the Field House, the Gym-Armory, and an enlarged football stadium with dormitories attached."[16]

If Governor Long's enthusiasm had been confined to football, Louisiana State University could have been dismissed as an expensive indulgence that shortchanged both citizens and higher education. That dismissal is inadequate because his interest in the monuments of LSU generated resources to bring established scholars to the faculty and to increase student financial aid. Every dimension of university activity was enhanced. The service mission of agricultural and home economics extension programs was expanded. All the more remarkable was that this took place in an impoverished state with a weak tax base and an established political elite.

The vision of the great state university was not exclusive to Huey Long. One reason for Long's success at Louisiana State University was his hand-picked appointment as university president, James Monroe Smith. Smith knew how to defer to Long, to work with the impatient governor, and to sublimate his own administrative ego for the benefit of the state university. Thanks in large measure to President Smith's understated savvy, investments in LSU were not confined to the glamour of football, marching bands, and campus architecture. Long's support extended to academic personnel and resources. Along with enrollment increases there was growth in the size and quality of the faculty. Whereas in 1925 the LSU faculty numbered 168, this more than doubled to 394 by 1935 and was characterized by nationwide recruitment. Long's efforts also included funding for such academic projects as the *Southern Review* journal.

Long as governor in the 1930s was acting much like the industrialists and philanthropists who took on the self-imposed role of heroic (and unregulated) "university builders" of the 1890s.[17] His example showed that a governor could combine generous support and love of monuments with meddling, a public sector equivalent of a Mrs. Leland

Stanford at Stanford University or reminiscent of a zealous president William Rainey Harper at the University of Chicago in the early 1900s. At Louisiana State University, along with the increased appropriations and superb facilities came the worry among faculty and students that they faced censorship if they disagreed with the governor. Often over-looked is that since he was primarily a promoter and builder, Long had little interest in the curriculum and usually deferred to President Smith. Eventually, however, Long's episodic clashes with the academic units (usually over censorship) meant that by 1935 the university was being reviewed by such groups as the Association of American Law Schools, the American Civil Liberties Union, the American Association of University Professors, and the Southern Association of Colleges and Schools.[18]

The usual interpretation is that at the time Long was assassinated in 1935, LSU's academic infrastructure was about to collapse because the campus was soon to inherit a full slate of indictments of its policies and procedures from national academic groups. Of all the investiga-tions, the concern by the ACLU was the most volatile. How seriously one should take expressions of concern by the AAUP and other aca-demic groups is less clear. Did the national groups show any concern about Louisiana State University when it was at best a small, third-rate, provincial institution that was socially exclusive and academically dor-mant? No doubt Long was self-serving, perhaps a demagogue; and he went too far in viewing the university as his pet project. At the same time, his interest in expanding higher education in his home state was genuine and generous.

The temptation is to see Huey Long as an academic interloper who "used" the state university. His demise, then, takes on the character of a morality play in which the death of Long the abusive intruder spares the state university from further excesses. But where would LSU have been without Long's interest and antics? Had national groups shown interest in academic standards and excellence at this compla-cent institution in the 1920s? Were foundations supporting educational reform in Louisiana? If the regional accreditation commission was con-cerned about an overzealous governor-senator in 1935, where was com-parable concern about lack of government support for higher education a decade earlier? Despite the concern by national organizations, LSU was a more formidable university than it had been prior to Long's involvement.

After Huey Long's death, succeeding governors and legislatures tried to continue his commitment, and for several years LSU sustained its place as an ascending comprehensive public university. Following World War II, the inordinate state resources characteristic of Long's pioneering effort dried up. On balance, Long's initial interest did elevate Louisiana State University to legitimacy in size and resources among modern state universities, especially in the South. The limit was that the glimpses of academic excellence that were part of Long's vision were for the most part not sustained. One innovation that did persist was Louisiana State University's commitment to national excellence in football; the "Bayou Bengals" football team endured as a source of state pride.

The University of Georgia

The University of Georgia, like its counterparts in most states throughout the South, was small and underfunded. Football was one of the first of its few ventures to gain national exposure, as university officials in the 1920s sought games with historic colleges in other regions. These included games against Dartmouth and Harvard in 1921 and against the University of Chicago in 1922, with all three being played away from home—and all ending in losses for the Georgia team. More important than winning was that Georgia had moved away from being a totally insular regional institution. Football as a tool for public relations escalated in 1923 when Georgia and Yale agreed to play each other.

For several years, this meant that the University of Georgia team and its supporters journeyed to the Yale Bowl, where, for several years, they lost. A watershed event took place on October 12, 1929, when for the first time the Yale football squad traveled to the South. The Yale team's arrival at the Athens railroad station put into motion a remarkable celebration and hospitality that demonstrated good feelings between the universities. Part of the historic symbolism was that the two institutions acknowledged a common bond: Yale alumni in 1785 had founded Franklin College, the forerunner of the University of Georgia. Scrutiny of souvenirs from the 1929 game indicates that both institutions were proud of the ties: tickets and programs included engravings of historic campus buildings from both universities; and it was pointed out that both teams claimed the bulldog as mascot. The game was played in the new Sanford Field on the Georgia campus, before a crowd

of thirty-three thousand. The final score of 15 to 0 marked the first
time that Georgia had defeated Yale. This heroic event in the saga of
the University of Georgia overshadowed that university community's
interest in Howard Savage's Carnegie Foundation report, released a few
weeks later.[19]

How did the move of the intercollegiate athletic department into
major league football connect with the total university mission, if at
all? Unlike Louisiana State University, there was no direct link
whereby football success was part of a coordinated plan of institutional
advancement. Administrative reorganization rather than expanded resources was the genesis of institutional transformation at Georgia.[20]
During the 1930s, the University of Georgia underwent modernization,
although in a version markedly different than Louisiana State University experienced with Governor Huey Long. The primary change was
structural—in 1932, the state created a consolidated Board of Regents
of the University System of Georgia.

Fortunately for the University of Georgia, the new Board of Regents
was dominated by university alumni. The university also gained by
having the state Agricultural and Mechanical College merged into the
University of Georgia as its College of Agriculture. The university also
absorbed the State Normal School and acquired a school of commerce,
all indicative of a new presence as a comprehensive university. There
were some trade-offs: the university closed its veterinary school and
lost its engineering program to Georgia Tech. Intercollegiate athletics
did tie into the new university system to the extent that the university's teams, along with those from Georgia Tech, remained the strongest in the state; and the University of Georgia demonstrated its commitment to big-time football as a founding member of the Southeastern
Conference in 1933.

Football's prominence within the University of Georgia became
increasingly evident during the lean budget years of the late 1920s and
continued over the next twenty years. According to the university's
bicentennial historian, Thomas G. Dyer, the pivotal event was the incorporation of the Georgia Athletic Association in 1929. Although the
Georgia-Yale game received public acclaim, it was this inconspicuous
and seemingly unspectacular organizational change that exemplified
the increasing influence and sophistication of intercollegiate sports in
higher education. As historian Dyer noted, "The establishment of the
independent Georgia Athletic Association in 1929 in many ways took

authority over intercollegiate athletics out from under the umbrella of the university administration and the renewal of the charter for the association in 1949 confirmed that extra-institutional forces would for another twenty years shape the development of intercollegiate athletics."[21]

Reading through the history of the University of Georgia, one finds a recurrent pattern where an administration and faculty committed to enhancing the academic offerings of the institution in the face of limited resources were required to defer to intercollegiate athletics in general, and the Georgia Athletic Association in particular. As Dyer commented:

> Dominated by influential alumni and dedicated to the achievement of national recognition for Georgia athletics, the association controlled substantial financial resources which it made available to the intercollegiate athletic program. Although faculty representatives sat on the board of the association, its independent status rendered their influence minimal. President Caldwell, torn between the desire for the public relations benefits which accrued from the football program and the difficulties which arose from dealing with the independent association, repeatedly faced problems which called into question once again what the relationship of intercollegiate athletics should be to the university's total mission.[22]

The University of Georgia case contrasted with that of Louisiana State University, where there was reasonable evidence that between 1930 and 1935 large-scale football was not in competition with state appropriations for university educational programs. Huey Long wanted a visible, winning football team to trigger increased funding for the entire campus. For Georgia, since there was no comparable mechanism, football prospered while the university as a whole remained financially malnourished. The University of Georgia enjoyed no windfall or generosity from its legislature. Nor did winning teams spin off support for the educational programs. To the contrary, by the late 1930s financial data indicated that the University of Georgia was falling behind in state support compared to flagship universities in other states throughout the South.

Whereas LSU was the object of a governor's pride and indulgence, the University of Georgia suffered a governor's neglect. A feud between Georgia's governor, Eugene Talmadge, and President Franklin Delano

Roosevelt meant that federal funds from the Public Works Administration Program that might have been used for campus construction were delayed until 1935. By 1937 the coincidence of a new governor (who was on good terms with President Roosevelt and the New Deal programs), a veteran chancellor (former university president Sanford), and a new university president (Harmon Caldwell) put the University of Georgia in position to follow through on sorely needed construction projects to accommodate an expanded curriculum. Between 1937 and 1940, the Athens campus received more than two million dollars in state and federal funds for construction of new dormitories and buildings for science, a demonstration and laboratory school, fine arts, and agriculture, along with renovation of historic buildings. The University of Georgia had expanded rapidly but in 1940 was still relatively underfunded; it was also small (with a total enrollment of thirty-seven hundred students) and at the same time overcrowded.[23]

Talmadge, who had been the university's nemesis when he was governor in the 1930s, resumed this role when he was reelected governor in the early 1940s. This time the University of Georgia was the object of his wrath when he heard a rumor that the dean of the College of Education had spoken in favor of campus racial integration. This led the governor to try to purge the campus. As historian F. N. Boney described it, "Talmadge pressed the Board of Regents relentlessly. Some ugly overtones of anti-Semitism and Yankee hatred emerged, together with a few wild charges of communism and sexual misconduct. Finally the beleaguered regents yielded to the pressure."[24] The regents dismissed the accused dean and several university employees. As a result, "in December 1941 the Southern Association of Colleges and Secondary Schools, denouncing Talmadge for 'unprecedented and unjustifiable political interference,' withdrew the accreditation of the University of Georgia and the other white schools in the University System, effective September 1942."[25]

The university regained political and academic strength only after a new governor worked to have the legislature pass a state constitutional amendment that put the university regents in control, while removing the governor as a member ex officio; the Southern Association eventually restored the university to its accredited status.

The crises that plagued the educational programs of the University of Georgia were different and disconnected from those of the varsity athletic program. It is this gulf that dramatizes the university's contrasting fortunes. The football team started to win more games and consolidated its popularity as the state's favorite team. When the university's academic situation reached a low point with the loss of regional accreditation in September 1942, the Georgia Bulldogs were enjoying their most successful season ever, an undefeated record of ten victories and one tie. This led to unprecedented national recognition: an invitation to play in the Rose Bowl game, culminating in a victory over the University of California, Los Angeles.

The football program also exhibited an alarming capacity to spend more money than it brought in from gate receipts. This was a drain on the university president's time, since in the early 1940s he had to deal repeatedly with the athletic director, football coach, and athletic association about expenses. Here was the classic predicament of institutional investment in big-time football: the University of Georgia team drew large crowds and played a schedule of major Southern universities and selected intersectional teams; it gained press coverage and statewide public interest; yet it still ran a deficit. The most glaring irony was that the Georgia Athletic Association, created to enhance football fund raising apart from regular state appropriations to the university, habitually fell short. Intercollegiate athletics under the Georgia Athletic Association had a dream arrangement: the association was virtually autonomous from university administrative control in its operation of varsity sports, yet somehow it was not required to fulfill its charge of raising sufficient money to run the varsity sports program! To apply a concept from economics, the Georgia Athletic Association was effective but not efficient.

The university's alumni and representatives aggressively recruited athletes within Georgia and in such distant, unlikely locales as Louisville, Kentucky, and Youngstown, Ohio. The program took on increased intensity in 1938 under a new coach, Wallace Butts. Statewide alumni support and recruiting started to pay off, and the team excelled, including two seasons in which the Georgia Bulldogs were national champions. One sign of national recognition came in 1942 when the Georgia quarterback, Frank Sinkwich, was awarded the Heisman Trophy as the outstanding college football player in the country. Between 1941 and 1948, the record in regular competition was sixty-five victories, sixteen defeats, and one tie. The team also played in six major postseason bowl games: the Orange Bowl (1941), the Rose Bowl (1942), the Oil Bowl (1945), the Sugar Bowl (1946), the Gator Bowl (1947), and the Orange Bowl (1949).

Football provided a bonanza for publicity, not for revenues. Officially a "student activity," Georgia's varsity program was increasingly subsidized for the benefit of alumni fans and the statewide public. Big-time football was not merely apart from university life, it was a burden that ultimately cost the University of Georgia time and trouble, as well as money. There was little wonder that the program was expensive, as it carried seventy to eighty players per year on athletic scholarships. Road trips were characterized by high hotel bills. Recruiting costs rose each year. Finally, according to Dyer, "In mid-1942 university comptroller J. D. Bolton took drastic measures to deal with overdue bills charged to the athletic department and cut off credit to the football program." Eventually, the athletic association's financial morass led the athletic director to resign. Despite mounting athletic debts, the head football coach insisted that the president of the university honor an agreement to pay him a performance bonus. The president became trapped by the football program's success: the university repeatedly had to bail out the expensive program, since the Georgia Athletic Association ran an annual deficit of seven thousand dollars for several consecutive years. The university administration reduced this deficit by dedicating half of each student's annual activity fee (ten dollars of a twenty-dollar fee) to the Georgia Athletic Association. Meanwhile, student fees and other university funds for such student activities as literary societies, clubs, and the student newspaper were drastically reduced.[26]

Sports threatened to get out of control when attempts by the University's president and even by some of the athletic association board members to curb athletic spending failed. To deemphasize or to eliminate the sport was out of the question, because no president could risk alienating enthusiastic alumni, fans, and sportswriters. The coaches and athletic officials were behaving like aristocratic officers in the czar's army as depicted in a Tolstoy novel: arrogant, disdainful of thrift, and believing that they were expected to run up bills. The coaches saw themselves as entitled to this subsidy. For the financially strapped American state university to support such habits indefinitely meant that the university administration was forced to pay a steep price for football prestige and publicity. In an understated appraisal that could well stand as an epitaph for academic control of big-time intercollegiate football nationwide, historian Thomas G. Dyer summed up the University of Georgia situation as follows:

> By the end of World War II intercollegiate football had achieved a special status both in the university and the state. Although its place in the university's total mission had not yet been resolved and would soon be questioned, the football program continued to offer the institution visibility that few if any of its academic programs could, and in the process presented President Caldwell and his successors with a series of complicated and often perplexing dilemmas.[27]

The University of Southern California

The University of Southern California (USC) showed that the booster college need not be a state university. In fact, it was the powerful University of California's neglect of the Los Angeles area that created a vacuum in which a private campus defined its own mission. Founded by Methodists, USC exchanged religion for region as its primary identity and became the de facto "public" university for the Los Angeles area. It was no accident that the institution's name reflected its constituency: it served a sprawling metropolitan area.[28]

In researching the pattern of institutional development at USC, the interesting finding is that varied historians agree on both the events and the emotions associated with the institution as it reached a student enrollment around nine thousand in the early 1930s. Whether one looks at the official house history or the more critical social histories that treat USC as part of regional development, there is consensus: the campus history from 1920 to 1946 follows the themes of growth and campus building. The long-time president of the university, Rufus von Kleinsmid, tied the institution's destiny to the economy and character of the region. It was an agenda in which he used intercollegiate athletics to foster institutional advancement. Everyone agrees that by the mid-1920s USC was known as a "football school."[29]

By standards advanced by Carnegie Foundation representatives Abraham Flexner and Henry Pritchett, USC embodied much that was suspect about the immature American university. To be president of USC in the 1920s demanded emphasis on fund raising and public relations. Using a strategy that the president of the University of Georgia probably would have envied, USC's president von Kleinsmid counted on varsity football as a source of both money and publicity. USC, as a private institution, could not count on an annual state appropriation, and von Kleinsmid apparently had little confidence in philanthropy or major gifts to build a university endowment. Even as USC evolved as a large, complex service university, it was confined by dependence on the same traditional source of income used by small, private liberal arts colleges: tuition dollars. Although tuition might suffice for business as usual, it was an unlikely source for seed money to finance construction. Without a large endowment, USC needed money to pay for new professional schools and programs to fulfill its plan to be a regional university. President von Kleinsmid's risky solution was to rely on national-caliber varsity football. His strategy worked—so well that it fostered distrust, even envy and avoidance from other universities.

USC gained a measure of both academic and athletic legitimacy when in 1921 it was admitted to the Pacific Coast Conference. Its athletic reputation soared when it played in (and won) the 1923 Rose Bowl. Success, however, brought scrutiny, and in 1924 USC was suspended from the Pacific Coast Conference after the University of California and Stanford raised questions about USC's admissions and academic eligibility standards. That unpleasant episode brought into the open rivalries between institutions and regions. It was a manifestation of the deep rivalry not only between the state flagship university and the private USC but also between northern California and southern California. USC was seen as young and aggressive, an embodiment of the new wealth and booming growth that characterized Los Angeles; in contrast, the University of California was seen as established, academically eminent, and enjoying national stature in football and other sports. Even if Berkeley and Stanford's concerns about USC's academic standards were warranted, the two northern California universities were not above reproach for their resentment of USC's threat as a rising institution, especially in athletics. Whether one favored Berkeley or USC in the rivalry, the institutional tensions confirmed that California was in fact two states, and the single University of California campus in Berkeley was not able to command statewide loyalty when the bulk of the population was in southern California. The resolution was that each section claimed its own booster campus.

Eventually, USC was restored to membership in the Pacific Coast Conference. Meanwhile, being quarantined from the conference gave

USC a chance to carry out a football and funding coup: President von Kleinsmid negotiated the deal that would consolidate USC's football fortune—and that would rankle the Carnegie Foundation's president, Henry Pritchett. USC and Notre Dame agreed to meet annually in football, starting with the 1926 season. When USC won the invitation to play in the Rose Bowl game (as it did frequently, with eight appearances between 1930 and 1948),it asserted its place among West Coast universities. When it played against Notre Dame, it gained national fame.[30]

This was no exaggeration. The first game, played at the Los Angeles Coliseum, filled the stadium to capacity. The 1927 and 1929 games, played at Soldiers' Field in Chicago, each attracted over 100,000 spectators.[31] On November 21, 1931, in Chicago, USC pulled out a thrilling 17 to 14 victory, which prompted college sports to transcend both the playing field and the campus: 300,000 local fans—about one-third of the Southern California area population—joined with the mayor, city council, and university administrators to greet the returning USC football team at Los Angeles's Union Station in one of the largest civic and university celebrations and parades on record.[32]

The blending of campus and civic aspiration was reflected in construction of elaborate local athletic facilities in the 1920s and 1930s. Los Angeles showed its support for competitive sports and its ability to organize large-scale sporting events when it successfully hosted the 1932 Olympics. Such events and projects brought campus and community together. The magnificent Los Angeles Memorial Coliseum, completed in 1927, was adjacent to the USC campus and a natural site for a national championship team, since it could hold crowds as large as 100,000. It was, of course, the home field for the University of Southern California. USC was also unlike many other "football schools" in that it did not neglect other sports. To the contrary, its varsity teams in track, baseball, swimming, and tennis enjoyed a benefit from football, and each achieved national stature. The paradox of athletic success, however, was that despite the popularity and loyalty football engendered, it also interfered with academic reputation. Once or twice every decade, USC was charged, even if not convicted, by other universities of sports overemphasis and weak admissions requirements.

USC, unlike the state universities in the South, did not suffer the chronic underfunding that came either from dependency on an indifferent legislature or from a weak regional economy. The Los Angeles area was affluent, ambitious, and growing. Whatever campus shortages or hardships the university endured during World War II were offset over the long run by the fact that Southern California had become the new hub of such industries as aircraft and defense production that were quickly built up during the war and that continued to flourish afterward. The USC plan as an extended university, with emphasis on professional schools of engineering, education, dentistry, medicine, business, public administration, and cinema, meshed well with this region's economic development. Yet preoccupation with growth tended to leave the university and its constituent schools underendowed and always a little hungry. Perhaps the biggest question mark about von Kleinsmid's institutional strategy to combine structural expansion, civic pride, and football publicity was whether the Los Angeles area might also have been receptive to endowing a high-powered scholarly campus. Historian Kevin Starr has pointed out that in 1922, early in his presidential tenure, von Kleinsmid's $10 million community-wide fund-raising campaign failed, prompting him to rely on "the cultivation of individual donors and football as sources of revenue."[33] Had he given up too soon on the proposition that Los Angeles wanted a markedly academic institution?

Were one to seek the antithesis of the USC model during the same years in Los Angeles, it would be California Institute of Technology, located in nearby Pasadena. Starting in the 1920s, the former Throop Institute pooled a concentration of national-caliber talent in the sciences in concert with a board and administration who cooperated with local government, regional industry, and federal and industrial research to create a small, well-endowed institution that consciously resisted large size. Cal Tech devoted itself selectively to areas of science and engineering where its teaching, research, and development would be in demand within the state and also would be among the best in the world. The Cal Tech approach even permitted some interesting athletic claims; although its varsity sports were low key, Cal Tech arguably set the record for having won the most football victories in the Rose Bowl. This was so because for several years the Rose Bowl facility, located in Pasadena, served as Cal Tech's home field. Without discounting this achievement, Cal Tech's distinctive contribution was the ability to poke fun at big-time football with its student tradition of pranks that played havoc with the scoreboard and card stunts of the major league teams from the Pacific Coast Conference and the Big Ten who met on New Year's Day for the "real" Rose Bowl.[34]

Meanwhile, in central Los Angeles, USC's president von Kleinsmid, known as "Rufus Rex" because of his imperial style, authoritarian administration, and love of pageantry, masterfully combined his plan for a growing, extended university with civic boosterism for over twenty-five years. When the editors of *Life* magazine showcased the American campus in 1937, their profile of von Kleinsmid noted, "At his sports-minded institution 10,000 males and 5,000 females, living in adjacent fraternity and sorority houses, get their higher education." Von Kleinsmid was described as "a dapper and friendly man with a genius for raising money."[35] Such favorable publicity did not totally cancel out the charges that USC was a football factory. This characteristic, coupled with President von Kleinsmid's devotion to publicity and construction, meant that the institution did not build a well-endowed, national-caliber infrastructure that would support either faculty scholarship or selective student admissions. The impression that USC was preoccupied with football and external appearances, whether accurate or not, became part of the image that denied the school a reputation for academic excellence.

In some ways, USC was a transplant of the midwestern state university to the private sector of the West Coast. Von Kleinsmid's perennial friction with the academic leaders eventually came to a head—and the traditionally deferential faculty revolted in 1946 after prolonged complaints of low salaries, heavy teaching loads, lack of resources, and absence of opportunities for scholarship. USC, then, was on the whole a success story that personified the appeal of the booster campus that fused civic pride and winning football. It simultaneously showed the limits of that strategy for improving institutional reputation. Not until after 1960 would USC work out the refinements and resources that allowed its academic programs, especially in its graduate professional schools, to claim a place among the nation's major research universities.

Notre Dame

Whereas the University of Southern California exemplified a campus that played down its religious connections to become a regional university, Notre Dame during the same period demonstrated an opposite strategy. Its emphasis on religious affiliation as a central part of its mission, combined with a phenomenal varsity football program, transformed this small college in South Bend, Indiana, and led it to capture the American imagination as a truly national institution. For Notre Dame, the time between World Wars I and II was a "period of stunning growth and change for a provincial sectarian college of modest reputation. It was Notre Dame's Golden Era," according to alumnus and retired newspaper editor John J. Powers.[36]

The transformation was started quietly by President James Aloysius Burns, a priest whose lasting contribution was to introduce systematic fund raising. His presidential successor, Father Matthew Walsh, continued public relations, construction, thoughtful hiring of new faculty, and a persistent shoring up of academic standards. Although known as an undergraduate college with no claim to be a major research university, Notre Dame was home for a succession of accomplished scholars in the physical sciences.[37] Most memorable was Father Julius Nieuwland, a chemist whose research led to the discovery of synthetic rubber. Academic gains, although important, were dwarfed by the popular energy generated by national-level football. As Powers summarized, "The new dynamism prompted them to reach for excellence in several ways. The most spectacular had nothing to do with scholarship. It was football, of course."[38]

Notre Dame, then, illustrated another variation on campus boosterism. Instead of state or geographical ties, it emphasized its role as the flagship Catholic university. As such, it symbolized the American faith in education as a means of social-economic mobility. At a time when anti-Catholicism was strong, Notre Dame provided a rallying point of achievement and pride that imbued its constituency with a sense of being All-American. Often forgotten today is that Notre Dame's football power was shared with other Catholic institutions, usually located in cities. One litmus test of this presence was that if one were to name a city, and attach "college" or "university," usually it was a Catholic university. Examples included the University of Detroit, University of San Francisco, Seattle University, University of Portland, Saint Louis University, Georgetown University, Providence College, Boston College, Santa Clara University, and the University of San Diego. The Jesuit influence on urban higher education was strong, as suggested by the founding of various Loyola colleges and universities in Los Angeles,

Chicago, Baltimore, and New Orleans. To these one must add such important Catholic institutions as Fordham and Holy Cross, which also took football seriously.

Notre Dame's contribution to American culture went beyond Catholicism. Sociologists Christopher Jencks and David Riesman pointed out in *The Academic Revolution* that religious affiliation in American higher education often was more fully explained as a sign of ethnic affiliation.[39] So, although Notre Dame brought increased respectability to Catholicism, it also did so for many immigrant families of Irish, Slavic, Italian, and Polish roots whose children represented the first generation to go to college. College football was part of the social-economic-educational elevator in twentieth-century American life. As David Riesman and Reuel Denney noted in their 1951 analysis of football as part of cultural diffusion in America, "A variety of sources, including letters to the sports page, indicate that a Notre Dame victory became representational in a way a Yale or Harvard victory never was, and no Irish or Polish boy on the team could escape the symbolism."[40] To reinforce the point, elsewhere in the same article they cited Notre Dame's famous coach, Knute Rockne, who succinctly stated, "After the church, football is the best thing we have."

By World War I, Notre Dame had become known as a small college that was a national power in football. The crucial episode in the organizational saga was the 1913 upset victory over a strong Army team. Since the game was played in New York, major newspapers gave the game special attention, transforming Notre Dame into a popular team—and its star players Knute Rockne and Gus Dorais became mass culture heroes for having perfected the forward pass. Sportswriters kept adding to the lore, best exemplified by Grantland Rice's 1924 praise for the "Four Horsemen" imagery of the Notre Dame backfield. More so than any other institution, it succeeded in gaining football victories and fame, and that permeated the campus fabric. Thanks to press coverage and radio broadcasts, the "Fighting Irish" football teams acquired a national following, including a "subway alumni": tens of thousands of Catholic fans claimed Notre Dame as alma mater. It was a bond that was not impeded by the facts that a loyal fan might not have finished high school, never have set foot on the Notre Dame campus, or never even have left New York City.

Notre Dame was selected as national champion ten times between 1919 and 1947. Between 1918 and 1930, its famous coach, Knute

Rockne, had a record of 105 victories and 21 defeats. Often it played home games at Chicago's Soldiers Field, either to accommodate crowds of over one hundred thousand or while waiting for completion of its new campus stadium in 1929. For several years Notre Dame attracted around four hundred thousand to five hundred thousand spectators, an average of about fifty thousand per game.

Popularity brought some problems. For example, Notre Dame was conspicuously absent from the Big Ten Conference long after it had achieved a sustained reputation as a power in the Midwest and the nation. Its petition for conference membership was denied in the mid-1920s. Most football histories allude briefly to the episode, leaving unclear whether this rejection was due to a combination of anti-Catholic sentiment and the allegation that Notre Dame's academic requirements for athletes were below conference standards. And, as mentioned in earlier discussion of the Carnegie Foundation reports, Henry Pritchett focused on Notre Dame along with the University of Southern California as the foremost examples of football overemphasis among American colleges and universities.[41] Notre Dame officials usually responded that outside critics had failed to note the institution's academic gains—and the supportive role football played in enhancing the entire campus. In citing these accomplishments, Notre Dame administrators and alumni probably did protest too much.[42] Who could deny that football dominated its institutional presence? Big-time football served the campus well and provided Notre Dame an identity and leverage unsurpassed in American higher education.

Knute Rockne and the College Coach as Culture Hero

Notre Dame had national importance beyond illustrating a variation of the booster campus because its campus saga featured Knute Rockne, foremost personification of the modern ideal of the college coach. As newspaper editor and Notre Dame alumnus John Powers recalled in 1991, "Football and Knute Rockne. The man and the moment. They were one of life's perfect matings. Pious sentimentalists saw the hand of God; skeptics called it coincidence. It was an immeasurable benefit to Notre Dame."[43]

A college or university committed to using big-time football as a part of its organizational strategy depended on charismatic leadership, whether from a friendly governor or from an energetic president. Above all, it required a professionalization of the position of college coach. Howard Savage and Henry Pritchett had emphasized in the 1929 Carnegie Foundation reports that the appearance of the professional coach was one of the most controversial additions to the campus cast. The transformation had significance beyond the playing field, for it was the coach who was college spokesman, celebrity, and even culture hero.

By 1930 there was a first generation of famous coaches, including Glenn "Pop" Warner, Andy Smith, Amos Alonzo Stagg, "Hurry Up" Fielding Yost, Bob Zuppke, and Howard Jones, who all had careers in which they were highly recruited, well paid, mobile, and honored. Grateful fans and alumni presented victorious coaches with automobiles and other gifts; some coaches, like Wallace Butts at Georgia, had incentive clauses in their salary contracts. All were dedicated, even obsessed, with the details of the game—and were allowed to be idiosyncratic so long as they won. Within the ranks of college football coaches, Knute Rockne of Notre Dame was the most famous coach of his day— and of all time. Every roster, poll, listing, anthology, or memoir about great football coaches ranks Knute Rockne at the top.[44] The awe Rockne inspired at Notre Dame was shared by a national audience. As David Anderson wrote in the 1991 *New York Times Book of Sports Legends:* "Rockne. The name itself provides strength—character as well as muscle. Until his death in a 1931 plane crash, Knute Rockne projected the image of Notre Dame football that all its other coaches have been burdened to maintain. Even now he remains college football's most famous coach."[45]

According to Anderson, in 1970 Rockne's son discovered a previously unpublished list of Rockne's twenty-five commandments, "the correct mental qualifications of an athlete." It was Rockne's counsel on scholarship, cooperation, obedience, habits, ambition, attendance, morals, sportsmanship, conduct, unity, service, leadership, patience, loyalty, self-sacrifice, determination, confidence, remarks, responsibility, concentration, losing, winning, the past, the present, and the future. His concern with such themes brought him respect as an educator and character builder. Today a small public library probably has in its holdings no fewer than four or five Rockne biographies. He is popular with aging, nostalgic sports fans from the 1920s as well as with new generations of juvenile readers. The number of articles and books about Knute

Rockne is staggering. For example, Michael R. Steele's 1983 work, *Knute Rockne: A Bio-bibliography*, itself a massive 318-page extensive study of Rockne, lists fourteen pages of bibliographic entries.[46]

The common thread among the assorted biographies is that Rockne, Notre Dame football, and American values were inseparable. His life reads as if it were a twentieth-century version of a Horatio Alger novel: the son of immigrants from Norway, this "sturdy Viking lad" grew up in the rough-and-tumble melting pot of Chicago, excelled in high school studies and sports, then worked in the post office for several years to save money so that he could afford to go to college at Notre Dame. As an undergraduate he overcame self-doubts about his talents to become an honor student and an All-American football player, as well as captain of both the football and the track squad. His "problem" as a graduating senior was a guidance counselor's dream: he had to choose between teaching chemistry or coaching football for his vocation. His decision to enter coaching disappointed his famous chemistry mentor, yet appealed to American boys. Rockne was not only a winning coach, he was a teacher, student, disciplinarian, motivator, and family man. Today the portrait may strike us as saccharine, even suspect. Despite some reservations (and exaggerations), historical records indicate that Rockne was indeed an impressive man, a worthy sports hero.

Most interpretations associate Rockne's fame with the 1920s, the so-called Golden Age of American Sports. He would fit well with Warren Susman's profiles of such influentials as advertising pioneer and inspirational writer Bruce Barton, automobile manufacturing leader Henry Ford, and legendary baseball player Babe Ruth as the memorable public figures of the 1920s.[47] His tenure as Notre Dame's head coach from 1918 until his untimely death in 1931 makes him chronologically closer to the 1920s than the 1930s. The limit of this conceptualization is that it relies too much on Rockne's public accomplishments, masking attention to his ideas and plans for the future that put him in the vanguard of sports and culture characteristic of the decades from 1930 onward. Had Coach Rockne's influence been limited to sports and to his own era, he would be interesting as a transient period-piece celebrity. He was more, an authentic culture hero who was no less than a secular saint.

In March 1988 the U.S. Postal Service honored Rockne with posters announcing, "Legends Live . . . On Stamps." It was the first time a sports coach had been featured on a United States stamp, and one of the few times a college sports figure had been honored. To unveil the stamp, President Ronald Reagan visited the Notre Dame campus and delivered an address that was covered by major television networks. Reagan's invocation of the legends of Notre Dame and their implications for Americana compressed politics, sports, legends, and mass media imagery. Art and life were blurred, given that Ronald Reagan himself had played the role of the famous Notre Dame student-athlete George Gipp in the 1940 movie *Knute Rockne, All American*.[48]

The Hollywood movie is important for ascertaining Rockne's place in American culture for generations after 1940.[49] Even though Rockne died in 1931, near the start of the era pertinent to this chapter, he remained as familiar a name to ensuing decades as he was in the 1920s. Nine years after his death, he commanded sufficient recognition to warrant investment by Warner Brothers studio in a major film production. For a nation known for its commercial culture, such faith in box office appeal was testimony to Rockne's enduring cult of personality. And, long after this popular and financially successful film stopped being shown in theaters, it enjoyed revivals on late night television broadcasts and eventually was released as a video cassette in the 1980s. The temptation is to dismiss the popular movie as "dubious history," an embellished fusion of fact and fiction. Even if the charge of superficiality were warranted, it begs the question of Rockne's legendary influence.

Rockne's contribution to modern American culture is that he pioneered the role of the college coach as entrepreneur. Unfortunately, most biographies are silent about this entrepreneurial role, leaving gaps and contradictions in their portraits. In the movie and juvenile biographies, Rockne rejects offers to endorse products. In one dramatic scene, he is going through paperwork at his office desk before a game and laughingly discards the invitation to promote a liniment, "Rockne Rub," dismissing such commercial opportunities as detracting from football's real worth. Contrary to such images, Rockne did devote himself enthusiastically and lucratively to endorsements and promotions. He was in demand as a motivational speaker to business and industry. At one time he supplemented his Notre Dame job with employment as sales promotion director for a national automobile manufacturer, the Studebaker Corporation. He devoted a great deal of time to public speaking, to the stock market, to making deals. Here is where the legend and the facts of his values get confused.

The circumstances of his death indicate uncertainty about Rockne's priorities. According to the movie, *Knute Rockne, All American*, in March 1931 while on vacation with his family in Florida he was called on short notice to join a meeting of coaches on the West Coast. Other accounts state that it was a commercial venture, not a coaching commitment, that beckoned him to Los Angeles. For example, according to Gene Schoor's 1987 history of Notre Dame football, Rockne was on his way to Hollywood to work out the details of a movie deal for *The Spirit of Notre Dame*. Rockne supposedly was to receive a $75,000 payment for his advisory role.[50] A similar, slightly different version comes from Jack Clary's 1990 book, *Great Football Coaches:*

> He had regained his health in 1930, and after a second straight national title, he was at the peak of his popularity, with his own newspaper column, supervising movie short subjects, running a football camp, making countless speeches, working for Studebaker, and becoming athletic director at Notre Dame—and still the offers poured in. One was to represent a chain of sporting good stores, so on March 31, 1931, he was in Kansas City to fly to the West Coast for some store openings.[51]

The puzzling combination of values that Rockne contributed to American culture was that his coaching built character while at the same time he embraced commercialism and professionalism in college sports. He stood for all that was "good and clean" in American life and education—yet was at odds with the amateurism and educational priorities presented in Howard Savage's 1929 reform report on intercollegiate athletics. After publication of the Carnegie Foundation report, he gave a speech in Buffalo in which he argued that the problem with college football was that it was not commercial enough.[52]

Rockne's responses to the Carnegie Foundation reports were important because he was influential. An interesting feature of the *Knute Rockne, All American* movie is that many famous coaches made cameo appearances and played themselves; in one scene, Amos Alonzo Stagg, Pop Warner, and others make a pilgrimage to Rockne's Notre Dame office, pleading with Rockne to be their spokesman before the Carnegie Foundation's hearings on intercollegiate sports. Rockne is convinced to participate when his fellow coaches bemoan the unfairness of the

Carnegie inquiries, with the sad comment that the reformers were not really "bad men," simply misinformed about the contributions college football has made to the national welfare.

Rockne, of course, was the coaches' choice to set things straight. In reluctantly accepting his colleagues' invitation, he warned that he would "mince no words" at the foundation's hearings. Rockne's subsequent testimony was oratorically thrilling. However, his impassioned remarks about the dangers of rushing to judgment on the impact of college sports on the student-players or his monologue about football's contribution to the "national intelligence" were polemics that were neither logical nor pertinent to the Carnegie Foundation's inquiries.

The fascinating feature of Rockne's power to elevate the professionalized college coach into the ranks of contemporary celebrities and national culture heroes was the extent to which the American public— and American leaders—deferred to Rockne's opinions on topics outside football or coaching. His eulogy included tributes from the president of the United States, senators, governors, the king of Norway, and national business leaders. The radio broadcast of his funeral service attracted the largest listening audience of the era. He was friends with General Douglas MacArthur and enjoyed associating with him and other national figures. One irony was that Rockne was fond of invoking military metaphors about the lessons taught by football even though he never served in the military, let alone saw action in combat. More puzzling is that his military homilies were contradictory. At one time he argued that college football was a good crucible for preparing future military leaders. At another time he argued that one reason the United States had not become embroiled in wars (as had European nations) was that the United States had college and school football as an outlet where young men could defuse their militaristic aggressions.

Did Rockne have lessons for American management? He was celebrated as a great motivator whose locker room talks and strategies led to heroic performances by players. The implication was that the methods developed by Rockne as an inspirational coach were applicable to American industry. This was all conjecture because, ironically, during the time he did serve as the paid sales promotion director for Studebaker, that company's automobile sales declined. No matter, either way college football was what America needed!

Rockne is perplexing because he may well have reconciled commercialism with character building in his own mind. But to reformers and educators, the resolution was either unclear or unconvincing. Had Rockne been a villain or a fraudulent opportunist whose abuses were sanitized by public relations campaigns, his reconciliation of education and commercialism could be understood and then rejected. He could be dismissed as an inflated charlatan, unworthy of hero status. However, since he was a remarkable educator, a family man, and a hero, he cannot be ignored. Was it all right—even desirable—for a professional coach at a college to be highly paid? Rockne himself received a salary of ten thousand dollars per year from Notre Dame in the mid-1920s—an extraordinary amount compared to faculty salaries of the day. And, contrary to the depiction of Rockne as steadfastly loyal to Notre Dame, he once planned to leave, having signed a contract for a twenty-five-thousand-dollar salary with Columbia before Notre Dame officials pointed out that he had not honored a permission clause in his Notre Dame contract.

Rockne, by his own example, demonstrated that the big-time college football coach had drifted far from the company of professors. From time to time a university received publicity for having conferred faculty rank on a football coach, as was the case with Amos Alonzo Stagg at the University of Chicago. Such actions usually were gratuitous because they further denigrated the status of bona fide professors who already had little in common with a charismatic coach when judged by standards of salary, facilities, and authority. The activities of recruiting, promoting, and public speaking, along with the lures of endorsements, indicated that by the 1930s the role of the big-time college coach had evolved very differently from that of university faculty. Illustrative of this widening gap in power and perks, Rockne was one of the first football coaches who simultaneously served as athletic director.

When Rockne died in 1931, American colleges and universities were left with unresolved questions: Were the values Rockne espoused exclusively gained by playing football? And how did virtues associated with football relate to winning? Indicative of this tension was how Americans went about selecting "best coaches" and "greatest coaches." Rockne's winning record and his commitment to high educational and spiritual values made him special. The dilemma was that most polls to select great coaches were dominated by one criterion: success at winning games. Victory regardless of values was a better route to coaching greatness than was the reversed proposition. When commercialism and professionalism were fused with intercollegiate athletics between

1930 and 1946, the lesson was that without victories, even Knute Rockne would soon be out of a coaching job and ignored by the public.

Legacies of the Booster Campus, 1930 to 1946

One of the most significant organizational developments during the period between the world wars was the incorporation and refinement of the campus-based athletic association. Along with the emergence of the NCAA and the maturation of the various athletic conferences, intercollegiate sports had acquired both an infrastructure and a super-structure. The appearance of the athletic association at Georgia and other universities was not completely new, since booster clubs and fund-raising support groups had been around for years. The athletic association, however, was different because it became a legal corpora-tion that was a part of, but apart from, university structure. It often had its own board, power to hire and fire employees, its own payroll, and its own facilities. At the same time, an athletic association enjoyed use of the university name, logo, facilities, and other resources. Given these advantages, there was little wonder that it became the organiza-tional model for big-time college sports.

There were numerous variations on the booster campus theme other than Louisiana State University, the University of Georgia, the University of Southern California, and Notre Dame. The University of Minnesota and the University of California, for example, were two significant cases because they provided the model for a campus to com-bine, although not necessarily integrate, national championship foot-ball with national-caliber scholarship. The University of Minnesota was especially interesting because its varsity teams drew the attention and support of Governor Harold Stassen as a symbol of state pride.

One commonality among the four highlighted booster campuses was that regardless of their academic standing around 1946, each had made an irrevocable commitment to big-time sports. It was almost impossible to think of any of these institutions without mention of varsity football. Indicative of this institutional commitment was the rise to power and prestige of the college football coach as a campus and culture hero.

. . . .

CHAPTER FOUR

Schools for Scandal, 1946 to 1960

After World War II, intercollegiate football flourished as public entertainment; attendance reached a record 14.7 million in 1947–48. Eager
to accommodate spectators, universities added new seating to stadiums
built in the 1920s. In 1949, the University of Michigan enlarged its
Ann Arbor stadium from 72,000 seats to 97,239. The same year, Purdue
expanded the capacity of its football facility more than threefold, from
13,500 to 51,000. Michigan State College added 33,000 seats to its original 14,000.[1] College athletic programs also satisfied the public's appetite for sports with postseason games. In 1946, college football teams
played in seventeen bowl games whose attendance totaled 478,000.[2] A
year later, two more major bowl games were added to keep pace with
spectator demand.[3]

Intercollegiate basketball joined football as a "cash cow." The popularity that basketball teams in the New York City area acquired in the
1930s spread to other regions. A major football game with attendance of
75,000 fans was still the biggest single draw, and basketball attendance
was limited by small auditorium size. Nonetheless, basketball was a
healthy source of revenue because the size of large indoor arenas had
increased, with some seating 13,000 fans. Also, college basketball com-
pensated for relatively limited seating by playing more than twenty
games per season. The economy of basketball appealed to athletic directors: athletic scholarships for a team of fifteen players cost considerably
less than athletic scholarships for a sixty-player football squad. College
basketball's appeal included Christmas holiday tournaments and such
postseason events as the National Invitational Tournament and the

National Collegiate Athletic Association championships. When one adds exhibition games and all-star games to the list, it became clear that college basketball had arrived as a lucrative spectator sport.[4]

Intercollegiate athletics paid a price for this popularity as the safeguards constructed over the preceding fifteen years by conferences and the NCAA collapsed in the postwar period. They were overwhelmed by an unprecedented popular interest and pressure to win. But external forces did not create the problems in collegiate sports; they merely exposed the weakness of the colleges' safety provisions.

The popular pressure on college sports was part of a phenomenon that taxed all higher education after World War II. Retooling curricula and enrolling large student constituencies created unavoidable difficulties. College administrators and faculty lacked precedent for flexible admissions and accommodating a new generation of college students. And the character of the student-athlete changed after 1946 when college athletic programs gained an expanded talent pool of veterans who enrolled in colleges under the Servicemen's Readjustment Act, popularly known as the G.I. Bill: students who had delayed or interrupted college education for military service as well as students who, after high school graduation in the late 1930s, would not then have had either the expectation or the financial aid necessary to go to college.

A good example of the veterans' impact was in the sport of boxing, which in the 1930s had a tradition of intercollegiate competition. Its bouts brought to mind the controlled violence and decorum of the gentlemen's club, exemplified by the University of Virginia's prewar championship teams whose home matches included student crowds wearing formal attire; the only applause allowed was between rounds and when decisions were made.[5] The atmosphere changed after World War II; by 1950, the college sport had become semiprofessional because coaches inherited a cohort of army veterans who had boxed competitively on service teams. Their intercollegiate competition against eighteen-year-old-high school graduates led to a disastrous mix of mismatches and injuries, even deaths. Semiprofessionalism in boxing caused a once thriving campus sport to inflate briefly, then to be abolished.

If the new professionalism engendered by military veterans hurt intercollegiate boxing, it stimulated football by allowing open recruitment with few restrictions on squad size or athletic scholarships. Admissions and hiring at colleges moved quickly when the war ended, as illustrated by the experience of the newly appointed head football coach at the University of Maryland. He signed his university contract on September 7, 1945, about ten days before being discharged from the naval station in North Carolina, where he had been coach of the pre-flight football team. Before leaving the service, he asked players on his Navy squad if any would like to play for him on his university team. Seventeen accepted his invitation without having even applied for admission. The new coach, worried that his veterans might not be eligible, was told "not to fret" by the university president (himself a former head football coach at Maryland) because, after all, the president made the rules. The Navy players were discharged on September 18, enrolled at the University of Maryland on September 19, and played in the opening game of the season on September 27.[6]

College sports showed adaptability and enterprise. Some athletic directors and coaches sensed the opportunities of a commercialized and media-oriented culture. In addition to campus stadium expansion, colleges and conferences were negotiating broadcast contracts with radio stations. Arguments within the NCAA now were seldom over amateurism versus commercialism. After 1946 the question was more likely to be, Which arrangement of broadcast and live attendance would maximize college athletic revenues?

After World War II, reform in intercollegiate athletics no longer meant deemphasis. There was a simultaneous need to corral the big-time programs and generate revenues, illustrated by the contradictory tensions at the 1948 NCAA convention. In the morning session on January 10, conference delegates endorsed a code to curb abuses in inducements and scholarships for athletes. Later that day, the NCAA also decided to continue holding the annual NCAA basketball tournament at Madison Square Garden in New York City. Karl E. Leib, of the University of Iowa and NCAA president, explained at the business meeting that there was "some sentiment for the return of the NCAA basketball championships to campus courts," and that "this may be done in the future as acceptable campus facilities become available." According to the reporter, "However, the need for revenue was paramount at the present time." He elaborated, "We owe a big debt to the [Madison Square] Garden for saving basketball during the war years when we had to take the game to the public because transportation difficulties kept the public from seeking out the game."[7] That financial considerations were driving the NCAA decision was now accepted as normal because the "regional basketball playoffs at Madison Square Garden and Kansas

City's Municipal Auditorium and the championship playoffs at Madison Square Garden were the NCAA's chief source of income last year, contributing a total of $57,635 to the coffers."

College sports, like the mythical beast from Dr. Doolittle stories, had become a "Push-Me-Pull-You," trying to go at once in the different directions of amateurism and commercialism. The lesson forthcoming was that college sports were not going far at all—except, perhaps, downward, soon to be mired in bad publicity and corruption. While the academic leaders who held NCAA office felt indebted to Madison Square Garden for having "saved" college basketball in 1948, their gratitude to this New York City arena would vanish in the near future. In 1951 Madison Square Garden would gain infamy, especially among the universities of the Midwest and South, as the symbolic site of the evils of big city life that corrupted college sports.

The NCAA's "Principles for the Conduct of Intercollegiate Athletics," 1946 to 1952

In 1946, college presidents, athletic directors, and NCAA officials took initiative to oversee intercollegiate athletics. One indication of interest in collective solutions was the increase in NCAA membership, which grew from 216 in 1945 to 317 in 1949. An issue, along with the financial health of college sports, was how to codify amateurism among such a large, diverse constituency. After two years of discussion, NCAA members adopted constitutional revisions called the "Principles for the Conduct of Intercollegiate Athletics" at the 1948 convention. It was a concise declaration of principles of amateurism, institutional control and responsibility, sound academic standards, financial aid, and athletic recruitment; its intent was to state in general language for all member institutions that varsity athletes were genuine students. It sought to give college presidents and athletic directors incentive to rein in booster clubs and alumni groups. And, by establishing a three-member compliance committee, the NCAA took on an enforcement role, with power to suspend or expel violating institutions.[8]

The striking feature of the "Sanity Code" was its terms. Essentially an honor code, it avoided overspecification. Its most controversial section was on financial aid, which prohibited athletic scholarships, limited a student-athlete's aid to the amount of tuition and fees, and required that awards be based on a student's financial need. To dispel worries about centralization of power, the NCAA's compliance committee made clear its intent to avoid direct intrusion into a campus's decisions about need-based financial aid.[9]

Despite adoption at the NCAA conference, the Principles for Conduct were not implemented effectively. The University of Virginia, known for having a clean program, opposed the Sanity Code, to the point of risking its membership in the NCAA. Virginia and its fellow plaintiffs objected to the Principles because they transferred authority to the NCAA, away from the institution or conference; further, restraints on financial aid penalized a strong academic institution while favoring ones with elaborate job programs. Virginia's objections were in part a jab at the Big Ten, which did not have athletic scholarships but was alleged to benefit from a network of alumni job programs for varsity athletes. Virginia was joined by a number of institutions, and its defiance became a test case in the early 1950s.

Virginia's complaints made it an unwitting ally with those who favored minimal restraints on big-time sports. Several universities in the South contended that they were at a disadvantage against the universities of the Midwest and Northeast that had large stadiums and jobs for student-athletes. Hence, the maligned Sanity Code was doomed to face revolt. Resistance caused the NCAA to forfeit an opportunity to be ahead of abuses, rather than to respond to offenses. The failure to resolve the concerns raised by Virginia prior to the Sanity Code's passage at the 1948 convention is puzzling. If, for example, the NCAA had allowed scholarships to include a student's expenses beyond tuition and fees, would Virginia have been placated?

The usual chorus among coaches was that the Sanity Code was an insanity code because it was impossible to enforce—the same rationale that led conferences in the 1930s to rescind their constraints on recruitment and training tables. This argument disguised the real reason for its failure: many NCAA institutions, whether through their presidents or their athletic directors, did not really subscribe to the ideal of amateur sports by and for athletes who were genuine college students. One cynical interpretation is that colleges with commercialized programs stood to gain by the ploy of approving a code they never intended to honor. Should reformers in the NCAA have anticipated this? If so, it meant that the organization was not fully committed to academically sound intercollegiate athletic programs. If many colleges were going to feign compliance while actually seeking a competitive edge, the NCAA faced two options: either to abdicate any claim to a substantive role in carrying out collective reforms, leaving regulations exclusively to conferences and institutions, or to build a regulatory machinery based on the premise that campus athletic programs were characterized by deceit.

If colleges and universities had subscribed to creating reasonable college sports programs, the Sanity Code might have been salvaged. Its principles allowed athletic excellence, even financial aid. However, provisions to enforce the code were problematic—penalties were too severe, and the NCAA committee had too much responsibility and too few resources.

Finally, in 1950 members refused to expel Virginia and others who challenged the code's terms. This led to further retreat at the 1951 NCAA conference, where members narrowly passed, by the necessary two-thirds vote, an amendment to the code that gutted the "Principles" by eliminating the section about NCAA involvement with financial aid. They also eliminated the rules and the statement of purpose that would have given enforcement powers to the NCAA compliance committee.[10]

Economist Paul Lawrence has argued that whatever the merits of the Sanity Code for restoring amateurism, there was another agenda: the NCAA sought to limit competition for student-athletes, acting as a cartel that controlled college sports by restraining expenses and competition. And, as Lawrence points out, despite its limits, the Sanity Code was a landmark in NCAA enforcement: it set a precedent for the NCAA to punish individual student violators and to suspend institutions that did not comply.[11] By initiating the Sanity Code, the NCAA members acknowledged conditions that could plague intercollegiate sports. It was the right instinct at the right time. That the Sanity Code for all intents and purposes died in 1951 was unfortunate, for events soon indicated how sorely a nationwide code of principles was needed.

Gambling and the College Basketball Scandals of 1951

At about the time that the delegates to the NCAA annual convention were gutting the Sanity Code, a story broke about the New York City District Attorney's investigation of "point shaving" in college basketball games. Whereas in 1948 the NCAA had praised Madison Square Garden for saving college basketball, this site was now blamed for having brought corruption into college sports. The integrity of intercollegiate athletics reached a low point in 1951 with the exposé of connections between organized crime and college basketball.

The facts are familiar, having been the subject of several books: varsity basketball players at seven universities, mostly in the New York City area, were found guilty of point shaving. The foremost offenders played for Long Island University, City College of New York, and Brooklyn College. As depositions were taken and cases pursued, the net spread to include some players from the University of Kentucky, Bradley University, and the University of Toledo. Since these were among the best teams in the nation, the charges were volatile.[12]

The 1951 gambling scandals were the tip of an iceberg, because point shaving had been going on for several years. Rumors among bookies had been circulating with sufficient influence to alter betting patterns. Discussions among college presidents at NCAA meetings in the late 1940s alluded to concerns long before the exposé. A 1945 claim that Brooklyn College players had fixed a game against Akron had not led to an investigation.

After the scandals story broke, news articles placed blame for the corruption.[13] FBI director J. Edgar Hoover revised his earlier praise of the value of competitive sports for the national welfare, then fumed about the breakdown of the family and the rise of urban gangs. The Carnegie Foundation's president scolded college faculty for not having been more forceful in teaching moral values. Scapegoats included physical education departments, accused of harboring athletes by enrolling them in easy courses. "Phog" Allen, the famous basketball coach from the University of Kansas, said college sports needed a national czar to clean up abuses.

What about the corrupted college players? Their tragedy warrants compassion: they were young men in over their heads, tangled in the temptations of an unregulated enterprise. Although they were guilty, each paid a tremendous price by forfeiting professional careers, losing college athletic eligibility, leaving college, and suffering lifelong humiliation.

College officials had overrated the sanctity of their institutions by ignoring the historic association of gambling and college sports. Accounts from the 1920s, including memoirs from the famous Centre College football team, show that college players often gambled, sometimes on their own games.[14] Historian James Cox, writing in the December 1985 issue of *Smithsonian* magazine, pointed out that George Gipp at Notre Dame acquired fame in town as a pool player and card player, "the terror of the parlors" who often gambled. Sportswriters called him "Notre Dame's Cool Gambler." As James Cox said, "The latter was most apt, since Gipp was the team's bookie."[15] Gipp was not alone in the 1920s, according to Cox: "Betting was common in college football at the time. Wagers, for example, between Army and Notre Dame, were often made on the eve of a game when, as was the custom, the two teams met for dinner. Players bet on their own team, or on themselves as individuals, an end claiming he would catch a certain number of passes next day, a back betting he would plunge for so many yards."[16]

Another historical fallacy is that the indictments in 1951 cleaned up college sports by eliminating ties with organized crime. This was not true, since comparable episodes surfaced in 1961, at North Carolina State University and the Dixie Tournament, and in the 1970s, at Boston College.[17] When point shaving did fade from college sports, it was not due to policing by the NCAA but because college basketball was not attractive to gamblers. One syndicate member recalled, "Betting lots of money on college basketball is a very difficult thing to do. Very few bookmakers get into the baskets seriously. In fact, most bookies will handle college basketball action only as a favor for someone who is also betting a lot on football or baseball."[18]

Gamblers had little trouble enlisting a player or two, especially if the arrangement was not to play to lose but to win within a point spread. The risk was that gamblers thought college players were unreliable eighteen- and nineteen-year-olds, whose physical maturity usually was far ahead of their judgment. Gamblers had to consider the uncertainties of a college player who had a change of heart and decided to play to win. After one game in which cooperating players failed to lose by the negotiated point spread, one fixer said in disgust, "That was it. No more. The end of the point-shaving scheme. Jimmy was so mad at losing the cash that he said he wanted to shake those kids up. At one point during the night he said, 'Let's go up to Boston and put their heads through hoops,' but we never went anywhere. By then Jimmy had bigger problems than money."[19] And college and university presidents now had bigger problems than gambling if they were to reform college sports.

Responses to the Scandals

The 1951 trials meant that the courts, not the colleges, dealt decisively with the serious college sports problems. The NCAA's failure to amend the Sanity Code or to implement some comparable measure left a vacuum. If college sports had grown to be a big business, it was an unregulated industry; colleges were shown to be unable to police themselves. Questions emerging from the trials were less about the basketball scandals and more about the condition of "legitimate" intercollegiate athletics.

It was the business-as-usual aspect, not the point shaving, that suggested how far college sports had drifted from the 1929 debates. Saul S. Streit, judge of the Court of General Sessions in New York City, led the probe and presented independent findings that made him despised among sports boosters because he had taken initiative where they had failed and had broken the college officials' conspiracy of silence about problems endemic to athletic programs. The 1951 counterpart of Howard Savage's 1929 Carnegie Foundation report was not written by a higher education group; it was written by Judge Streit in his sixty-three-page commentary, which documented the commercialism and professionalism that had gotten out of control.[20]

Another feature of the basketball scandals was the denial syndrome, often along regional lines. The booster colleges of the South and Midwest initially dismissed the scandals as confined to the urban Northeast. The abuses could not be explained away as a "city" problem, however, after Bradley University, in Peoria, Illinois, and Kentucky were implicated. Now coaches and athletic directors at the university sports factories had a real problem: to gain control of their own players and programs. This latter revelation was traumatic to the college athletic establishment. Gambling was anathema to the famous coaches simply because they wanted their teams to win. Point shaving revealed their own professional impotence, contrary to their public image and self-image as disciplinarians who covered all details to assure winning. Nowhere was this more evident than the boast by Coach Adolph Rupp of the University of Kentucky, who had told reporters that the gamblers "couldn't touch my boys with a ten-foot pole."[21] Rupp was echoing his mentor, Coach "Phog" Allen of the University of Kansas, who had claimed in the late 1940s that the midwestern players and teams were not like the city teams of New York.

Another lesson that college coaches might have learned was that any college team was vulnerable. College officials suddenly were sensitive to this point, and the higher education community scrambled to restore public confidence with belated studies and statements. Trials involving the Madison Square Garden point-shaving scandals were not the only bad news for college sports in 1951. In the same year, there was front-page coverage of transcript alterations by coaches at the College of William and Mary.[22] At the United States Military Academy, over ninety cadets, including a large number of varsity football players, were dismissed when they were found to be involved in an exam-cribbing ring.[23] Given such episodes, not surprisingly there were numerous responses to the ills of college sports. Charles Grutzner wrote a series of articles on athletics and education for the *New York Times* based on his survey of forty colleges and universities.[24] The commissioner of the Pacific Coast Conference continued his track record of being ahead of exposés by lobbying for deemphasis since 1946. He recommended eliminating broadcast of conference games and participation in postseason bowl games.[25] But his exceptional initiative was ignored: most reform efforts were reactive and showed that there was neither a unified voice nor a coherent policy within American higher education to guide college sports.

The American Council on Education's Presidential Committee

Newspaper articles on the point-shaving trials were placed alongside articles announcing the creation of a special committee to consider ethics and college sports. In October 1951, the American Council on Education (ACE) turned attention to the sports problem; on November 10, 1951, Dr. Arthur Adams, president of the ACE, announced appointment of ten university presidents to a committee charged to make recommendations to the ACE's 979 member institutions.[26] Over the next month, the ACE Special Committee on Athletic Policy showed the

American public that college and university presidents had convened to address the problems of college sports. They received favorable press coverage, including front-page headlines that announced, for example, "College Presidents Ready to Hurl Flying Block at Football Scandals."[27] The ACE committee invited Judge Streit to advise them. Streit initially was interested, but by December 6, 1951, he had begged off meeting with the ACE group in Washington, D.C., concluding that "it would be indiscreet and do violence to the Judicial Canons of Ethics should I make any public or quasi-public appearances or pronouncements in connection with any of my judicial decisions or statements from the bench."[28]

The committee met between December 1951 and February 1952 to listen to various groups and to draft their special report. At the December 12 meeting in Washington, Coach Lloyd Jordan of Harvard, speaking as president of the National Football Coaches Association, argued that football should be considered a regular part of the institution's program and that coaches be made members of the faculty. After suggesting some ways to combat pressures toward overemphasis, Coach Jordan told the ACE special committee, "We must recognize that colleges are in the entertainment business. The only question is, How far shall we go? But if we do it at all, shouldn't we do it well?" President Millis of Western Reserve University, a member of the ACE committee, "opposed the notion that colleges are in the entertainment business, saying that he has yet to find a college charter that includes it as a legitimate objective."[29]

One revelation was that football coaches had no code of professional ethics. Attention then shifted, as President Butterfield of Wesleyan "argued at some length for the preparation of a statement that would move all colleges, on a long-range basis, away from the present situation toward intramural sports for all, with intercollegiate contests strictly limited to those growing naturally from the intramural program." This led to talk about reducing postseason bowl games, spring practice, and recruiting. The ACE group was briefed on parallel developments with accrediting commissions, especially the North Central Association of Colleges and Secondary Schools.[30]

The ACE report caused some concern among its supporters when it was presented to the ACE Executive Committee and released to the public on February 16, 1952.[31] Milton Eisenhower, president of Pennsylvania State College, advised, "I am in accord with the philosophy and most of the recommendations of the Special Committee on Athletic Policy. I am wondering, however, if it would not have been wise to submit the report to all member institutions for a vote of approval or disapproval. It just seems to me that a highly favorable vote would have been obtained and such a vote would have strengthened the hand of the American Council on Education in its negotiations with the NCAA, regional accrediting associations and others that might be interested."[32] After an explanation by the ACE president, Eisenhower agreed, with one reservation: "However, we are going to get an improved athletic situation only if most of the good institutions want it. There is need for an educational program for a high degree of agreement. My guess is that athletic directors and coaches will try to have the recommendations weakened at many points. In newspapers everywhere I am reading words to the effect that the recommendations are idealistic, not practical. I am for the report 100 percent and want to do what I can to bring about its general adoption."[33]

Eisenhower was correct about opposition from coaches. John Hannah, president of Michigan State College and chair of the ACE special committee, learned firsthand that presidents could be countered by coaches at their own institutions: Michigan State football coach Biggie Munn told an audience, "I would rather have my son be a football player than a Phi Beta Kappa" because "you learn democracy and Americanism in the game of football."[34] A more sobering perspective was that of the former head coach at the University of Texas, who reminded presidents that presidents and boards—not fans or alumni—fired coaches who failed to win, despite presidents' alleged pleas for athletic reforms.[35]

One source of discord among college presidents and the ACE special committee dealt with ACE's relationship with the NCAA. Many thought that the ACE committee was to act independently, even to react to the NCAA's alleged failures to reform college sports. In May 1952, several university presidents expressed concern to the ACE. One wrote, "I was, frankly, very much disappointed in the seeming reversal of attitude on the part of the American Council on Education in turning back the policing of athletics to the National Collegiate Athletic Association. It has been the failure of that body to police adequately athletics that has resulted in large part, for the present abuses."[36]

Similar concern came from presidents of small colleges. The president of Allegheny College, located in Meadville, Pennsylvania, wrote to Hugh Willett of the University of Southern California and NCAA president, saying he had seen no visible signs of anything fundamental being done to implement the ACE recommendations. Instead of eliminating postseason bowl games, the NCAA had endorsed nine such games. And, he noted, the "subsidy and commercialism evils exist also in small colleges." He wanted to give the NCAA some "tangible reassurance that a few college executives are interested in doing something more than making pious proclamations. I can well appreciate that with millions of dollars invested in athletic facilities no great changes can be expected very soon. But the beginnings ought to make themselves evident if changes are ever to come."[37]

The ACE thus had to placate presidents, reminding them that from the start the ACE had been working closely with the NCAA and other associations. Walter Byers, executive director of the NCAA, for example, had been invited to early meetings of the ACE special committee and was included in the presentation of the final report to the ACE Executive Committee. The chair of the ACE committee wrote to the president of the NCAA, "I am sure that you appreciate that we are all trying to accomplish the same general objective in spite of the newspaper efforts to make it look as though we were engaged in a civil war with the athletic directors and coaches and the NCAA on the one side and the college presidents on the other."[38]

Despite such tensions, the president of the ACE remained optimistic about college sports reform. He thought that major bowls were having difficulty attracting top teams yet conceded that conferences were having mixed results in stopping rule violations. The Big Seven had controlled overemphasis at the University of Oklahoma, but the Southern Conference's efforts to curb Maryland made no headway and collapsed.

Milton Eisenhower's warnings proved to be perceptive, since the committee's public relations problems continued. Raymond F. Howes, staff associate for the ACE, complained to the Associated Press sports editor that articles were emphasizing the ACE committee's "frowning on post season bowl games and spring practice" as a "step in the right direction." The ACE objected to the slant, emphasizing that "the recommendations with regard to bowl games and spring practice were subordinate items in one recommendation of ten. . . . It is no wonder that some of the sports writers who replied without having seen the report of the Committee charge that 'The college presidents have side-stepped the cause of their program's evils—recruiting and subsidization.' As a matter of fact, of course, the fundamental recommendations of the Committee were on precisely those points."[39]

The ACE committee was being whipsawed unexpectedly and unfairly. Harvard's sports information director offered yet another loyal dissent: he felt that the ACE should emphasize elimination of postseason bowl games and spring practice because there was a need for action: a "lack of leadership, or perhaps the absence of good examples, is causing public opinion to sink what was launched not only as a soundly-endorsed program, but also a sane and practical one." It would have "indicated that the presidents 'meant business.'"[40]

In public addresses, committee chair John Hannah remained confident that "sports de-emphasis was sure to come," and that "athletic directors and football coaches probably wouldn't like it," but that the ACE presidents would ultimately prevail. "We have announced our principles and we will give the various conferences and the NCAA two or three years in which to adopt and live up to our proposals. Then, if they refuse, we will come back with police powers and force, if necessary, to see that our principles are adhered to."[41]

The short shelf life of press coverage in the aftermath of the court cases meant that the university presidents and the ACE had to gain public support promptly. The promising start in November snagged on the confusion over issues. The second task was to insure that the special committee set into motion actions that would lead to structural reforms. This was hampered by the ACE's lack of power to mandate regulation or cooperation. The special committee never had any intention of being or constructing a new enforcement apparatus. On April 3, 1952, the ACE staff associate wrote to Henry Johnston of the Harvard Athletic Association:

> There have been numerous indications in the press that sports writers are losing interest in the committee's recommendations merely because they have not, by some miracle, been completely adopted within eight or ten weeks. For example, Mr. Marsh of the *Herald Tribune* was very much disappointed to learn that three of the regional accrediting associations had not taken, and cannot take, immediate action. As a result, an Associated Press dispatch reported that those three associations had refused to cooperate. The actual fact is that official representatives of all of the regional associations sat with the committee and

promised to work for full cooperation as rapidly as their respective procedures would permit.

The implication was that "those of us who sincerely desire to see significant reforms in the conduct of intercollegiate athletics must have sufficient foresight and stamina to continue to work over a period of several years. After all, this situation has been building up for more than forty years, and in some places some abuses are very firmly entrenched. No conceivable agency or group of agencies could accomplish a complete reform in a few weeks."[42]

A favorable legacy of the ACE special committee's report was that it showed presidential and institutional concern. The limit was that the concern was late; had it been in 1946, it would have shown proactive leadership. According to an Associated Press interview, the committee felt underappreciated in its effort to "try to introduce a little sanity into college football. [It] feels that it has accomplished a good deal more, in a broad sense, than might be generally realized." Raymond Howes, ACE staff member and committee secretary, concluded, "If the committee has done nothing else, it has succeeded in bringing the nation's college presidents together in the common cause and convincing them that they must take an increasingly active hand in regulating their sports program." Further, "There has been intense activity during the past year and a half in every athletic conference. In most conferences there have been movements by presidents of institutions either to assume direct control or to exert greater influence on policies approved by their representatives." The new guideline in the Big Ten was that the commissioner "will make his reports directly to the college presidents instead of to the faculty representatives." Why this was an improvement remains unclear, since a president was likely to be a sports booster, and since it marked a muting of the collective faculty voice.

Howes was confident that "a start has been made on a unified national program, and that it will become increasingly productive as procedures are perfected and places where abuses exist are isolated and dealt with. . . . As far as spring practice and bowl games are concerned, progress toward abolishing them has, indeed, been slow. The committee didn't promise any miracles. But it is also true that if those were the only problems football faces, the committee never would have been formed."[43]

Favorable publicity, good will, overtures of cooperation, and the symbolism of presidential concern gave the ACE committee its day in the sun. But its limits were soon evident. Even concerned university presidents had difficulty leading athletic departments in their own institutions. One illustrative embarrassment was that shortly after release of the ACE special report, the committee chair, President John Hannah of Michigan State College, learned that his own institution had been exposed for having an elaborate slush fund. According to Mervin D. Hyman and Gordon S. White, Jr., Michigan State College was put on probation by the Big Ten Conference "for its delinquencies in permitting to exist an organization, the Spartan Foundation of Lansing, known to have solicited funds for the assistance of Michigan State athletes."[44]

More problematic than the Michigan State episode was that the ACE presidents' committee lacked means to implement its observations and recommendations. During the drafting of the report, some press coverage suggested that the ACE was challenging the NCAA—perhaps as a swipe at the failure of the Sanity Code. The NCAA inherited from the ACE committee much of the enforcement charge and during the rest of the decade would gain membership approval for an enforcement code and machinery. In the meanwhile, such nascent enforcement powers did little to change the organizational culture of the booster college, where big-time sports continued as a part of institutional advancement.

The Booster Campus, circa 1950

Attempts by the ACE special committee to draft a forceful statement encountered resistance among university presidents. An example of the occasional awkwardness came after talk about eliminating bowl games, when one committee member reminded ACE president Adams that the football team from *his* university was, indeed, going to play in the Sugar Bowl.[45] The president of Southern Methodist University, also a committee member, wrote on January 2, 1952, to Adams that he could not sign a proposed statement made by President Butterfield of Wesleyan that called for a five-year deemphasis plan. The SMU president went on to observe, "I do not believe that corruption is that widespread, nor do I agree with his remedies."[46]

Even within the ranks of reform-minded university presidents, there was strong support for big-time sports. SMU, for example, pro-

vided 154 athletic scholarships, compared to 141 academic scholarships, 20 pre-theology tuition wavers, and 20 band scholarships. Athletes lived and ate together in a "beautiful dormitory," which the SMU
president claimed helped athletes' academic performance. Differences
often were along regional lines. On January 16, 1952, President Adams
wrote to John Hannah:

> I am not at all surprised to learn that sports writers in the South are
> critical of the Committee's recommendations. That is the section
> where the most serious trouble lies and where the greatest amount of
> spade work must be done, if bad practices are actually to be corrected.
> The encouraging and to my mind by far the most significant develop-
> ment, however, is that the most thoughtful and influential sportswrit-
> ers are generally sympathetic to the work of the Committee and feel
> that you and the other Committee members have made an important
> contribution to the eventual solution of the athletic problem. When
> the editor of the *New York Times*, and such sports writers as Arthur
> Daley, Irving Marsh, Shirley Povich, and Allison Danzig are with us,
> we need not pay too much attention to some of the small fry in the
> provinces.[47]

Adams underestimated the local and regional character of American higher education. The small fry in the provinces were far more
influential in shaping public opinion within a state or campus community than were the nationally circulated newspapers. This was reinforced by the president of West Texas State College, who told the ACE
committee that the alumni of his region "want a good intercollegiate
athletics program—want it badly enough that they're willing to put
their money into it and still leave the control to the administration of
the institution." For example, he rejected alumni offers to contribute
to athletic scholarships, restricting help to one item: "a supplement to
the salary of the head football coach, though I should be glad for any
of the other coaches or academic faculty members to receive such a
supplement to their institutional salary." The alumni agreed with the
president that this was necessary to hire an excellent coach. "I know
this policy will seem to most of you who read this questionnaire a very
dangerous one and probably also a rather sinful practice, but permit me
to say in all candor that I think it is an excellent policy and that it has
proved so in actual operation." He justified the high salary of a coach
in terms of the "emotional atmosphere" and demands from local and

regional audiences for a winning team. Any proposals by national committees that ignored that situation appeared to have been written "either by children or by barn owls from the ivory towers." His problem was that "it's hard to find people who are sufficiently interested in a better program in anything except athletics that they will actually put money into it."[48]

Regionalism continued to be a strong force in the postwar period. Southern universities still lagged in gate receipts, due to smaller stadiums than those possessed by their counterparts in the Big Ten. But stadium construction increased as teams from the Southeast and Southwest persistently claimed national prominence in football. An example of a successful newcomer was the University of Oklahoma, whose football team was the best in the nation and held the longest winning streak—thirty-one consecutive victories. Meanwhile, the president of the University of Oklahoma observed, "It seemed to me that a winning team had done a great deal for the state of Oklahoma, but not nearly as much for the university." His state budget request for $10,600,000 for the biennium was substantially more than the governor's recommendation of $6,950,539. In February 1951, the university president appeared before the Oklahoma state legislature's joint House-Senate Appropriations Committee and presented a thirty-minute case for why the university warranted increased appropriations. One state senator remained unconvinced. The president's final effort at persuasion was to reply, "I hope to build a university of which our football team can be proud."[49]

Although this episode has worked its way into the folklore of higher education, some of its significance has been missed. It is most famous as a comment on overemphasis on athletics. In fact, the president's candor was refreshing; furthermore, his proposal was an interesting funding strategy that, if implemented, would have helped academic programs. Often overlooked is that his presentation was unsuccessful. The legislature did not approve his request for additional funds. Hence, those who justify big-time sports as a way of helping academics must consider the revised conclusion that in some cases intercollegiate athletics can be an end in themselves, not a means to helping the university. At the same time, the examples from West Texas State College and the University of Oklahoma indicate a regional environment of politics and popular interest with which presidents had to work, regardless of the views of the ACE special committee. An important variation on this theme came from the University of Kentucky after World War II.

Campus Profile of the University of Kentucky

The temptation in discussing the University of Kentucky's athletic program is to dwell on the point-shaving scandals of 1951 because it was sensational news when the indictments were extended to include this outstanding team, which had won the NCAA championship in 1948, 1949, and 1951. To do so is misplaced emphasis that overlooks the University of Kentucky's greater significance for understanding the place of sports in the American university. That Kentucky players were involved in point shaving shocked the Kentucky officials, coaches, and alumni because it was uncharacteristic of their program. The enduring issue was raised by Judge Streit's criticism that Kentucky's teams were "highly systemized and commercialized enterprises."

Streit's condemnation elicited a spirited rebuttal signed by the governor of Kentucky, the university president, members of the Board of Trustees, and several members of the Athletics Board. They did not deny that their varsity sports program was highly commercial and professional, but they did take issue with the evil connotations that Judge Streit attributed to these characteristics. Furthermore, they argued, the public—not the university—had to accept much of the blame for the excesses of college sports.[50] The result was a stand-off marked by harsh feelings on both sides.

Sorting through the records to referee the dispute between Judge Streit and the University of Kentucky representatives yields an unexpected bonus: it constructs a profile of the American booster campus in the postwar period.[51] If American college sports had had their own Rip Van Winkle who went to sleep in 1930 and awoke twenty years later, his biggest surprise would have been the athletic program of the University of Kentucky. Kentucky showed how a newcomer could ascend to the top ranks of college sports. Also, its primary vehicle was basketball, not football.

Kentucky had no Governor Huey Long. However, in the 1930s Lieutenant Governor Albert B. "Happy" Chandler was supportive of college sports at the state university. Chandler, governor from 1935 to 1939, later would serve as U.S. senator, commissioner of baseball, and then again as governor of Kentucky from 1955 to 1959; he was also a longtime University of Kentucky board member. He provided the continuity in state leadership that befriended the university's athletic program for several decades.

If football had its Knute Rockne, then college basketball's own legendary figure was Adolph Rupp, longtime coach of the University of Kentucky basketball Wildcats.[52] Rupp was inspiring and influential in his emphasis on winning. He found a receptive university and state-wide constituency in Kentucky from 1930 until his retirement in 1972 as the undisputed "Baron of the Blue Grass" who acquired a presence equal to any public figure in the state. No statewide or campus follow-ing surpassed devotion to Kentucky basketball, and the team became integral to both university and state culture. Rupp promoted basketball in Kentucky schools, and boosted it by hosting the state high school tournament in Lexington, home of the university. Kentucky teams were home-grown talent, with some allowance for a recruit from Ohio or archrival Indiana.

Kentucky's intercollegiate athletics found a crucial source of uni-versity support in Herman Lee Donovan, the new president who took office in 1941. Kentucky fans wanted a football team to go with Rupp's basketball tradition. According to Donovan's memoirs, he was continu-ally asked by the governor and legislators about the future of University of Kentucky football.[53] World War II interrupted immediate plans, but gave Donovan time to develop a strategy by which to use athletics as the vanguard for building a great state university. In 1946, Donovan spelled out his proposition to businessmen and alumni: the university administration was interested in a strong athletic program, but it would require substantial donations from supporters. Donovan got his money quickly, raising about $120,000 for an endowment.[54]

The companion step was to create an effective structure for running the sports program. President Donovan's key innovation took place in November 1945 when he gained approval for the University of Ken-tucky Athletic Association, a corporation with its own board. This sep-arated athletics from the university while keeping the two organiza-tions in partnership, with some overlapping board composition.[55] The state also authorized bonds to expand the football stadium's capacity from about 20,000 to 38,000. The capstone was the state's commitment to build a new Memorial Coliseum that seated 13,500 for basketball.

Meanwhile, the governor's office showed interest in connections between education and economic development. Governor Simeon Willis arranged for Griffenhagen Associates of Chicago, a consulting firm, to analyze the place of the University of Kentucky in plans for the state's future.[56] The 1947 Griffenhagen Report is an intriguing document for tracking the combination of outside expert analysis with state politics that provided a blueprint for a modern public university. Their report coincided with the rising optimism and economy of post–World War II. It gave university officials data with which to make a case to the legislature and citizens of the state.

The Griffenhagen case was that higher education in Kentucky was an underutilized resource. Compared to institutions in midwestern states such as Minnesota, the University of Kentucky was underfunded by its state legislature—and the state's economy suffered due to this neglect. A modern state university could benefit the state if it had expanded research and development, rationalization of structure and procedures, and upgrading of teaching and services. The report on the university was consistent with earlier studies, because since 1924 the Griffenhagen firm had frequently been under contract for recommendations to modernize various Kentucky state agencies. Governor Willis, an advocate of educational improvements, was not an unabashed booster for the university. How he envisioned the university's role in the state was uncertain. His influence was limited because his term ended in 1947. President Donovan, however, seized the report's momentum to promote the university.

The Griffenhagen Report was important because its tone was moderate, its analysis based on systematic data, and it dealt with the University of Kentucky in a comprehensive manner. Its publication four years before the 1951 scandals makes it invaluable as an informed outside source on Kentucky athletics apart from the emotions associated with Judge Saul Streit's 1951 court opinion. The Griffenhagen research team cautioned that although athletics could be part of the university vision, the imbalance was already detrimental to education. It recommended that "as soon as practicable, intercollegiate athletics be returned to an amateur sports basis."[57] It had reservations about the University of Kentucky Athletic Association, but found some consolation that inclusion of the university president and five faculty members on the UKAA board meant that "the university is almost in complete control." Even the Griffenhagen researchers acknowledged that rational analysis was insufficient to understand the University of Kentucky's situation:

Still, it is really impossible to put football and basketball in its proper place in university education because some of the alumni, other fans, and sports writers demand winning teams with such force that their demands cannot be resisted. It can be assumed that the university faculty in general is not proud of the position of university athletics among the university's activities. But in viewing the situation realistically, it must be concluded that the university administration, in establishing the University of Kentucky Athletic Association, Incorporated, took a step toward making the most of a bad situation, from an educational stand-point.[58]

The UKAA's separation from the university had two redeeming features: it acknowledged that physical education and varsity sports had nothing in common, and it confirmed that athletics was "operated as a business enterprise and, as such, its fund should be kept separate from university funds." The problem was that the consultants found two areas where the UKAA was at odds with its justification. The nominal one-dollar annual fee that the UKAA paid to the University of Kentucky meant that it was not charged sufficiently for use of university property; further, the UKAA received inordinate benefit at little expense from the state's construction of a new field house. A second inconsistency was that grants-in-aid were "made to athletes from a portion of the regular student fee." The Griffenhagen Report's logic was that "athletics is, primarily, an entertainment rather than an educational enterprise, and should be entirely self-supporting." The section concluded: "Athletics in the University of Kentucky, as in other universities, has become professionalized, though it is still considered to be amateur. As such, athletics has no worthy place in a university. The University of Kentucky and other state universities, as soon as possible, should return intercollegiate athletics to its amateur standing."[59]

At the September 27, 1947, meeting of the University of Kentucky's Board of Trustees, the executive committee responded to the entire Griffenhagen study. It gave great support to President Donovan's campaign to increase statewide interest in higher education, exemplified by the brochure, You Cannot Have a Great State . . . Without a Great University.[60] The motto was, "The State of Kentucky Is the Campus of the University of Kentucky," as university officials cited data to show legislators that their institution lagged behind flagship institutions in the Midwest.

But the president and the board accepted only some parts of the Griffenhagen Report. Recommendations on intercollegiate athletics were in the category that "may be theoretically sound but are not feasible because of the particular situation at the university, or for other reasons." The board, for example, rejected without comment the recommendation that "the University of Kentucky . . . , as soon as possible, should return intercollegiate athletics to its amateur standing." The recommendation that "the compulsory student fee for grants-in-aid to athletes be discontinued" led the board to reply, "The student is not, as a matter of fact, compelled to pay a fee for athletics. He pays a general incidental fee for which he receives a great many privileges beyond direct instruction. One of these is that of attending athletic contests. It does not seem practical to make one part of this general incidental fee optional."

The board dodged the concern that the issue was propriety, not just practicality. Nor did it answer the question of why scarce university resources were being dedicated to athletics, the one activity that could be self-supporting through gate receipts and donations. Technically, the UKAA did not receive state tax money; it did, however, receive 15 percent of its annual income from the mandatory student fee transfer. In 1953, for example, the university's Board of Trustees allocated $62,716 in student fees to the UKAA as part of the association's $417,417.51 total income.[61]

The university's board also rejected as "impractical" the Griffenhagen recommendation "that, after the new field house has been constructed the state be reimbursed, over a period of years, from the earnings of intercollegiate athletics, for the proportionate part of use devoted to intercollegiate athletic practice, contests, and other collegiate athletic uses." Contrary to the "separation" function cited by the Griffenhagen Report, the UKAA was attractive because it allowed the university to pay a football coach above the salary cap for a state employee. The 1946 fund-raising letters sent out by the alumni association made clear that the aim was to "hire the BEST FOOTBALL COACH IN THE UNITED STATES that we can procure; give him a free hand to do what is necessary to get us winning football teams. (Yes, we can pay over $5,000 through this new corporation.)"[62]

The University of Kentucky now had the elements of an athletic powerhouse: an endowment of alumni and business donations, a supportive president, a connection with a total university vision, a subsidy from the student fees, and the structure of the athletic association. The combination worked. After being known as the "graveyard of football coaches," in 1946 the University of Kentucky hired a young coach who had been successful in his one season at the University of Maryland. When the young coach, Paul Bryant, arrived on campus, he was greeted by a crowd who saw him as the savior of Kentucky football. Notorious for firing staff and driving off uncommitted staff, his impact on Kentucky football from 1946 to 1953 marked the greatest transformation of any football program in the nation.

By 1950, the University of Kentucky Athletic Association had an incredible concentration of coaching talent: Rupp in basketball and Bryant in football, whose combined impact on university morale and statewide loyalty was tremendous. The basketball team won national and conference championships and had a winning percentage of over 90 percent. During the same years, the football record went from modest seasons to championships; in eight years, Kentucky football teams were invited to four major bowl games, of which they won three. The 1950 football team won ten games and lost one; was champion of the Southeastern Conference; and in the Sugar Bowl, defeated the University of Oklahoma in a game ranked as one of the biggest triumphs in the history of college sports.

Kentucky coaches Bryant and Rupp were famous for their demanding programs. One player estimated that Bryant's football squads practiced eleven months per year. There were no restrictions on the number of players on a squad, or on scholarships. It was not unusual to find over one hundred players at Bryant's August football camp for three workouts per day weeks before classes started. Rupp's basketball teams were considered to be the most disciplined, best-conditioned squads in the nation, known for teamwork and defensive play. This reputation explains why the 1951 basketball scandal at the University of Kentucky was a shock to the university and to the national athletic establishment.

When the NCAA suspended the University of Kentucky basketball team for the 1952–53 season, university officials suffered humiliation without admitting guilt. The University of Kentucky's response to the scandals was not resolve to clean up its program (which it claimed was already clean) but to endure what they thought was unfair punishment that made them a national scapegoat. Coach Rupp, with a vote of confidence from the governor and the university president, vowed to return with a program that was even stronger than before. The University of Kentucky basketball team accomplished this goal in 1953–54 by going undefeated in twenty-five games and winning the NCAA championship.

Historian Charles Gano Talbert observed that "following the war, Donovan became convinced that the University of Kentucky would never receive proper financial support until it satisfied the desire of a highly vocal portion of the population for a football team."[63] And, the athletic fund-raising letters of 1946 claimed that one aim was to "help the University generally." Did President Donovan's two-part strategy work? Did commitment first to big-time football and basketball then stimulate total development of the university? During Donovan's tenure, intercollegiate athletics received first attention. In campus construction, although the postwar enrollment boom created a need for classroom buildings, laboratories, and dormitories, these became secondary to building the new Memorial Coliseum.

Donovan, in his memoirs, *Keeping the University Free and Growing*, had an entire chapter entitled "The Athletics Program of the University," in which he emphasized that the "tale of the University of Kentucky Athletic Association is a great success story." Later, he concluded, "After twenty-eight years as a college president, it is my considerate [sic] judgment that no other activity of a college or university is as difficult to administer as the athletics program. Unfortunately, more people have an interest in athletics than in education, and in their desire to have a winning team, they sometimes do things that disrupt an institution."[64] Presidents such as Donovan did not succeed in altering this mind-set. One troubling feature of the rationale cited by Donovan and other booster-university presidents was their inconsistent position on institutional self-determination. When a nationally respected outside source, such as Griffenhagen Associates, noted that the University of Kentucky's disproportionate commitment to athletics was departing from norms of highly regarded state universities in the Midwest, the university board and administration rejected the caution. However, when Kentucky was called to task for the eventual problems associated with overemphasis and big-time athletics, Donovan conveniently invoked "national trends" to justify his local situation. For example, he wrote, "If we were overemphasizing athletics at the University of Kentucky, we were only keeping in step with an overwhelming majority of the great American universities."[65] His explanation failed to acknowledge that many great American universities managed to supplement their "big athletics" with "big academics." Some, including the University of Chicago and Johns Hopkins University, achieved greatness without major athletic programs. In contrast, for the University of Kentucky during Donovan's presidency, even though the educational programs did gain resources, the gap between athletics and academics remained wide. When Donovan concluded, "It is easy to see why I hold that the most trying problem of a college administrator is the athletics program," the glories and leverage he gained from the Kentucky athletic program suggest that he was shedding crocodile tears. The University of Kentucky between 1946 and 1960 was the institution its president and alumni wanted.

How did events in college sports in the late 1940s and 1950s fit into the University of Kentucky's institutional heritage and mission? A revealing document is the 1960 self-study that the University of Kentucky prepared for the Southern Association, which includes a section entitled "A Genuine University Atmosphere."[66] In contrast to the publicity associated with football and basketball, there were signs of an underestimated source of university strength and commitment: a dedicated faculty, well aware of the limited resources it faced as a state university in a relatively modest economic environment where academic and educational programs tended to be overshadowed by athletics. The outstanding feature was faculty commitment to the cultural and intellectual life of undergraduates in both the classroom and the cultural, artistic, and literary activities of the extracurriculum. The faculty persevered in making the emerging state university a beacon, both "utilitarian" and a cultural force within the lives of students and in the life of the state, even though public commitment was foremost to intercollegiate athletics.

The University of Kentucky's rebuttal to Judge Streit's critique absolved the campus of some charges. It also confirmed that the university itself accepted commercial and professional athletics as a central part of the campus. In building a top-rank intercollegiate athletic program after World War II, the University of Kentucky was also acquiring a source of recurrent problems. The legacy of athletics was a tradition of championship teams—and a tradition of controversy. Over the next four decades, the University of Kentucky attracted publicity that alternated between national championship celebrations and national notoriety. Each time a Kentucky team was charged with improprieties, investigation would be followed by alumni and fan denials. "Reform" usually meant a renewed commitment to sustaining a formidable athletic program.

The University of Pennsylvania

Boosterism after World War II was not confined to the state universities of the South. The University of Pennsylvania, a private mid-Atlantic urban university, was notable because its administration advanced a novel institutional mission between 1950 and 1952. The plan failed in part because the Penn administrators' ideas about the potential for promotion were ahead of their time, and also because Penn was unable to maintain the precarious balance of academics and athletics.

Penn was caught between two worlds. Its heritage included nationally ranked football teams as well as association with the historic universities of the so-called Ivy League grouping. As discussed earlier, one obstacle to creation of a formal Ivy League in the 1930s was the reluctance of the presidents of Harvard, Yale, Brown, Columbia, and Dartmouth to enter a formal alliance with Penn. In 1937, Penn's president, Thomas Gates, worked to gain the presidents' confidence and to encourage formation of an Ivy League. Gates gave his assurance that Penn's football program would veer from big-time competition.[67]

From 1937 to 1949, Penn had a solid football program of winning teams and large home crowds. Penn was dominant in play against Ivy teams, with a record of fifty-two victories, seven defeats, and three ties between 1935 and 1950. To wary Ivy institutions, Penn already was close to overemphasis. Even after Penn had signed the 1945 Ivy Group presidential pact, there was uncertainty as to the direction of Penn football and its adherence to the eight-member agreement. In the late 1940s, under its new president, Harold Stassen, Penn's athletic policy as part of its total institutional plan shifted emphasis. Stassen, who had been governor of Minnesota for several terms, was influenced by the public support that the national championship University of Minnesota football teams had brought to the university and state. In August 1950, he presented a comparable vision for the University of Pennsylvania, as he announced, "This date will be a milestone in Pennsylvania athletics. . . . We want victories with honor. We want to improve our schedules. We want to be able to appeal to star high-school athletes. . . . I foresee a remarkable future of strong teams."[68]

The presidents of the other Ivy League institutions saw a dismal future in which Penn would probably extend its dominance over Ivy teams. Stassen's "Victory with Honor" meant that the Pennsylvania plan was to combine the prestige of Ivy League academic affiliation with the power of Big Ten football. For a while, Penn did manage this precarious balance. It frequently attracted crowds of seventy thousand at its home games at Philadelphia's Franklin Field and played successfully against such teams as Army, Navy, California, North Carolina, Virginia, Wisconsin, and Notre Dame as well as its traditional Ivy League foes.

To carry out the "Victory with Honor" plan, President Stassen hired a new athletic director, Francis Murray, whose charge was to restore attendance (which had dropped to about forty thousand per home game) to seventy thousand. Murray did this and more. Not only did the large crowds return to Franklin Field, but Penn also captured a new audience: local television viewers. Early on, Murray understood the power of broadcast sports and made Penn's athletic program the nation's most innovative in negotiating contracts for televising home football games. According to historian David Goldberg's analysis, Penn had the formula for athletic department success: "The 1952 football team generated revenue in excess of $500,000 for the university and football netted a profit of well over $300,000, enough to subsidize all of Penn's other athletic teams and leave the school with a $75,000 athletic surplus to boot."[69]

Ultimately, however, Penn's athletic policy balancing act was upset by opposite forces. Foremost was the pressure of prestige in which Penn opted to deemphasize big-time football to be in tune with the presidents of the Ivy Group.[70] Penn's compliance meant that it became a charter member of the 1956 Ivy Group conference. The second force was Penn's lonely battle against the National Collegiate Athletic Association. The NCAA, fearing that televising college football would deter game attendance, moved in the early 1950s to ban live television coverage of all college football games.[71]

Penn protested in vain that the NCAA had overstepped its authority by intruding on an institution's right of self-determination. Only Notre Dame and a few other institutions sided with Penn. When Penn resolved to defy the NCAA television ban, the NCAA countered by declaring that Penn was "not in good standing." Penn eventually backed off, grudgingly forfeited its television program, and steered its athletic policies toward the Ivy League philosophy.

Whereas the University of Kentucky withstood external pressure to deflate its athletic program, Pennsylvania withdrew its novel strategy of combining powerful athletics with powerful academics, opting to emphasize its educational priorities. Most historical interpretations hail the resolution as a wise institutional choice that stood for a strong academic university and a sane, balanced varsity sports program. David Goldberg, however, has recently presented a provocative revision, arguing that by the mid-1950s Pennsylvania (and its fellow members of the Ivy League) had forfeited "a position of leadership on the national intercollegiate front." According to Goldberg, "Universities such as Duke, Stanford, and Michigan—which combine outstanding academic curricula with nationally successful athletic programs—have emerged through the past three decades in the national consciousness as the models and outstanding examples of how academics and athletics can and should be integrated."[72]

One counter to Goldberg's conclusion is that since 1956 the Ivy League has constituted a model of academic and athletic excellence that ought be emulated, not denigrated, by other conferences. Whether or not one agrees with Goldberg's conclusion, he provides a good reminder that in the early 1950s neither presidents nor athletic directors knew how the college football debates were going to be resolved. Nor was it predestined how institutions were going to define their programs or align themselves in conferences. Penn's decision to drop its "Victory with Honor" program was not inevitable. Why, for example, did Pennsylvania not continue its distinctive plan and dare to be an independent institution (as did Notre Dame)? Why did not Penn join a conference with like-minded universities who wanted to be of national caliber in both athletics and academics? This might have been membership in the Big Ten, in the new Atlantic Coast Conference established in 1953, or some other alliance that offered an alternative to the Ivy League's deemphasis.

Penn's decision to conform to the Ivy League philosophy was important for reshaping its own institutional identity. However, its enduring national contribution to the business of college sports derived from a role it rejected when finally it affirmed its Ivy League allegiance: namely, as a pioneer in television. First, Penn had demonstrated the potential that college football games held for drawing large television audiences. Second, Penn was influential in defeat: as historian David Goldberg and economist Paul Lawrence have shown, Pennsylvania's ultimate setback in its clash with the NCAA over broadcast policies signaled the maturation of the NCAA as a cartel controlling media markets and revenues, with a collective power that henceforth surpassed the prerogative of a single member institution.

Reform Reassessed

Even though the 1951 scandals led to an enforcement system, large-scale, commercialized college sports were able to persist. The American Council on Education's special committee report indicated that college and university presidents lacked an effective means by which to implement reforms. This void benefited the NCAA, which by 1960 had two power sources: it overcame the initial setbacks of its 1948 "Sanity Code" and acquired license to police athletic programs; and it gained as a promoter and protector of commercial interests, whether it be in television contracts or in bowl games. Between 1946 and 1960, intercollegiate athletics coalesced into recognizable clusters, as big-time conferences stood in bold relief. Within major conferences, commissioners started to police and penalize member institutions for rules violations. Such efforts did little, however, to impede those institutions committed to commercialized programs. Creation of the Ivy League in 1956 was probably the most important instance of athletic reform. At the other extreme, one finds at the University of Virginia a 1952 faculty report that made a case for reform but had little impact.[73] The life cycle and limits of collective reform after World War II are best illustrated by the peculiar and complex episode of the Pacific Coast Conference.

CHAPTER FIVE

Faculty Control and the Irony of Reform

The Pacific Coast Conference, 1946 to 1959

During the nationally televised broadcast of the 1991 New Year's Day Rose Bowl Game, the PAC 10 Conference announced that it was "celebrating its seventy-fifth anniversary." Tracing its roots back to 1915, it saluted itself as the "Conference of Champions" and claimed the most NCAA champions in men's and women's sports.[1] The PAC 10 had a long association with the Rose Bowl (the first college bowl game) plus a remarkable record of individual and team performances in Olympic competition. Conference membership, consisting of the University of California at Berkeley, UCLA, Washington, Washington State, Oregon, Oregon State, Arizona, Arizona State, Stanford, and the University of Southern California, represented a notable American achievement in bringing together excellence in academics and athletics within the large research university setting.

If the record was right, the history was wrong. The conference was scarcely more than twenty-five years old, having been created as the PAC 8, with two members added in 1978 to become the PAC 10. To celebrate a seventy-fifth anniversary meant that the PAC 10 had taken liberty to link itself to the old Pacific Coast Intercollegiate Athletic Conference (PCC), founded in 1915. This glossed over a rough historical edge: the PCC was dissolved in 1959. What now stands as the PAC 10 has a different charter than did the PCC. This is no antiquarian quibble, because dissolution of the PCC in 1959 was one of the most bitter incidents involving the politics and philosophy of intercollegiate athletics.

The PAC 10's selective memory imposes a misleading cohesion on the history of college sports. If the PAC 10 wishes to trace its beginnings back to 1915, one must then reopen the books to examine the issues that led to disruption of the historic PCC.

The Context of the Conference

Why study a conference? The case of the PCC after World War II is significant because it illustrates the complex academic diplomacy of intercollegiate athletics, including the ironies of reform and the changing place of the faculty in the governance of college sports. The conference is the crucial unit in shaping and regulating intercollegiate athletics because it can have more impact on shaping athletic policies than the NCAA and certainly more than occasional reports such as those issued by the Carnegie Foundation or the special committee of the American Council on Education. It also allows insight into the role of conference commissioner, an important but relatively understudied figure. The conference is the locus where a small group of institutions in voluntary association agree to work together, to compete while showing some sign of mutual respect and comparable academic standards.

The Conference Crisis of 1956

The PCC crisis took place in 1956. Just as college basketball teams had their conspicuous scandal in 1951, five years later so did college football with the Pacific Coast Conference episode. Revelation of major offenses at four member institutions—the University of Washington, the University of Southern California, the University of California at Los Angeles, and the University of California, Berkeley—created what one journalist called "Football's Biggest Stink." Another writer said, "College football never has experienced quite so shameful a mess as the current Pacific Conference scandal."[2]

Press coverage focused on the four offending institutions' reliance on slush funds for systematic, unauthorized payments to college football players. Violations of the conference code led to major penalties: tens of thousands of dollars in fines, forfeited eligibility for the postseason Rose Bowl game, and loss of one year's eligibility for underclassmen and half a season's for seniors. It also brought the NCAA into a strong enforcement role. Although the 1956 events were dramatic, they were merely a snapshot of an extended film of the operation and control of big-time college sports between 1946 and 1959.

The Conference and the Commissioner

The crisis of 1956, then, was not an isolated event. Instead it was the culmination of long-term developments following World War II. The PCC was relatively strict, with a regulatory record that included suspension of the University of Southern California from the conference in 1924, the conference's critical self-study of 1932, and its voluminous Atherton Report of 1939.[3] The PCC had a paid commissioner, an elaborate constitution, a formal code of conduct, a system for reporting student-athlete eligibility, and regular meetings of institutional representatives and conference staff. Its most distinctive characteristic was that its power was vested in its faculty athletic representatives (known as FARs). They *were* the conference. Even though there was a strong Presidents' Council and a council of athletic directors and coaches, conference authority ultimately was with FARs. Although there were variations from one campus to another, a FAR was usually appointed by the president, often upon recommendation from the campus faculty senate. Another key feature was that the Conference itself did not declare offending student-athletes ineligible: each institution did so for its own athletes found guilty of conference violations.

The commissioner after World War II was Victor O. Schmidt, a 1923 alumnus of the University of Wisconsin who received his law degree in 1928 from the University of Southern California. He continued the conference tradition of strong enforcement and set up the conference office in Los Angeles. Schmidt's leadership in the NCAA after World War II gave the PCC a conspicuous place in national debates. As Paul Lawrence described in *Unsportsmanlike Conduct*, at the 1950 NCAA Conference Schmidt stood firm for enforcement of the Sanity Code once it had been adopted:

> Besides two members of the Compliance Committee, only one person spoke in favor of terminating the memberships. Victor O. Schmidt, Commissioner of the Pacific Coast Intercollegiate Athletic Conference, . . . noted that all members had agreed to the Sanity Code when it had been formulated two years earlier, fully aware of the punishment due a member who failed to comply. To Schmidt, retreating before actual

violations seemed sadly ironic, and he colorfully summarized the choices for the voting membership: "Are we going to wear the red badge of courage [vote for termination] or are we going to show the white feather of surrender and despair [vote against termination]?"[4]

Although the NCAA may have retreated from its 1948 Sanity Code, the PCC persisted in drafting its own Athletic Code of Conduct. Between 1947 and 1951, Schmidt encouraged FARs and presidents to discuss the athletic policies they wanted, recommending that the prospective code be congruent with their universities' educational philosophies. Once the conference was clear on that, then the commissioner could administer appropriately. In 1949, he told the conference that "collegiate athletics is the orphan in the huge family of higher educational activity in this country" and urged academic leaders to rethink the proposition that intercollegiate athletics be expected to bear the burden of being financially self-supporting.[5]

Schmidt's preference was for strong institutional self-determination, with the conference taking a secondary role. In 1950, he made a case for observing the law rather than enforcing the law within the conference and argued against a system of fines for violations. He observed, "We are thinking of the Conference and the member institutions in exact reverse," warning university leaders that they could not and should not expect the conference to solve essential institutional problems. The universities ultimately were to be responsible for sound practice because "the Conference cannot control where it has no control"; Schmidt cautioned that the "institutions are playing a game of hide and seek with the conference."[6] The commissioner acted as a catalyst, challenging faculty and university presidents to take initiative for responsible athletic policy and academic philosophy.

Contrary to Schmidt's personal preference, the conference adopted a system of fines. In the late 1940s, the PCC was an example of a conference in which there were simultaneously strong restrictions and dramatic violations. Keen competition for athletic talent was illustrated by one famous player, Hugh McElhenny, halfback for the University of Washington who had been recruited by over sixty colleges when he was a high school player in Los Angeles and, later, a student at Compton Junior College. According to one sportswriter, "he had found his way to Seattle by following a trail of twenty dollar bills" when he enrolled at Washington. An All-American halfback, he earned a place in the lore of college sports, becoming known as the first college player "ever to take a cut in salary to play pro football."[7]

To Commissioner Schmidt, such incidents meant that by 1951, "our policy thus far has been a gradual but continuing capitulation to pressure for a professional-type program, by which I mean a program seeking perfection and excellence in athletic techniques the likes of which was never intended for amateur sports or for part-time or leisure participation by regular college students carrying a normal study load. We are trying to perform an impossibility: to operate a professional program on an amateur basis."[8]

A turning point came in 1951 when the conference investigated charges that the University of Oregon football coach had violated the conference code for financial aid and athletic subsidies. When violations were confirmed, Commissioner Schmidt came down severely on the University of Oregon, noting to FARs and presidents, "If the members individually prevent the Code from being enforced, how can the collective whole accomplish something that the aggregate of the individuals oppose?" Moving from general principle to the specific case, he said:

> The Commissioner has informed the University of Oregon that unless rebuttal could be made of the violations reported against its head football coach, the members of the Conference might well inquire how they could continue confidence in the performance by the University of Oregon of its responsibilities under the Athletic Code, so long as the head football coach continued as a member of the athletic staff. It seems to the Commissioner that if the members abdicate their responsibility of enforcement of the Code to the Conference, that the Conference should assume authority to make that enforcement effective even to the extent of making recommendations concerning the institution's internal athletic affairs, and where those recommendations are not followed to proceed with consideration of canceling schedules or of suspension from membership. The Commissioner has not made any such recommendations to the institutions in this case. The membership will recall that two years ago the Commissioner made a recommendation concerning a head coach at another member institution and that the Conference denied him the authority.[9]

The University of Oregon complied with conference sentiment and fired the violating coach. Then Oregon's coaching staff and FAR urged the PCC to look at what they thought were serious abuses by the UCLA football coach, Red Sanders. Although the conference took no action against UCLA, the Oregon case set a precedent for strict enforcement. Conference attention then shifted to problems of alumni booster clubs. According to the *New York Times*, the West Coast situation was as follows: "One West Coast educator, who has been close to the athletic scene for many years, said the attitude of college officials and observance of eligibility standards had improved in recent years, but that there was still much secret subsidization by alumni. 'The old graduate is often over-enthusiastic when he sees a good football or basketball prospect, and that seems to be the trouble all over the country,' he said."[10]

This situation was familiar to Commissioner Schmidt, who had faced pressure from alumni groups to ease conference restrictions on recruitment and financial aid. The president of the Pacific Coast Athletic Alumni Committees had recommended "certain changes in policy and rules, which we find will do much toward correcting the hypocritical situation facing all our schools relative to the subsidization problem." Schmidt responded that he was obligated to enforce conference rules, not to make policy. After 1952, charges of violations escalated. The conference affirmed that presidents were ultimately responsible for an institution's programs, so that booster clubs must be "under university control." And the PCC special committee on organized recruiting had each university file a report on its various alumni clubs.[11]

Schmidt's preference was for institutional self-regulation. However, with the approval of FARs and the knowledge of presidents, he reluctantly took on expanded powers of surveillance and fact finding. At the November 1952 conference meeting Schmidt noted, "Under present regulations there seems to be no real sincerity on the part of member institutions, or interested individuals to control the situation. . . . Adequate and effective enforcement seems impossible under present regulations, and has resulted in suspicions and lack of trust, which stimulate rumors undesirable to the best interests of the conference."[12]

The commissioner, concerned that the conference had strayed from its original intent, observed in December 1953, "The recruiting rules of the Conference have been cut and pruned so drastically over the last twelve years as to be unrecognizable from their original form when enacted in some detail . . . in January 1940."[13] Eventually the conference appropriated ten thousand dollars to be used by the commissioner in employing professional assistance to investigate abuses of financial aid.[14]

The PCC was in the vanguard of reform. As early as 1951, its FARs had formal discussion of dropping out of the Rose Bowl, eliminating spring football practice, and placing strict limits on financial aid and job programs.[15] Most important, in 1953 the presidents reaffirmed their 1951 commitment that PCC athletics "would go no further down the road of professionalism."

The next issue to surface was that of campus responsibility for athletic programs, as well as for alumni booster clubs. On June 6, 1954, the conference agreed "to recommend that each member institution require its Director of Intercollegiate Athletics to be under the direct control and supervision of, and with responsibility to, the university administration instead of any student association, board of control, or sub-governing body."[16]

Robert Gordon Sproul, president of the University of California, summarized the conference situation to the chancellors of Berkeley and UCLA as follows: "Taken as a whole, the report seemed to furnish a clue to the Conference's frustration in attempting to secure compliance with its code. In his role as investigator and 'prosecuting attorney' the Commissioner appears to have been and to be at a particular disadvantage when confronted by his employers when they choose to act as 'attorneys for the defense.'" Sproul proposed to give the commissioner more security and better status by having his hiring controlled exclusively by the conference council of presidents, so as to put the commissioner "in a stronger position to proceed vigorously against suspected violations and violators."[17] In fact, this would merely have shifted power from FARs to presidents. The faculty athletic representatives rejected Sproul's recommendation.[18]

Another jurisdictional matter was that the PCC faculty representatives emphasized that the conduct of athletics was to be left with institutions, "and the conference should intervene only when a member institution fails to discharge its responsibility." By spring 1955, however, violations had increased, indicating the need for more conference enforcement machinery. At their meeting of May 10, 1955, the presidents once again renewed their claim to be rightful employers of the commissioner: "In making the present proposal, the presidents have no desire to take over the day-to-day management of the Conference or otherwise to erode the authority of the faculty representatives."[19]

By June 1955, conference dynamics shifted as the FARs took more interest in commissioner reports and began to hand out sanctions.[20] Schmidt noted, "In the area of rules enforcement, it is my own inclination to place more emphasis on prevention," by relying on information and education before problems arose.[21] Finally, Schmidt's memo to all presidents expressed concern that FARs were not being informed of presidents' decisions or being sent minutes.[22]

Anatomy of the Scandal of 1956

Review of conference events from 1946 through 1955 demonstrates that there had been both a progression of reform and regulation and an escalating pattern of code violations. Commissioner Schmidt did have a formidable reputation for investigating offenses, having been praised by one national magazine as "college sport's top private eye." But his information did not necessarily constitute proof, especially when tracking the financial activities of booster clubs. Each club tended to dodge conference inquiries by replying that it would open its own financial records to inspection only if all others would open theirs. Also, there was wrangling among member universities over allowable academic standards and financial aid packages. For example, the two campuses of the University of California—Berkeley and UCLA—were expressly forbidden to offer athletic grants-in-aid. This was their own university rule, while the conference itself made no such restriction. Increasing power accrued to the commissioner, and within ranks of FARs and presidents, their growing awareness of code violations coincided with their dissatisfaction that enforcement was not yet sufficient.

The conference mood changed with a series of exposés of slush funds in early 1956. In four sensational cases, the stories first appeared in the press, as distinguished from having been uncovered by the commissioner. The exposed slush funds relied on euphemisms for their names. For the University of Washington, it was the "Greater Seattle Advertising Fund." At USC, it was the "Southern California Educational Foundation." For UCLA, it was the "Bruin Bench" and the "Young Men's Club of Westwood." Berkeley was involved with the "San Francisco Gridiron Club." Berkeley's athletic recruiting club in the Los Angeles area was known as the "South Seas Fund," appropriate for talent fishing expeditions outside the northern part of the state.[23]

As each of the PCC scandals was uncovered in the first four months of 1956, it had a domino effect. The first was at the University of Washington. In January 1956, several football players who were discontented with their head coach staged a mutiny. The athletic director fired the coach, who then retaliated at a subsequent press conference by raising rhetorical questions about an alumni club's alleged slush fund.[24] The Pacific Coast Conference followed up on the charges, found evidence about the illegal activities of the Greater Washington Advertising Fund, and in early May imposed sanctions on Washington. A month later, on June 9, University of Washington officials withdrew their request that the PCC reduce its penalties. In short, Washington took its medicine.[25]

In early March, allegations about illegal payments made by the Bruin Bench and the Young Men's Club of Westwood were published in Los Angeles newspapers. Commissioner Schmidt, who had been investigating these organizations for several months without their cooperation, arranged with UCLA officials on March 5 to interview 19 student-athletes and athletic staff members. Two days later, the UCLA chancellor refused to permit the commissioner to conduct the interviews, pending completion of UCLA's own internal investigation. Ten weeks passed before the PCC commissioner was given permission by UCLA officials to proceed. Conference inquiry led to UCLA's admission that "all members of the football coaching staff had, for several years, known of the unsanctioned payments to student athletes and had cooperated with the booster club members or officers, who actually administered the program by actually referring student athletes to them for such aid."

Soon thereafter other PCC universities joined UCLA in the conference review of subsidy violations. One key figure in the indictments was a UCLA alumnus and member of the UCLA Athletic Advisory Board who also was Los Angeles deputy district attorney. He told reporters that there was a secret fund for illegal payments to USC athletes. Over the next week, the Los Angeles Mirror-News reported that it was the so-called Southern California Educational Foundation. Most damaging was the claim that a key participant in the illegal program was an employee of the General Alumni Association of USC. A few days later, the same UCLA alumnus and deputy district attorney continued his exposé, charging that the University of California at Berkeley operated a phony work program for athletes. University of California officials initially denied the allegations. However, they conducted their own investigation and in June acknowledged that twenty-five players had received illegal aid. Eventually the NCAA looked into the offenses and imposed its own sanctions, marking one of the first great test cases for NCAA enforcement in football.[26]

Aftershocks

The real drama for the PCC came after the revelations of slush funds and the handing down of penalties. The shifting alliances among institutions after the scandals broke revealed the ugly side of the politics of higher education. The tensions among university presidents surfaced at a special meeting of the conference Presidents' Council in San Francisco on July 17, 1956.[27] The agenda was sufficiently sensitive that the chair, President Sproul of the University of California, arranged for a court reporter to make a complete transcript. Chancellor Allen of UCLA insisted that the conference ought to reconsider penalties. He claimed to have affidavits of wrongdoing at other conference institutions. Implicit in the discussion was that Stanford's athletic program was one of Allen's targets. Allen refused to present the documents, a defiance of standard procedures of evidence that irked the presidents of Stanford, Oregon, and Washington, who tried to convince Chancellor Allen that no conference could pursue charges without specific documentation. All the while, Allen worked to dilute the authority of the faculty athletic representatives.

Campus Animosities and State Rivalries

One by-product of the 1956 scandals was that some of the university presidents brought into the public arena intense animosities between institutions and states. Specifically, ill feelings between California and Oregon came to the fore. In this way the scandal precipitated the intrusion of university regents and board members, as well as state influentials, into conference affairs.[28] The primary example of extended participation was Edwin Pauley, a regent of the University of California who was formidable in the oil industry and was also part owner of the Los Angeles Rams professional football team. In correspondence with President Sproul of the University of California, Pauley stated his disdain for universities in the Pacific Northwest and advocated that the California institutions leave the Pacific Coast Conference to form a "California

Conference." Pauley's letters to Sproul reflected the influence of John Vaughn, president elect of the UCLA Alumni Association, who was a strong advocate for UCLA's right to freedom from the PCC in athletics and from the University of California system in institutional development.[29]

For a while, Regent Pauley encountered dissent from some University of California regents. Donald McLaughlin of San Francisco took issue with Pauley's proposed solutions to conference problems. If, for example, Pauley felt that University of California campuses deserved to play against colleges with comparably high academic standards, McLaughlin suggested that Pauley consider athletic policies elsewhere as models. McLaughlin saw Ivy League institutions as appropriate academic peers for the University of California and preferred their policies in contrast to those of the PCC. Nevertheless, McLaughlin felt that to withdraw from the PCC would be "a most serious mistake. It would surely expose us to the charge that we were condoning the violations of a code we had accepted; and that we were planning to open the door to the many doubtful procedures for which we were very properly penalized."

Regent McLaughlin believed that the PCC rules were too strict if Berkeley and UCLA desired to participate in "big football" and play such opponents as the midwestern universities and most of the southern universities. On the other hand, he wrote, "the rules are much too liberal if we are to be accepted as proper opponents for teams from the colleges of highest academic rank, with which, in my judgment, we should desire to be rated."[30]

Pauley, whose base was in southern California, received favorable editorials and coverage in the Los Angeles newspapers but fared less well with the San Francisco press. On May 28, 1957, an editorial in the San Francisco Chronicle lambasted Pauley, charging him with wanting intercollegiate athletics to be a money-making venture. His intervention in Pacific Coast Conference matters was depicted as a "wide end run by regents [that] threatens UC standards."[31]

By this time, relations among the member institutions were sufficiently strained that the conference was starting to unravel. Eventually the three University of California members of the Presidents' Council (President Robert Sproul, Chancellor Clark Kerr of Berkeley, and Chancellor Raymond Allen of UCLA) drafted their own "Five Point Plan" that emphasized academic eligibility standards; it essentially set UC campuses apart from the Pacific Coast Conference and laid the groundwork for their departure from the conference. The plan, which supported Regent Pauley's point of view, appeared to be a show of unity among the University of California campuses. However, some other conference members argued that this was misleading. Their interpretation was that the UC plan actually was the product of family quarrels and compromises within the UC ranks.[32]

Sproul's View of the PCC's Dissolution

Robert Sproul, president of the University of California, has been depicted by his biographer George Petit as the influential figure among the PCC presidents. Petit's account of Sproul's role in the conference includes Sproul's insinuation that the faculty athletic representatives often sided with athletic directors—a curious charge, since FARs were usually appointed by their respective university presidents. Sproul's enduring complaint was the failure of the PCC to adopt tougher academic eligibility requirements. Obviously, Sproul as a university president was predisposed to push for greater presidential control.

The questionable part of his view of conference events was his tendency to ignore a volatile situation that underlay the athletic policy issues: there was strong UCLA alumni discontent about both the PCC penalties and the larger issue of UCLA's lack of autonomy within the University of California structure. In addition, Sproul was sensitive about Berkeley's own unexpected humiliation in the scandal. The upshot was that for Sproul, the PCC dispute was not just about athletics. At stake was the ideal to which he had long been devoted, a unified University of California that enjoyed statewide support.[33] The idea of maintaining one great university even as it added statewide campuses and centers was Sproul's passion, but it collided with the aspirations of UCLA alumni who believed that Sproul's vision would always favor the Berkeley campus at the expense of the younger UCLA campus. Both the success and the scandal of college football at UCLA were fuel for the volatile UCLA alumni who were increasingly adamant about wanting football success and campus autonomy.

To understand the cluster of governance issues emanating from the Pacific Coast Conference, it is helpful to balance Sproul's perspective with the interpretation of events made by the president of Oregon State College, A. L. Strand. Strand wrote to Sproul upon receiving word that the University of California institutions were leaving the PCC, prefacing his letter with the statement, "When the 'paper rubbish of our lives' is being examined by some future historian I want him to find this reply attached to your telegram" about UCLA and Berkeley withdrawing from PCC. According to Strand:

> The actual reasons for California [Berkeley] and UCLA dropping out of the PCC are as different as day and night. The latter's part in the conference trouble, which began with the revelations of dishonesty on a wholesale basis at UCLA, USC, and Washington, nearly two years ago, has been despicable from start to finish. Pressure from within and without the Los Angeles institution brought about the action of the California regents on December 13. The reasons for the parent institution [Berkeley] getting out are various—political to save unity in its organization and to protect UCLA from expulsion—athletic and academic because its officials, its faculty senate, and student leaders are out of sympathy with the seemingly inescapable practices of highly competitive intercollegiate athletics. The significance and gambit in the whole affair was the union of Berkeley with UCLA.

The University of California's "Five Point Plan" skirted the real issues and put forward conditions that everyone knew the conference could not accept. Strand continued,

> Admissions and scholarship had nothing to do with the withdrawals, although they constituted the point of emphasis in the official action of the regents and in the publicity given to the exodus. Berkeley's desire to schedule athletic contests only with academic equals, or near equals, is real, although in the 42-year history of the conference, this expression was seldom, if ever, expressed before last June. The marriage of this desire on the part of Berkeley with the known ambitions and necessities of its sister institution has produced a bastard that has the bark of a purebred but the innards and hair of a mongrel. Everyone recognizes it for what it is.[34]

The president of the University of Idaho echoed Strand's concerns and expressed displeasure with the president of USC and the chancellor of UCLA at Presidents' Council sessions:

I am getting awful [sic] sick and tired of the spouting off that both Fagg and Allen are resorting to in the press. Myself, I see no reason whatsoever for any special meetings of the Presidents' Council. I think the faculty representatives have followed the dictates of their conscience as well as the instructions given them by the presidents. The point that both Fagg and Allen ignore is that we had regulations referred to as the PCC Rules which all institutions were obligated to comply with. Knowingly and wittingly their representatives did not comply and Heaven knows it wasn't unwittingly but with full premeditated aforethought that they committed the violations. They were caught, and now why should they scream and insist that other people be involved and complete investigations be made before penalties are invoked upon them? . . . If this is the attitude that they are going to maintain, I believe personally that it might be a blamed good thing for them to withdraw from the conference since it is quite evident that either they expect special consideration to be given to them because of the size, prominence, and the fact that they are located in California where there are a lot of rabid sports writers and fans; or perhaps they just don't intend ever to comply with any kind of regulations if they are not according to their desires. . . I am much disgusted. Do we or do we not abide by rules and regulations until they are changed—if not, why have rules and regulations?[35]

The University of Southern California had been fairly reserved through much of the conference discussions, but this changed when USC was dragged into the maelstrom by the UCLA alumnus's exposé of the Southern California Educational Foundation. USC's president Fagg had tended to align with Chancellor Allen of UCLA; but, along with this united front of Los Angeles institutions, according to USC coach John McKay in his 1965 oral history for the USC archives, USC felt betrayed by UCLA in 1956. USC now had to deal with charges. Its responses included seeking assistance from state legislators. In addition, USC alumnus Asa Call obtained a legal opinion about whether the PCC had violated the California state constitution. USC officials even worked with Assemblyman Frank J. Bonnelli to see about creating a California State Commission, instead of the Pacific Coast Conference. These efforts accomplished little beyond galvanizing popular opinion in Los Angeles in favor of USC. For example, beyond the furor of public controversy, the Association of Independent California Colleges and

Universities (of which USC was a member) advised that to involve the state government in control and regulation of college sports was a wrong move.[36]

Campus Profile of UCLA

The center of the storm was UCLA. UCLA's institutional history during the period 1946 to 1960 illustrates yet another important variation on the modern American booster campus. Founded in 1929, it is an example of a young branch campus that asserted its own identity apart from the historic flagship university—in this case, Berkeley. Its ecology within the metropolitan Los Angeles area that it shared with USC suggests an interesting symbiosis: the two universities were archrivals. Their competition for local support was fierce and sometimes bitter, but their fates were always interdependent and usually of mutual benefit. It was a situation where a growing city and region supported both institutions. Los Angeles also happened to be a football-crazy city after World War II: its fans and press enthusiastically supported both UCLA and USC teams, as well as the professional Los Angeles Rams.

After World War II, UCLA's ascent created an unprecedented organizational structure, the multicampus system, which raised an important question: how does a public university in a state as large and diverse as California retain its hold on the public's imagination? The University of California provided American higher education with the prototype of a new entity: the multicampus system. This distinctive structural arrangement was reflected in the composition of the PCC's Presidents' Council: the University of California, technically a single institution, had three members: the system's president, plus the chancellors of two major campuses. Yet among the faculty athletic representatives, it acted as two distinct institutions, with Berkeley and UCLA each having a representative, although there was none for the University of California system as a whole. By any measure, UCLA was a thriving, successful campus in the 1950s with high undergraduate admission standards, ascending graduate programs, an outstanding faculty, and highly regarded professional schools. Yet it still wanted to shake off the perception of being Berkeley's "southern branch," the junior campus of the University of California.[37]

One way to gain campus stature was through intercollegiate athletics. Playing in the local shadow of the powerful University of Southern

California football teams in the 1930s and 1940s made this a difficult assignment. By the early 1940s and after World War II, UCLA competed with and even surpassed USC in its won-lost records and local support. Throughout the 1950s, however, the UCLA athletic program displayed a sustained capacity to attract and generate controversy over intercollegiate athletics. For example, in the early 1950s UCLA alumni tarnished the public image of cohesion within the University of California system with intermittent complaints that Berkeley could stockpile more athletic talent than UCLA because UCLA's admissions requirements were especially strict.

Between 1951 and 1956, UCLA had problems of irregularities in its campus work program, which employed a large number of UCLA football players. Quite apart from any conference investigation, UCLA's own business manager repeatedly alerted the chancellor and the dean of students to suspicious conditions: a lack of supervision of athletes doing campus work; a budget that rose from about five thousand dollars in 1947 to over fifty thousand dollars in 1953.[38] At UCLA, the athletic program, including the athletic staff and coaches, was under the auspices of the Associated Students of UCLA (known as ASUCLA). ASUCLA expressed concern over its inability to supervise all the student employees, especially those who were associated with the athletic program. Eventually the conference became concerned about the inadequacy of supervision of work by athletes at the University of California at Los Angeles.[39] Hence, one issue that emerged in the conference and in university discussions was whether intercollegiate athletics should be removed from ASUCLA control and placed more formally under the university administration.

Contrary to President Sproul's vision of a cohesive University of California, by the mid-1950s substantial mistrust had developed between the athletic officials at Berkeley and those at UCLA. The national notoriety that UCLA gained in the mid-1950s from the Knox affair did not help. Ronnie Knox, a highly publicized football player who was being groomed by his father for a career in professional football, transferred from Berkeley to UCLA, precipitating a storm of charges and countercharges about illegal payments.[40]

UCLA's perspective on the reasons for the dissolution of the Pacific Coast Conference differed from Sproul's. The main issue for UCLA was that its alumni were threatening to campaign for a split from the existing University of California structure to become an autonomous institution. President Sproul stepped into a hornet's nest because the civic pride of Los Angeles in the 1950s swayed overwhelmingly in support of UCLA's right to self-determination. UCLA officials were able to use the PCC football disputes to claim that their institution was being held back by both the conference and the larger University of California. Once again, regional conflicts such as those that characterized USC's disputes with Berkeley and Stanford in the 1920s reappeared, although this time they were confined to public higher education. City pride, state politics, college sports, and university structure became intertwined when, for example, on May 26, 1956, the Los Angeles City Council asked for a statewide investigation of the PCC situation. According to one article, "Councilman Ernest Debs charged that northern schools couldn't beat UCLA on the field, 'so they beat them this way.'" Athletics were tied to educational policy, as the reporter went on to say: "The UCLA group was honest. They turned over the information and Dr. Robert Gordon Sproul, head of the University of California whose first love is Berkeley, used it against us. Dr. Sproul has often tried to stop expansion of UCLA. He tried to sabotage the medical school here. . . . 'UCLA is big enough to have its own president, independent of Berkeley control.' Councilman Gordon Hahn also accused Dr. Sproul of not favoring the UCLA group."[41]

A few months later, in northern California, the *Oakland Tribune* of July 11, 1956, said, "In Los Angeles, State Assemblyman Joseph C. Shell pointed out that many UCLA alumni and students feel President Robert Gordon Sproul of the University of California 'sold them down the river' in recent conference sessions."[42] Shell declared that he was prepared to introduce legislation at the 1957 session of the legislature to give UCLA and possibly other southern campuses freedom from Sproul's control." Public outbursts from the Los Angeles area prompted President Sproul to regroup with UCLA, supporting Regent Pauley's view that the University of California ought to bolt from the PCC.

Meanwhile, UCLA chancellor Raymond Allen was stumping the state to win public support for his own campus in the wake of the PCC slush fund controversy. In a speech to the Commonwealth Club in San Francisco, Allen said, "My program is to save the conference. But if this cannot be done, then we have to create a new conference along more realistic lines. In that event, I would strongly urge an alignment of institutions comparable academically and athletically. The presidents then should write a code that fits institutions involved and under which all can live comfortably with athletics."[43]

Allen's speech was based on a curious revision of conference history. For example, he overlooked the fact that faculty athletic representatives, not presidents, wrote the code and set conference policy. Allen also ignored the point that the proper sequence was to change policy before opting not to adhere to code when one voluntarily belongs to an association. There was nothing mandatory or coercive about UCLA's membership in the conference. Chancellor Allen's views about deemphasis of big-time college sports were puzzling for two reasons: first, he had been president of the University of Washington in the late 1940s and early 1950s when the Pacific Coast Conference code was being put into place, a role that had allowed him to be informed and influential; second, while Allen was president of the University of Washington he had served as one of ten members of the American Council on Education's special committee on ethics and college sports. Given such experience, it was disconcerting to have an academic leader contend that the aim for a university was to live "comfortably" with athletics. The enduring challenge was to live appropriately in making college sports part of higher education.

Some of the public outrage over the UCLA and USC scandal in Los Angeles was bluster. Petitions to the California state government had little substance. For example, by August 30, 1956, the California State Assembly Judiciary Committee announced that it was postponing its investigation of the PCC situation. Governor Goodwin J. Knight had responded to the Los Angeles City Council's request that he investigate the fairness of the PCC ban on UCLA, but this led to no enduring state action.[44] The immediate public outrage over the conference sanctions did provide a rallying point for city and regional pride in the Los Angeles area. It also brought attention to a figure in UCLA's local popularity: its charismatic, controversial football coach, Red Sanders.

Red Sanders: The Coach as Culture Hero

A pivotal character in the UCLA boosterism saga after World War II was head football coach Henry "Red" Sanders, who joined the coaching staff in 1949. He was the person most responsible for UCLA's football success—and UCLA's reputation for conference code violations. A hero in Los Angeles, Sanders was regarded with distrust by universities in the Northwest. To the Los Angeles sportswriters, Sanders was devoted to his athletes and to the community. When he turned down lucrative offers to leave UCLA for a new position at Texas A&M, one reporter observed, "It was very tempting, but Sanders cared about more than material goods." His success and popularity were so great that he received a ten-year coaching contract from UCLA.

One Los Angeles sportswriter wrote, "He was the greatest coach, teacher and leader of men I have ever known." In a similar vein, a photograph caption stated, "Red Sanders Doing What He Loved Best— Teaching." Along with selection as national college football coach of the year in 1954, Sanders won numerous civic awards, was selected as the Los Angeles Citizen of the Year in 1950, was in demand as a public speaker, and gave the keynote address at events such as an Eagle Scouts awards banquet.

The Los Angeles press and alumni glorified him. When the news of the Bruin Bench and Young Men's Club of Westwood slush fund was published, the Los Angeles writers portrayed him as a martyr, unfairly criticized by envious coaches, especially those at the conference schools in the Northwest. One partisan chronicler of UCLA football credits Sanders with having brought about the self-destruction of the conference, praising Sanders's relentless fight against the Purity Code. The UCLA chancellor saluted Sanders, especially for having won the national college football championship and being named coach of the year in 1954.

When Sanders died at age fifty-three of a heart attack on August 14, 1958, "Westwood went into shock. Even today, more than three decades later, his former players and coaches still dearly miss Sanders. They miss the man whose magnetic personality turned young boys into mature men. He never won a Rose Bowl, but he won practically everything else." Beyond the eloquent eulogies, even the partisan Los Angeles sportswriters had difficulty reconciling some of the circumstances of Sanders's death with his stature as an outstanding citizen.[45]

The truth was that Coach Sanders had been an embarrassment to the UCLA administration for several years. His public misbehavior and failure to reform despite numerous warnings from campus administrators had become a serious concern that resisted harmonious resolution. At one time Sanders rejected recommendations from the UCLA administration on the grounds that he was employed by the ASUCLA. The

UCLA chancellor, despite his public praise of Coach Sanders, grew weary of Sanders's criticisms of university and conference athletic policies and asserted that the regents of the University of California and the administration of UCLA, not the ASUCLA, were the final authority on employment matters. And despite the Los Angeles newspaper writers' praise of Sanders as an educator, the irony was that Sanders and his attorney did not see the role of coach as analogous to that of teacher. They saw no compelling reason why a coach's conduct should be subject to the same scrutiny and expectations as that of teachers. University officials disagreed, stating, "We consider a college athletic coach to be in the same category as a teacher." Their concern led them to add a "good behavior" amendment to Sanders's contract.[46] Sanders's death, however, rendered these issues moot. What UCLA officials called the "Sanders Problem" did illustrate the power of a charismatic coach and the potential for conflict between the coach and the policies and leadership of university presidents and chancellors.

The Ledger Sheet after Dissolution of the Conference

By 1957 the conference had fallen apart, leading to the decision to dissolve in June 1959. There were other casualties. Two members of the conference Presidents' Council—Chancellor Allen of UCLA and President Fagg of USC—left their jobs. On January 11, 1957, "Dr. Fred D. Fagg, Jr., resigned as USC president for reasons of 'ill health' although speculation is that the conference athletic scandal and alumni opposition to his leadership" was "a prime cause."[47] According to one UCLA chronicle, "One of the casualties of this three-year hassle was Raymond B. Allen himself. He came into office in 1952 with the full confidence of the Regents and alumni, but such support was badly eroded during the PCC squabble. He was also considered a possible successor to Sproul [to be president of the University of California system], but that hope was dashed when the Regents picked Clark Kerr for the position in 1958."[48] Allen resigned as chancellor on June 13, 1959, to work on projects in Indonesia and with the World Health Organization in Washington, D.C.

During Allen's last year as chancellor, he tended to unfinished business from the PCC. With the PCC gone, a paramount question was, Who would UCLA identify as peer institutions for college sports? Soon after the PCC was dissolved, several of its former members (California,

Washington, UCLA, USC, and Stanford) created the Academic Association of Western Universities (AAWU). Eventually Oregon, Oregon State, and Washington State would join this loose coalition, but members were under no obligation to play all other members.

Indicative of the strains that intercollegiate athletic controversies had imposed on academic diplomacy were the discussions between Chancellor Allen of UCLA and President Wallace Sterling of Stanford two years after the PCC scandal. Allen wrote Sterling a candid "Dear Wally" letter reminding the Stanford president that UCLA officials had not forgotten that Stanford had voted for expulsion of UCLA from the PCC. If Stanford wished to play football against UCLA in the future, then UCLA expected an "expression of confidence from Stanford."

UCLA's Faculty Senate Committee on Athletics had already advised Allen that UCLA ought to break off all athletic competition with Stanford. The UCLA athletic director was upset about Stanford's alleged misinformation about the structure and character of UCLA's athletic program. Allen himself thought that such a rupture would be a tragedy: "But our people feel a need for positive assurance that we are competing with a *friendly* institution, and I must say, Wally, that I share this feeling. I think the only way the storm raised by Stanford's expulsion vote can be dissipated is by a statement from you (not for press release, of course) indicating that after consultation with me and with others, you understand our athletic program and have every confidence that it will be administered with all honesty and integrity." Allen then proposed a meeting of faculty representatives and directors from both institutions so that any lingering doubts Stanford might have could be resolved. Allen told the Stanford president: "It is my thought that at the conclusion of this meeting you would be in a position to give us the kind of endorsement we feel we must have if we are to understand each other and pursue in good spirit our future athletic relationship. If this is done, we shall proceed to the 1963–64 schedules forthwith." The UCLA chancellor's closing remark to the Stanford president was: "Your written statement to me of confidence in the administration here would be for limited circulation to a few of our people. With it, this whole sorry business can be brought to a successful termination."[49]

Despite the hard line that Chancellor Allen took with Stanford, UCLA was having problems arranging competition with what its administrators considered to be suitable institutions. The Ivy League schools refused to play UCLA. Many large universities had already booked their football schedules years in advance. Others were wary of playing UCLA while it was on NCAA probation. The critical situation was summarized in the following memorandum from the UCLA athletic director to the UCLA faculty athletic representative on June 10, 1958:

> All of this points up the fact that we have not taken a very realistic view of our position. The Regents' policy decision stated that we would strive to achieve association with institutions of comparable academic standards. I am of the opinion that they certainly did not expect a complete metamorphosis immediately. We should all realize that when game schedules are arranged four or five years in advance it is just not possible to meet all the factors involved within the immediate future. . . . Another factor, which may or may not enter into our present situation, is that perhaps some institutions prefer not to schedule us while we are on "probation." . . . It should be apparent to the Administration that my position is most untenable. . . . Repeated questions from alumni and press relative to my success, as compared to U.S.C.'s success, are becoming embarrassing. We cannot issue statements that institution x, y, or z fails to meet the academic requirement of our policy, or we will be courting disaster from a public relations standpoint. Our present position calls for a little common sense.[50]

Even the other major California universities were making football scheduling plans without UCLA. On March 9, 1960, presidents Kerr (UC), Sterling (Stanford), and Topping (USC) met at the San Francisco airport, where "it was agreed that Sterling should sound out Ivy League presidents as to the possibility of scheduling games between the member institutions of their league and the member institutions of the AAWU."[51] President Topping of USC was a bit wary of scheduling many games with Big Ten institutions, a caution that later was put aside. He did for a while show interest in a suggestion by President Harnwell of the University of Pennsylvania that USC and Penn consider playing each other in football, although this failed to reach fruition. USC was not receptive to a proposal by the president of the University of Houston that the two Los Angeles universities join the universities of Pittsburgh, Miami, and Houston to form a conference of large, urban universities.[52]

One institutional legacy of the PCC discussions throughout the

1950s was that the University of California had to tend to an internal structural issue: namely, the control of intercollegiate athletics, which entailed reforming and clarifying the role of such student organizations as the ASUC and the ASUCLA in the governance and finances of university programs.[53] This reform marked once and for all that big-time intercollegiate athletic programs could no longer accurately be called "student activities."

The Conference and the Irony of Faculty Involvement

At the 1991 annual conference of the American Association of University Professors, Creed Black, chair of the Knight Foundation Commission on the Future of College Sports, made the following observation about higher education governance and intercollegiate athletics:

> Of all the people testifying before the Knight Commission, the most disappointing, the least impressive, were the faculty [athletic committee] reps. They seemed to have no idea what their role was. Their role is obviously to represent academic interests, but they seemed to have been co-opted by the athletic departments. I can't remember a single instance where a faculty rep ever stood up and said, "The whole thing is a shame and I'm not going to take it any more."[54]

The principle of faculty control of college sports has often been invoked; yet, whenever the principle is put into practice, it is maligned. Was the depiction of faculty representatives posed by Creed Black historically accurate? The Pacific Coast Conference from 1946 to 1959 represents a case where the faculty athletic representatives did, indeed, take charge.

A composite profile of the PCC faculty representatives during the 1950s suggests a group of talented, responsible individuals who were respected by both faculty and administrators at their respective universities. It included Berkeley's Glenn T. Seaborg, professor of chemistry and a Nobel Prize winner in 1951; later, he would serve as chancellor of the Berkeley campus. From the University of Oregon, there was Orlando John Hollis, dean of the School of Law; Hollis had also served as acting president of the University of Oregon in 1944–45. Stanford's Rixford Snyder was professor of history and director of Admissions; he also served on the Executive Committee of the College Entrance

Examination Board. Hugh Willett of the University of Southern California was professor of mathematics, director of Admissions, and director of Archives; in 1950–51, he was president of the NCAA. The University of Washington's faculty athletic representative was Prof. Donald Wollett, a specialist in labor law. For UCLA, the conference representative was Prof. Joseph Kaplan, a distinguished physicist. Washington State University was represented by Professor Emmett Moore, chair of the Department of Civil Engineering. Oregon State College's representative was Glenn Holcomb, professor and chair of the Department of Civil Engineering. Dean Ernest Wohletz of the College of Forestry represented the University of Idaho.

The faculty athletic representatives were established scholars, of which several had held administrative positions. Nonetheless, the newspapers (especially in southern California) placed a great deal of blame for the conference controversy on them. They were accused of being unrealistic, indicted for having drafted an unenforceable code. Dean Orlando Hollis of Oregon was repeatedly criticized by the Los Angeles press; another view of his work, however, came from the *Portland Oregonian* of June 5, 1958, which praised him as standing for idealism over economics in college sports.

Far from being weak or indifferent, the faculty athletic representatives of the PCC were committed and informed. Early in the decade, they reached agreement with the Presidents' Council that the PCC would "go no further down the road of professionalism." Their reforms were appropriate, given the abuses after World War II. The irony was that the presidents and the public (especially in Los Angeles) criticized the FARs because they endorsed a strong code of amateurism and made hard decisions about penalties. On balance, a major characteristic of the dissolution of the Pacific Cost Conference was the continual effort to dilute the power of the faculty. As PCC commissioner Schmidt noted in his December 1956 report:

It appears that important policy decisions are being considered, and may be made, at the level of the Presidents' Council, which, we are informed, has met or is meeting today. Whether their decisions, in turn, may be dictated to some extent at even higher levels, is something of which I have no knowledge. Nevertheless, the fact remains that the faculty athletic representatives and directors of athletics, either separately or jointly, have over the last few years engaged less and less authority in the policy area governing intercollegiate athletics among the member institutions of the Pacific Coast Intercollegiate Athletic Conference.

Schmidt went on to say that the FARs had been sensitive to recommendations by the presidents and had "tried to hold tight to the repeated injunction of the Presidents' Council that the Conference 'go no further down the road of professionalism'; that they enforce the Conference rules against subsidy without reluctance toward imposing severe penalties, including ineligibility of students; that they strengthen and attempt to equalize competition among Conference member institutions and draft schedules to accomplish this." The problem, according to Commissioner Schmidt, was that the presidents had drifted apart from the FARs: "Much information which customarily is received in the usual course in documented form is no longer available with respect to policy direction in the conference." Schmidt felt that the presidents' desire to scrap round-robin play "would appear to be attributes of a weaker Conference, while what is needed is a stronger one."[55]

Another casualty along with the conference was the commissioner himself. Schmidt was the conscience of the conference; he was educated and articulate, and he brought professionalism to his office. He devoted a great deal of time to speaking to civic groups throughout several states about intercollegiate athletics issues. He understood jurisdictions within the organization and deferred to presidents and faculty as appropriate, yet stood his ground in his position. The key to the decade's controversies was the presidents' resolution that the PCC "go no further down the road to professionalism." Schmidt took that charge seriously. Even though he had graduated from USC's School of Law and had chosen to have the conference offices in Los Angeles, he avoided favoritism toward local institutions. To the contrary, his firm stand for amateurism in college sports tended to make him unpopular in Los Angeles when the 1956 scandals surfaced. Schmidt's legacy was to show that despite the rhetoric of reform in academic circles, not all presidents truly wanted a strong conference commissioner who carried out the letter and spirit of conference policies.

From PCC Crisis to PAC 10 Conference

As the Pacific Coast Conference disbanded, many of its member institutions faced identity problems about the kind of football program they wished to pursue. As one University of California regent had said, the dilemma facing the Pacific Coast Conference in 1956 was that its philosophy of intercollegiate athletics floundered between the Ivy League and the Big Ten.

The fact that a few years after dissolution of the PCC, a new conference (the AAWU) was reconstituted with virtually the same membership of the old PCC indicated that the conference was not the horrible idea its detractors had claimed in 1956. Despite their real and imagined differences, the great universities of California needed their counterparts in the Northwest. Subsequent creation of the AAWU and then the PAC 8 Conference brought together institutions that were success stories. One way to look at the fifteen-year period after World War II was that it was a "great experiment" that was rejected. Whereas the presidents claimed that they wanted amateur athletics, they actually were making an extended pit stop, not changing their earlier direction toward high powered and highly commercialized competition. It was a period during which these universities moved from the pretense of amateur athletics to creating an association with policies and programs that openly embraced the highest levels of athletic performance.

Universities that had been members of the PCC emerged from the 1956 scandals with scars, but then enjoyed a decade of success and prestige in academics and athletics. A legacy of the PCC scandal was that the intrigues of an intercollegiate athletics conference made ward-heeler politics look relatively reasonable and honorable. The usual interpretation was to say that college football purported to be a means to an end, while in fact becoming an end in itself. The PCC between 1946 and 1959 exemplified this latter situation: intercollegiate football became the vehicle that drove other political agendas in higher education, including power struggles within the University of California, keen campus rivalries within the city of Los Angeles, and pride that pitted California against the states of Oregon and Washington. Sproul's hopes for a great University of California were fulfilled, although the split of the university system into distinct campuses, each with its own claims to prestige, may not have been exactly what Sproul had in mind in 1950. The events of the decade meant for UCLA that a young university came of age—and in so doing lost its innocence.

In retrospect, the presidents and alumni of the member institutions of the Pacific Coast Conference were not really unified in their commitment to amateur athletics, regardless of their public statements. Nor were the university presidents always serious about faculty governance in college sports, especially if it curtailed their own presidential authority.

The PCC controversies involved some of the most famous academic leaders in American higher education, including Robert Sproul and Clark Kerr of the University of California and Wallace Sterling of Stanford. The bittersweet corollary is that the intrigue and animosities that characterized the presidents' actions did not represent these leaders' finest hour. In contrast, the commitment of the commissioner and the faculty athletic representatives tends to have been forgotten. Many of the university presidents within the PCC allowed, even encouraged, their institution's athletic programs to commercialize varsity sports between 1946 and 1960. Gains in publicity and alumni morale that accompanied a Rose Bowl victory or a national championship, however, coexisted with educational compromises. One harsh lesson for academic leaders who either embraced or acquiesced in the lure of big-time college sports was that the policies and problems of intercollegiate athletics in the Pacific Coast Conference cost presidents a great deal in terms of time, trouble, and headaches. In some cases, they cost university presidents a job.

• • • • • • • • • • • • • •

CHAPTER SIX

Critics and Controversies, 1960 to 1980

After 1960, intercollegiate athletics entered a period of consolidation and confidence during which serious consideration of deemphasizing sports dissipated. Athletic scholarships were accepted as standard practice, and post-season bowls flourished as an established part of America's New Year's Day celebration. There were no major scandals, and both the NCAA and the various conferences had enforcement officers to penalize teams and coaches found guilty of code violations to reassure the public from time to time that college sports were being regulated. More important than rules enforcement was that after several years of worry about college football's declining attendance, the college game enjoyed a surprisingly healthy financial outlook.

The NCAA skillfully converted old problems of television and professional football into new prosperity.[1] The longstanding fear that the National Football League was a competitor for sports fans was minimized by demographic avoidance: most big-time football universities were located outside major cities. NFL football franchises in, for example, Cleveland or New York had little consequence for a college football game in Lincoln, Nebraska, or Tuscaloosa, Alabama. Also, the NCAA and the NFL worked out truces to reduce conflicts. Unlike major league baseball, the National Football League resisted drafting players until after their college class was ready to graduate. This cooperation even gave some large-scale college programs an advantage in recruiting athletes because a college coach could promote his own program as a feeder to the NFL.

Scheduling conflicts were averted because college games were played on Saturday, professional games on Sunday. There was a different worry, however—that televised NFL games might reduce attendance at college games. This was a variation on an earlier problem: following World War II, NCAA officials had considered televised college games to be a parasite that fed on ticket sales. In 1961, the NCAA reversed its policy by choosing to cultivate television as a source of publicity and profits, leading the NCAA and the professional NFL to help each other acquire new markets. The NCAA, for example, benefited from the NFL's successful lobbying for federal legislation in 1961 that exempted sports leagues from antitrust laws. This allowed the NCAA to establish itself as the agent that would negotiate rights to telecast college games involving NCAA member institutions. This consolidated the NCAA's stance, first taken in 1952, when it opposed the University of Pennsylvania's attempt to pursue its own television contracts. The NCAA also gained invaluable protection when the same legislation was amended to prohibit broadcasting professional football on Friday evenings and Saturdays from a TV station located within 75 miles of an intercollegiate game.

The NCAA's coup was that it had defused external financial threats while increasing its internal authority over member institutions by controlling the selection of games to be televised. The move into television packages also gave the NCAA mass exposure as the "voice of college sports" during pre-game and halftime shows. Old fears about a saturated market had been dispelled because the NCAA enjoyed a multiplier effect in which televised games tended to expand, not reduce, popular interest in big-time college football. According to economist Paul Lawrence, the NCAA received a two-year contract from the National Broadcasting Corporation for $6.5 million for the rights to broadcast twenty-nine college games in 1964 and thirty-two games in 1965. During the same years, college football ticket sales showed record increases of more than 5 percent each year, bringing attendance in 1965 to 24,682,572. The biennial contract with a major television network for the right to broadcast college football games also jumped, going from $15.5 million for the 1966 and 1967 seasons to $24 million for the 1971 and 1972 seasons.[2] The television contracts provided revenues for running NCAA championship events and meeting NCAA operational expenses.

All this meant that intercollegiate sports of the 1960s became part of what has been called American higher education's "golden age."[3]

Recovery from the sports scandals of the 1950s was best illustrated by the resilience of USC and UCLA, two universities encumbered with NCAA penalties in 1958. Their outlook changed swiftly, as each experienced success in both academics and athletics. UCLA came to be known as the "Athens of Athletics," home of one of the most successful varsity sports programs, including numerous NCAA championships in basketball shaped by legendary coach John Wooden.[4] Its monument was the Pauley Pavilion, constructed in 1966 and named in honor of donor and University of California regent Edwin Pauley, who had been influential in the Pacific Coast Conference dissolution. Under a new chancellor, Franklin Murphy, UCLA ascended in research, campus building, admissions standards, faculty salaries, and graduate programs. UCLA also gained in academic prestige as a member of the Association of American Universities. Across town, USC enjoyed comparable gains in research, academic programs, and fundraising under President Norman Topping. And from 1961 to 1963, USC compiled one of the most impressive sports records for a single campus: an undefeated season and a Rose Bowl victory in football along with NCAA team championships in swimming, tennis, track, baseball, and gymnastics.[5] The PCC penalties and problems were dim memories.

Within this era of good feeling, when brush fires flared, the college sports establishment responded promptly with formidable public relations efforts. Major problems in the 1960s included a bitter jurisdictional feud between the NCAA and the Amateur Athletic Union and a dispute with the Ivy League presidents over the NCAA's proposal to set nationwide policy on academic requirements for varsity sports eligibility. And in the early 1960s, a number of articles revived public concern about the perennial abuses of big-time coaches: commercialism, overemphasis, a return of the "dirty play" issue, some charges of point shaving in the prestigious basketball Dixie Tournament, and scattered incidents of recruiting abuses.[6]

Controversies over the Coach as Culture Hero

The biggest assault on the self-confidence of big-time intercollegiate athletics came in an article in the March 23, 1963, issue of the *Saturday Evening Post*, "The Story of a College Football Fix." Author Frank Graham, Jr., contended, "Before the University of Georgia played the University of Alabama last September 22, Wally Butts, athletic director of

Georgia, gave Paul (Bear) Bryant, head coach of Alabama, Georgia's plays, defensive patterns, all the significant secrets Georgia's football team possessed."[7] Since Butts and Bryant were nationally known football coaches, the charges had both real and symbolic importance. Bryant, 1961 "coach of the year," whose Alabama team had won the national championship, was no less than a state and regional culture hero, already regarded as one of the great coaches in collegiate sports history.

The pivotal incident was an alleged telephone call that Butts made from an Atlanta insurance company office to Bryant's football office in Alabama on a morning prior to the Alabama-Georgia game. A businessman working in the same office where Butts (a director of the company) was visiting claimed that by chance he had picked up a telephone extension and overheard a fifteen-minute conversation between Butts and Bryant. His notes on the call were shown to the commissioner of the Southeastern Conference and then turned over to legal counsel. A few months later, the *Saturday Evening Post* picked up the story and published Graham's article.

Butts filed a libel suit against the Curtis Publishing Company. The jury awarded him $3,060,000, signaling to some that big-time college football coaches had been exonerated. Bryant had been especially impressive as a witness and gained national respect for his expertise and forceful testimony. After the initial celebration, however, it was not evident that the court decision had given college sports a clean bill of health. The jury's decision meant that the *Saturday Evening Post* had been found guilty of libeling Wallace Butts because its editors had printed unwarranted charges about a fixed game. Despite the verdict, the case left the American public with troubling questions about college coaches and their athletic enterprises. A careful analysis of the Butts-Bryant case was eventually provided by James Kirby, in his 1986 book, *Fumble*. Kirby's account was compelling because the author, hardly a sensationalist, had been dean of the School of Law at Ohio State University and, later, a professor at the University of Tennessee. He had served as the Southeastern Conference's official observer at the Butts libel trial. Were Kirby to have written an irresponsible account, he would have jeopardized his own professional reputation.[8]

The trial ended with Butts's attorney telling the jury: "You know, one of these days, like everyone else must come to, Wallace Butts is going to pass on. No one can bother him then. The *Saturday Evening*

Post can't get at him then. And unless I miss my guess, they will put Wallace Butts in a red coffin with a black lid, and he will have a football in his hands and his epitaph will read something like this: 'Glory, Glory to old Georgia.' "[9]

The attorney's closing statement, effective for its emotional appeal, left unfinished business because testimony by officials from the University of Georgia, where Butts had been coach and athletic director, did not say that he was of good character. The Georgia Athletic Board had called for him to step aside from his coaching job in 1961 and eventually demanded his resignation as athletic director. Nor did the court case disprove the businessman's claim that Butts had talked on the telephone with Coach Bryant about Georgia's players and plays.

The gist of James Kirby's 1986 study was that Butts's legal victory was muted. Although the jury awarded him $3,060,000, the court later reduced the record settlement to $460,000, with no contest from plaintiff Butts. Often overlooked was that Paul Bryant's companion libel suit never went to trial since both sides agreed on an out-of-court settlement in which Bryant received $320,000. Bryant understandably claimed this as his victory. In his autobiography, he wrote that he was bitter about "the fact that the NCAA and a so-called SEC executive committee investigated Wally and me, but never investigated the people who were to blame for all of it—the *Post*, and the eavesdropper, and the writers."[10]

According to Bryant, the University of Alabama's president and Bryant's attorney came by a week before the scheduled trial date of February 4, 1964, and asked him, "Paul, what would you settle for?" Bryant apparently was willing to settle out of court, because he told readers that he was "ripe for anything" because he already had "gone the gauntlet." Bryant's account, however, was silent about why the university president was inclined to have the case settled out of court. That decision was especially puzzling because Bryant had earlier stated that he was prepared to ask for a $10 million award, to cover both the charges of game fixing and an earlier *Saturday Evening Post* article that had claimed that his coaching advocated dirty play. One implication that followed from James Kirby's reconstruction is that had Coach Bryant gone to trial, he and the president of the University of Alabama would have had to face both scrutiny of the inconsistencies between their respective explanations of events and subpoena of numerous university records dealing with university procedures and practices. The out-of-court settlement meant that at the very least, serious questions about the episode remained unanswered.

Since social history is not confined to court decisions, the Bryant-Butts episode was important beyond the fresh insights that it provided about big-time football programs and their coaches. If one believed Butts and Bryant, it was acceptable for rival coaches to exchange information in the days before their teams were to play each other, even though the same coaches made elaborate provisions to insure that their practice sessions were closed. Furthermore, testimony in the court case indicated that coaching was a profession of perks and privileges as well as pressure. Package deals included high salaries, income supplements from outside groups, use of airplanes for recruiting, construction of new training facilities, large expense accounts, loaned cars from local dealers, club memberships, television and radio shows, investment opportunities, and commercial endorsements. Coaches used university offices for their own activities. Butts, for example, ran up $2,800 in personal telephone calls that he charged to the University of Georgia. While holding both the positions of athletic director and head football coach he had time for numerous business ventures. He had a history of extravagant hotel and travel expenses, also billed to the University of Georgia.

Coaches had direct, frequent access to university leadership, including both the president and the board. Who among the academic administration—a provost or a dean or professors—had the luxury of such amicable access? One irony in the libel case was that Wallace Butts's attorney claimed that Butts as athletic director and former coach was *not* a public figure but should instead be viewed as an institutional employee. Yet it was precisely the role as public figure, not as teacher or administrator, that dominated the coach's professional life. The amount of time that a university president spent dealing with the problems and pleasures of big-time college sports was substantial, even though it was allegedly a peripheral university activity. Head coaches often had media access, including their own weekly television and radio shows. When Coach Bryant wished to respond to the *Saturday Evening Post* story, he was given free air time on local television stations.

The Butts situation at the University of Georgia was equivocal. He had been asked to step aside as head football coach but allowed to continue as athletic director. Thus, he did not relinquish the football program after he ceased to be coach. This revived the question about the organizational wisdom of the university's having approved a dual appointment as head coach and athletic director in the first place, an arrangement that both Bryant and Butts had enjoyed at one time. Where were customary checks and balances? Such appointments, although not illegal, did illustrate the autonomy that university presidents and boards accepted, and often embraced, in the administration of college sports.

Coaching Ethics and the Illinois Episode

The other unsettling incident concerning the ethics of college coaching took place in 1966–67, when the Big Ten Conference documented slush fund violations at the University of Illinois and told the university that it would be out of good standing if it did not fire the football coach, the basketball coach, and an assistant basketball coach. The NCAA also imposed penalties on coaches and some Illinois athletes. The University of Illinois president protested that the conference penalties were too harsh, since other conference institutions had committed comparable violations without having been found guilty. According to conference historians, the protest was not persuasive because the Illinois case was distinguished by records that documented payments over several years. Apparently, a disgruntled assistant athletic director had turned over the records to the conference when the football coach, Pete Eliot, was given the added role of athletic director.[11]

Eliot's firing from both his positions was traumatic to the college sports establishment, given his reputation for high character and outstanding coaching. Yet, as one reads the accounts of conference penalties over several years, which place the Illinois case in context, there is an unmistakable tone of levity among coaches suggesting that each year after World War II several teams within the conference took turns being penalized for having violated conference recruiting and subsidy rules. Michigan State took its lumps in 1953, and Ohio State's athletic program was at loggerheads with its faculty a bit later and was placed on conference probation in 1958. Indiana University received severe penalties between 1957 and 1961. When the Big Ten opted for need-based financial aid instead of a jobs program or full athletic scholarships, Michigan State's football coach, Duffy Daugherty, told the press,

"Our grants-in-aid are based on academic achievement and need. By academic achievement, we mean can the boy read and write. By need— well, we don't take a boy unless we need him."[12] It was little wonder that such public statements caused concerned faculty to conclude that varsity sports and academics were in different orbits within the same institution. This, along with the court case of coaches Butts and Bryant, raised the question, how did big-time coaches view the university?

The Coaches' View of the University

Memoirs and guides written by famous coaches are a readily available source of insight about how they viewed the university. They indicate that coaches faced few constraints and were allowed practices and privileges that would have been grounds for expulsion had they been done by a professor. Coaches candidly acknowledged that their customary procedures in the 1950s included "raiding" other campuses for players and "baby sitting" prized recruits to evade rival coaches. A favorite approach to training was to hold summer camps (without a football, so as to comply with conference regulations) in which several hundred players started weeks of double practice sessions which were so demanding that each day busloads of candidates left the team. This approach would be perfected in the 1960s and 1970s at Arizona State University, where Coach Frank Kush held "Camp Tontozona."[13] In discussing these practices, there is little disagreement by either critics or supporters about the training regimen. The difference is in interpretation: was this educationally appropriate and effective? Coaches claimed that it instilled an essential work ethic that built character and winning teams.

What did coaches think about the academic dimension of campus life? Often there was ritual deference to the value of an education, including claims about the satisfaction of having players complete degrees. Such statements must be balanced with other accounts, including statistics on graduation rates. Often players were kept eligible through two or three seasons of varsity competition, after which they dropped out of school before having completed a degree. Many coaches liked to brag about their skill in getting around academic priorities. One recurrent bit of coaching lore about admissions requirements was the coach's claim, "Our football recruits graduated in the top five percent of their high school class," pausing to add in a stage whisper, "in height and weight." As Coach Bryant recalled in 1975:

I used to go along with the idea that football players on scholarship were "student athletes," which is what the NCAA calls them. Meaning a student first, an athlete second. We were kidding ourselves, trying to make it more palatable to the academicians. We don't have to say that, and we shouldn't. At the level we play the boy is really an athlete first and a student second.

He's there as an emissary of the school, paid with a scholarship to perform a very important function. He represents the students, the administration, the alumni, everybody. Sometimes before millions of people. The fact that he's a student, the second part of the deal, is the only meaningful way we have to pay him.[14]

Unfortunately, Coach Bryant's timing precluded the use of his remarks to help achieve any meaningful reform within the NCAA. Where were his candor and courage in 1950 or 1960 or 1970 when the issue was timely for NCAA policy discussions? As memoirs, such statements come across as humorous. When the incidents were current, however, the humor was at the expense of educational priorities because coaches routinely denied that academic standards had been skirted. The relation of coaches to academic policies often created a cat-and-mouse game in which, apart from gratuitous claims about curriculum and degrees, the custom was that academic rules were nuisances to be overcome. Faculty, of course, would have been naive to have expected otherwise because they lacked power to counter the coaches' denials.

Coaches learned from their mentors the hidden curriculum of dealing with faculty. New coaches typically hired tutors for student-athletes; a second obvious approach was to try to charm the faculty. The advanced lesson was to have the audacity to blame the faculty for athletes' poor academic performance. One young football coach recalled with awe how a famous basketball coach handled a faculty committee that had come to the Athletic Department office to register a complaint about varsity players' low grades. The veteran coach greeted his faculty visitors by saying, "'By gawd, come on in here! I been waiting for you bastards to show up! I wanta know what the hell happened to my basketball player over there in your English class,' and he threw out a name while some anonymous department head cringed. 'By gawd,' . . .

you expect me to take these pine knots and make All-Americans out of them and I send you a B student and he's making a hot-damn D!' "[15]

All this made for crowd-pleasing anecdotes at alumni gatherings and sports awards banquets. It also confirmed that academic critics had been justified in their concerns, despite denials by the athletic department. Nor was it evident that they could count on the support of the president in voicing their concerns that athletes be bona fide students. The institutional tendency was to tolerate such academic abuses as a necessary price to pay for doing athletic business.

How did the legendary coaches see themselves among the faculty and other university employees? When convenient, coaches claimed to be "educators," while always careful to justify their exceptional salaries and facilities as appropriate for the pressures of winning. One apocryphal tale attributed to a famous basketball coach in the 1960s was as follows:

> On this particular day the pumps at this particular gas station were occupied. At one, the chairman of the department of mathematics at the university filled his Ford, at the other, the university's basketball coach filled his Cadillac. "Coach," the professor said, "I'm the chairman of the math department at one of the country's greatest academic institutions and I drive a Ford. You're the basketball coach and you drive a Cadillac. How can that be?" "Professor," the coach said, "if you could square the hypotenuse before 14,000 people a night, you'd be driving a Caddy, too."[16]

In coaching manuals, faculty were portrayed as a public relations assignment. According to a 1963 advice book by Darrell Royal, the football coach at the University of Texas, it was important to learn how to win over the faculty by informing them about the realities of the football program. The proposed solution was to invite three faculty each week to team meetings, meals, practices, and to sit on the bench during games, leading the coach to explain, "We hope it gives the professors a new insight into the game and helps them to realize that the players are just students in one of the campus activities, no matter how much identity they lose when they climb inside that football equipment."[17]

According to the coaches, a major innovation intended to promote good academic practice in the early 1960s was establishing an "academic counselor to athletes." Popularly called the "brain coach," the position typically would be filled by a former high school teacher with a master's degree. Royal informed his readers that the 1963 football coaching manual noted, "The Brain Coach herds our freshmen athletes through the maze of registration and indoctrination with a careful and considerate hand. He takes them in a body on orientation tours and to indoctrination lectures. He sees that they are properly familiarized with the university before classes ever start. He helps with their registration and class schedules (this is not only for football players, but all athletes)."[18]

Royal went on to say that the brain coach also served as the athletic department's "goodwill ambassador," the "only person from the athletic department who contacts the professors or the administration." And, "Contrary to some beliefs, the Brain Coach is definitely not a crutch. He's not something for athletes to lean on. He's there to keep a fire blazing under their bottoms and to keep them putting out an effort to stay in school and eligible for athletics." What the athletic establishment saw as a bridge between athletics and academia was symptomatic of the chasm that was getting wider. Athletic officials were patronizing when they assumed that their brain coach was authorized to represent students to professors and to be involved in academic discussions, even though this individual was not a member of the instructional faculty or even a university staff member but, instead, an employee of the Athletic Association. Reciprocation also was unlikely. Would a coach or an athletic director be equally accessible to a faculty member?

Creating the academic athletic adviser position also raised a policy question about preferential treatment: why did athletes warrant a brain coach when other students did not? This rekindled questions about the propriety of using student fees for exclusive athletic association services. It also revived the conundrum about whether coaches wanted athletes to be seen as students who happened to play a sport. Coaches sent mixed messages on how they viewed student-athletes. The example of the University of Texas football coach represented the "integrationists" who wanted faculty to see athletes as "just students involved in an activity." At another extreme, Coach Bear Bryant was adamant that his football players were special both in their privileges and in their obligations, a view that some universities formalized by constructing athletic dormitories that separated athletes from campus life while increasing coaches' supervision of players.

Even without separate dormitories, integrating athletes with other students was often unlikely because the time demands of playing a major sport, followed by off-season conditioning and spring training, precluded a student-athlete from pursuing many options in studies and the extracurriculum. An extreme rationale to legitimize this commitment was offered by a popular football coach who told reporters in 1978 that those who go to college to play football ought be able to major in football as a field of study. He elaborated on his philosophy of education: "Look, a person who's a woodworker and is in school to learn to carve isn't interested in the guy working on computers in the engineering department. And the saxophone player who wants to become a music teacher couldn't care less about the law classes. If a kid wants to play football, with the idea of turning professional, then he ought to be allowed to earn a degree in college football."[19]

The coaches' views summarized here were, of course, selected from among all coaches nationwide. Whether typical or not, they represented a significant composite profile, resembling the composite "fictional" coach "Honest John Taggart," which James Michener created to describe the big-time college coach in *Sports in America*.[20]

The Counterculture and the Seeds of Criticism

The outstanding feature of intercollegiate athletics as part of academic affairs in the 1960s was the virtual absence of critical inquiry by leaders in higher education. One searches in vain for a commission report that addressed essential questions comparable to the 1929 Carnegie Foundation study. Scrutiny would take place outside the higher education establishment, led by a discontent from a small, scattered group of faculty and students. Its canon was the exposé from inside in which former players who had survived the harsh training camps and the authoritarian regimes of coaches told their stories in graphic detail to popular audiences. Such exposés included Dave Meggysey's account of the special privileges given to football players at Syracuse University in the early 1960s; Gary Shaw's *Meat on the Hoof*, an analysis of the high-powered football program at the University of Texas; and Jack Scott's anthology on the "athletic revolution."[21] Their critical theme was the exploited athlete, including sociologist Harry Edwards's studies of the black athlete as a victim in American schools and society.[22]

Not only were there no major commission reports in the 1960s, but there were few signs of scholarly study of the policies and missions of college sports in academic disciplines or in college courses. The curriculum changed slowly, exemplified by appearance of the course "Education and Athletics," taught by Jack Scott, a graduate student at the University of California at Berkeley. Scott's innovative course featured guest lecturers and panel discussions, often heated and polemical, which caught the attention of such major journalists as Robert Lipsyte and Joseph Durso of the *New York Times* and showed that the topic of college sports had potential for public interest and controversy.[23]

Critical analysis of college sports was limited in its immediate effects because it was countered by equally strong praise of coaches by other former players. And, since many of the critics of big-time college sports were associated with student radicalism of the left, college athletic officials garnered support by aligning their own mission and heritage with mainstream political values. The slogans of college sports became a conspicuous part of the vocabulary of American political rhetoric. Having the president of the United States congratulate winning teams at bowl games or inviting the governor of a state to be guest of honor at traditional rivalries gave the NCAA a formidable public image of patriotism. Mixing politics with college sports sometimes backfired, as California's superintendent of public instruction learned when he praised the football coach at Oregon State University for leadership and values comparable to those of Vice-President Spiro Agnew.[24] Eventually the coach was fired and Agnew resigned from public office, prompting a reevaluation of what was meant by a "winning tradition" and "fundamental American values." Such occasional gaffes did not, however, reduce the appeal that college sports held for politicians: three United States presidents—Richard Nixon, Gerald Ford, and Ronald Reagan— invoked the legacies of college football as part of their administrations' political roots.

Malaise in Higher Education, 1970 to 1980

While intercollegiate athletic programs were in political favor in American popular culture, colleges and universities were subjected to unprecedented critical analysis by both friends and foes. Such scrutiny had two sources: first, it surfaced in the aftermath of student unrest as an indication of the loss of customary public deference to higher education; second, by 1971 a sagging national economy and declining state revenues forced a rethinking of colleges and universities as a high priority in government budgets.

Economists Earl Cheit and Howard Bowen contributed thoughtful analyses of college costs that prompted college administrators, boards, and legislatures to reconsider college operations. In 1971, Cheit warned of a "New Depression" approaching for higher education, a projection that was soon confirmed in many states as disgruntled legislators departed from their customary support for higher education to show their dissatisfaction with college administrators' inability to squelch student unrest. Private colleges were hit by several years of inflation, along with demographic reports about regional shifts that projected declining enrollments.[25] Planning, whose watchwords were cost-benefit analysis, zero-based budgeting, and steady state growth, indicated declining funding and low morale as colleges and universities scrambled for strategies to insure institutional survival in the 1980s.

Serious analysis of higher education and its adaptation to a harsh new environment between 1970 and 1980 was best illustrated by the series of studies commissioned by the Carnegie Commission on Higher Education and the Carnegie Council on Policy Studies in Higher Education, both chaired by Clark Kerr, who enlisted scholars from a variety of disciplines to subject higher education to an unprecedented examination. The results were not grounds for optimism. One irony of the studies was that even though many presidents of major universities devoted a great deal of time to college sports, the Carnegie Commission studies included almost no mention of intercollegiate athletics.[26] How can this difference between institutional practice and policy research be explained? For some presidents and trustees, college sports truly were seen as a peripheral activity, a nuisance not worthy of much consideration in total campus planning. For others, college sports were not mentioned because they were inviolate, not to be subject to budget cutting like other activities. For many academic deans and professors, intercollegiate athletics was a topic to be avoided for reasons of indifference and disdain. Why give scarce time and attention to an activity that had privileged status?

Even though the planning research of the early 1970s urged colleges to prune expenses and review all programs, college sports never became a mainstream topic for reports commissioned by the Carnegie Council on Policy Studies in Higher Education. Eventually some foundations did pay attention to intercollegiate athletics: in 1973, George Hanford, vice-president of the College Entrance Examination Board, received two grants—$15,000 from the Carnegie Corporation and $57,750 from the Ford Foundation—to conduct for the American Council on Education a pilot study on the place of college sports in higher education.

George Hanford and the Systematic Study of College Sports

Intercollegiate athletics' holiday from critical scrutiny ended in 1974 when the American Council on Education published George Hanford's report, *An Inquiry into the Need for and Feasibility of a National Study of Intercollegiate Athletics*.[27] Hanford's *Inquiry* did not totally transcend the deference and compromise that often characterized the genre of commission reports, but it minimized them. As vice-president of the College Entrance Examination Board, Hanford understood the diplomacy of higher education, but also knew that the gravity of college sports issues required that his report get down to serious business.

Hanford's report differed from Howard Savage's 1929 study in some important ways: it was not triggered by any single spectacular episode; it was proactive, a kind of distant early warning system that anticipated a new set of problems outside public consciousness; it was written by analysts within the higher education community, not by an external group. Even though Hanford had knowledge of historical developments in higher education and athletics, he spent less time looking backward and more time trying to convince presidents to confront the future. And Hanford's recommendations provided a rationale for bringing such disciplines as economics, history, sociology, law, psychology, and political science to bear on the continual analysis of college sports. Its appendix, which contained studies by contributing authors, showed by example how such research might be done.

The heart of its discussion was that, contrary to conventional wisdom, intercollegiate athletics faced severe financial problems because "only big-time football is generally revenue producing."[28] Despite the boom of the 1960s, football was expensive and problematic; 151 colleges had dropped the sport since 1939. Nowhere was this more evident than among urban private universities, especially Catholic institutions.

The realities of financing college sports provided the wedge by which Hanford shattered the veneer of health and harmony. In truth, the image of college sports as an American success story masked the regional and institutional differences among athletic programs. Hanford warned that "national solutions to problems are going to be hard to develop in the light of regional differences." The incongruence between academics and athletics was most glaring when one considered colleges in the Northeast because "while many of them are nationally ranked academically, very few of them or their publicly supported brethren are nationally ranked in football. . . . Thus, the Northeast's outlook on the intercollegiate sports scene, where football plays such a nationally unique and dominant role, tends to differ from that of other sections of the country." Borrowing from David Riesman's studies of campus prestige, Hanford noted that in the United States there was an "academic procession" in which "higher education moves forward like a snake with the leadership at the head going through phases of developments at one point in time that those successively further back in the procession will encounter successively later in time under somewhat altered circumstances."[29] Was there a comparable snake for the athletic procession?

It was not an apt metaphor for intercollegiate athletics. Hanford hoped that perhaps the Ivy League would be the leader in the athletic procession, serving as a model of academic priorities and athletic proprieties. Although the Ivy League was successful, it was not being emulated by major universities elsewhere. What Hanford might have substituted for David Riesman's snake metaphor was one of intercollegiate athletics as a hydra: many serpents going in different directions. Or perhaps the image of a snake pit would better have described the fierce infighting among rival factions. If there were dominant institutions, they tended to be the universities of the Big Ten and the Pac Eight, not the Ivy League. Universities in the Southeastern, Southwest, and Big Eight conferences showed that institutions resisted a single national procession, opting instead for their own conference benchmarks and regional models.

Hanford claimed that faculty were relatively uninvolved in intercollegiate athletics governance. Where faculty policy committees did exist, they represented an "outward semblance of authority but no real clout."[30] Hanford called for an end to tiring debates about amateurism and professionalism, noting that the issue had been settled: "big time college sports are in fact in the entertainment business whether they like it or not."[31] He concluded, however, that commercialism was far from being a solution; on the contrary, college sports were going to face financial problems by trying to survive in the competitive realm of sports entertainment as big business.

Despite the box office success of bowl games, big-time conferences, and television contracts, Hanford warned that all college athletics, including the powerful programs, faced increasingly severe financial strains. His summary report was expanded in an appended study by Robert Atwell on the economics of intercollegiate athletics.[32] One response to financial differences among institutions was that the NCAA crystallized into categories known as Divisions I, II, and III. Even this failed to satisfy the large-scale programs, which successfully lobbied to set themselves apart via the finer distinction of "IA" and "IAA" categories. Within each Division I university athletic program there were tensions, as football coaches asked why their revenue-producing sport should be expected to subsidize the "minor" sports, forgetting this had been one justification for the construction of football stadiums in the 1920s.

Hanford's report highlighted the lack of debate among presidents as well as the scholarly inattention to policy issues surrounding college sports. Where could one go for comprehensive data on trends in college sports finances? Who was monitoring changes in student-athletes? Who was testing the claims of sports advocates? These questions were increasingly important because Hanford foresaw a changing legislative and legal environment; his own remarks focused on the changing role of the student-athlete and concluded that congressional investigation and litigation would dominate these issues in the coming years. In addition to the old issues, a new one had arisen, prompted by the 1972 Title IX legislation on equal educational opportunity: the issue of gender. According to Hanford, "The most important and far reaching recent development on the college sports scene has been the movement to achieve equal treatment for women in the conduct of intercollegiate athletics," because women's sports were "woefully underfinanced." Mary McKeown's appended study provided data that undergirded Hanford's statement.[33]

One weakness of many national reports was that they failed to suggest future action. To correct this, Hanford argued that the best sequel to his own study would be to incorporate evaluation of intercollegiate athletic programs into the self-study that each college and university was required to undertake for regional accreditation. Hanford's forthright proposal departed from established practice when he wrote, "Although all aspects of a college's or university's operations are presumably subject to review, there is one notable exception to this universality of attention. The regional accreditation associations have abdicated responsibility for sound standards of conduct in intercollegiate athletics and left it to the national athletic associations such as the NCAA and NAIA and to the regional and local athletic conferences such as the ECAC, Big 10, and Pac-8." He continued, "This disinterest on the part of the accrediting agencies, and more particularly on the part of the faculty members and administrators who comprise their visiting teams, would seem to be further evidence of the breakdown in the relationship between athletics and education."[34] Hanford's proposal forced an institution to explain its intercollegiate athletics program as part of its institutional mission, an exercise few institutions had taken time to do. Reliance on the NCAA as an evaluating agency was risky, given that organization's preoccupation with its television programs and championship tournaments.[35]

Hanford's report was distinctive because it built in some mechanisms to disseminate its message and promote future research and development. It had several positive results. First, the report caught the attention of James Michener and served as the base for his extended discussion of intercollegiate athletics in his best-selling 1976 work, *Sports in America,* providing Hanford's report an audience far beyond college presidents.[36] Second, in January 1977 the Ford Foundation awarded a $200,000 grant to the American Council on Education to establish a Commission on College Athletics.[37] Third, the NCAA showed signs of activity by commissioning Mitchell Raiborn to survey the financial condition of athletic programs in NCAA member institutions.[38] Fourth, the Hanford study and ACE provided the impetus for multidisciplinary study by devoting the fall 1979 issue of *Educational Record* to college athletics.[39]

A good example of applied research to correct what Hanford called "scholarly inattention" were analyses by Robert Atwell, an economist and president of Pitzer College in California, whose article in the *Educational Record* provided a primer of basic features of the economics and finances of intercollegiate athletics, with emphasis on institutional differences. These themes would be further developed in *The Money Game: Financing Collegiate Athletics,* which Atwell coauthored with Bruce Grimes and Donna A. Lopiano for the American Council on Education in 1980.[40] Over the next decade, Atwell continued to connect research to policy discussion and public debate in his role as president of the American Council on Education.

The Student-Athlete

After 1970, the definition of a student-athlete underwent official changes that would have astounded Howard Savage and the Carnegie Foundation researchers of 1929. First, the NCAA allowed freshmen to compete in varsity sports, except football and basketball; the measure was amended again in 1972, when freshmen were permitted on any varsity team. Forgotten was the reasoning that a new student needed time to adjust to college studies without the pressures of varsity play. Another concession to commercialization came in 1974 when the NCAA ruled that a student could compete as a collegiate player in one sport and as a professional in another.[41]

Such "reforms" trivialized any discussion about amateurism in big-time college sports. Capitulation to commercialism continued when the NCAA rejected a proposal to have athletic scholarships awarded on the basis of financial need, leading Hanford to call this "perhaps the saddest self-commentary by the athletic establishment about the state of its own morality" because it showed that "the big time intercollegiate athletics establishment on balance doesn't trust itself."[42]

The student-athlete's role in Division I and II institutions was also being changed by the rising expectation of both coaches and students that athletic grants-in-aid would be available for all sports and no longer restricted to men playing football and basketball. The nonscholarship athlete was an anomaly in Division I, known as a "walk on," because the understanding was that if a university was seriously committed to a sport, then its players would be awarded grants-in-aid. This standard raised the skill levels in all sports; it also brought a new, semiprofessional character to so-called minor sports. Athletic directors were now finding that it multiplied their expenses, since Division I programs were now committed to fielding teams in more sports, with more scholarships for each sport.

To trace this transformation of intercollegiate athletic programs, one need only compare a university's yearbooks of 1955 and 1975 to see changes in the number of sports and the size of squads. At the University of Kentucky, the first time a grant-in-aid was offered for a sport other than football, basketball, or baseball was for a varsity swimmer in 1967–68. This was indicative of a nationalization of Olympic sports in which for the first time universities in the South made serious commitments to teams in swimming, gymnastics, soccer, and wrestling. Some sports, such as hockey, remained regional, but these were upgraded in recruiting and financial aid. The trend would be compounded when institutions opted to be competitive in women's sports.

Changes in American culture were ahead of the campus because at a time when few major universities gave ample funding to women's varsity teams, there was a proliferation of sports camps and skill teaching for children. This often took place outside public school programs and included city leagues, summer camps, instructional clinics, AAU competition, and club sports that promoted numerous "new" sports (e.g., soccer, field hockey, and lacrosse) and, most important, included girls as athletes. A 1978 cover story for *Time* magazine announcing a gender revolution that would transform American athletics already was taking place for a generation of girls long before they would enroll in college.[43]

The popularity of summer camps and youth leagues eventually had another consequence for both men and women as college athletes: specialization, characterized by year-round training and early instruction in a single sport. It meant that parents were less likely to favor having their son or daughter play more than one varsity sport because the risks of injury and the dilution of effort were too great. So, colleges tended to lose a great many players who at one time might have, for example, played football in the fall and baseball in the spring. In addition, if parents had devoted years to supporting special instruction for their child's sports skills, this fed their quest for a grant-in-aid as a payback. An athletic scholarship became the goal for an expanded group of prospective students, cutting across sports and gender. Although colleges would benefit from this talent, professionalization and specialization would drive up operating expenses.

If women represented a disproportionately small percentage of varsity athletes, then the issue of race and college sports presented a markedly different and equally problematic profile. Hanford's report, along with Roscoe Brown's appended study, raised questions about possible abuse of black student-athletes, echoing James Michener's point that commercialization of collegiate football and basketball placed black men inordinately into the role of hired athletes, disproportionate to their numbers in the student population and in other student activities. The traditional rebuttal was that college sports were in the vanguard of social change by providing an escalator for socioeconomic and educational mobility. Such claims were tempered by relatively low graduation rates for black student-athletes and the commensurate underrepresentation of blacks among coaching staffs and athletic administrations.[44] College officials' claims about collegiate sports and educational opportunity for minority students also lost persuasiveness when one acknowledged the changes in federal student aid policy where such need-based programs as the Pell Grants and state scholarship awards, combined with institutional monies, made higher education at public and private institutions increasingly affordable. For a coach to claim that an athletic scholarship was the only or the best way for a black student to gain access to higher education was patently incorrect—and often dysfunctional, when one considers the tendency for big-time programs to isolate student-athletes from the general student body. It also did a disservice to those minority students who had educational aspirations apart from athletics.

Digesting the Data and Analyzing the Sports Enterprise

Mitchell Raiborn's studies of athletic revenues and expenses, conducted for the NCAA, were relatively straightforward summaries; taken in conjunction with his comparable study from the 1960–69 period, the 1970–77 report provided a historical database by which each institution could match itself against collective trends.[45] His statistics illustrate how the cultural trends discussed in the preceding section altered university athletic budgets and provide a clue to an important story: Group I (big-time football and basketball, comparable to the NCAA's Division IA) showed an incredible rise in both revenues and expenses, with revenues lagging slightly. Here was a graphic portrayal of programs operating at full speed, their powerful ascent matched only by their susceptibility to overextension. Were the subject a hospital patient rather than an intercollegiate athletic department, cardiologists would be on the alert for a massive coronary.

Except for the large-scale programs of a conspicuous, influential minority of large universities, most college athletic programs already faced a widening gap between expenses and revenues. Institutions absorbed athletic deficits as part of their educational program, an accommodation that was tolerable in prosperous times but which would eventually cause problems.

Raiborn's studies were also revealing about the surveyed institutions' resistance to scrutiny: there was a poor return rate of surveys among NCAA member institutions; Raiborn had to rely on self-reported data; and the data were of limited analytic use because they were confined to summaries by institutional group. The studies did show, however, that Division II and Division III were running deficits and were dependent on institutional subsidies. This should not have been surprising because, at this level, college sports (including football) were not expected to be self-supporting. The surprise was the revelation of differences within the Division I ranks. Hanford's 1974 finding would be central for the next decade: even the big-time programs in the NCAA's Division IA were showing signs of financial strain despite the bonanza of television revenues and high attendance.

From Confidence to Criticism in Higher Education, 1980

The strength of big-time college sports within American culture around 1970 was in large part a function of avoidance, indicative of an enterprise characterized more by self-congratulation than by critical self-analysis. Ironically, the significant problems that emerged after 1970 were products of the same policies that had fostered the commercial success of big-time sports between 1970 and 1980. It would be the relatively ignored questions about differences among colleges and universities in such areas as athletic funding, financial equity, and educational propriety that would converge in debate over the role of the student-athlete, with attention to race, gender, and educational opportunity.

Neither the NCAA nor the athletic directors and football coaches at major universities were in the vanguard of social and legal reform. During government hearings on Title IX legislation in 1975, the athletic director at the University of Maryland complained that the Department of Health, Education, and Welfare did not understand intercollegiate athletics. He then proceeded to "educate" inquiring officials and pointed out that implementation of Title IX, which mandated equal opportunity for women's sports, would destroy established activities, noting that "to me, this is poor business and poor management." He further pointed out that the university was "in competition with professional sports and other entertainment for the consumer's money," and he "did not want a lesser product to market."[46] In the same spirit, the football coach at a state university explained to reporters that a losing season and bad publicity hurt his program because "we're in the entertainment business and are susceptible to the whims of fans who may get upset with our performance."[47]

For an athletic director to invoke sound management and business practices was not compelling because most big-time college sports programs were seldom run without subsidies and privileges unknown to most businesses. The same circle of coaches and athletic directors who resisted the drain of resources that compliance with Title IX might entail were often completely indifferent to frugality, not least of all to the financial shortfalls most universities were facing. George Hanford's 1974 report had warned that the economic constraints facing higher education, combined with the rising costs of intercollegiate athletic programs, meant that eventually athletics and academic programs would be in direct competition for scarce available dollars.[48] Such concerns had little impact on athletic directors—in the same year, University of Pittsburgh athletic officials told *Time* magazine reporters that their football program included these expenses: $600,000 to operate the program, $350,000 for 140 scholarships, and $30,000 for the head coach's salary. Furthermore, the head coach had a weekly television show and was given a blank check for recruiting. In less than a two-year period, alumni donated $181,000 for varsity sports, none of which went for general university or educational use. The donations paid for enlarging locker rooms, installing carpeting, a lounge, and a stereo system, leading the coach to comment, "Carpeting floors doesn't win ball games for you, but it sure makes things more comfortable."[49]

The most significant feature of such public statements was that coaches and athletic directors no longer went through the ritual of deferential statements about educational purpose. The institution of college sports was sufficiently strong as an end in itself. Politically this was represented by formation of the College Football Association, an organization of universities with big-time football programs, whose sixty-one charter members did not include institutions from the Big Ten or PAC 10 conferences. At many universities, faculty members confirmed Hanford's observation about the erosion of faculty involvement in sports governance, illustrated by a 1976 faculty senate meeting at a state university. When one professor introduced a resolution that the university's proposed use of a donation fund roster for "allocating choice seating for University sporting events is in direct conflict with, and reflects unfavorably upon the fundamental academic role of the University," at the next meeting the senate council responded with the following recommendation: "The Governing Regulations clearly specify that the functions of the Senate include only matters that are pertinent to academic issues. . . . We believe that this policy of restraint should be maintained and we do not believe that the proposed resolution deals with a topic that is within the scope of traditional and proper Senate concerns."[50] The case was closed, and the faculty senate's action confirmed the divorce of academics and athletics.

By 1978, the national press had once again rediscovered problems with coaching and recruiting excesses.[51] And, once again, these familiar exposés could be deflected by the college sports establishment. More significant was the relatively inconspicuous development that while athletic directors and coaches were riding a crest of popular success, a new set of problems started to surface in the early 1980s: intercollegiate athletic programs finally had to acknowledge concerns about spiraling expenses and flattened revenues, conditions with which colleges and universities had been dealing since 1970. Despite the avoidance shown by some faculty senates and university presidents, academics and athletics eventually would be intertwined in institutional and national policy debates.[52]

CHAPTER SEVEN

From Sports Page to Front Page,
1980 to 1990

On October 14, 1980, the *Los Angeles Times* featured a story about a report from the University of Southern California which told how the "powerful athletic department usurped the authority of the admissions office and admitted 330 scholastically deficient athletes over the last decade."[1] The university's investigation was prompted by an earlier allegation that more than 30 USC athletes had been enrolled in a speech class for which they received academic credit without attending. The subsequent report documented how normal admissions review procedures had been bypassed, and how student-athletes were enrolled in extension classes and given grades for little or no academic work. One track star "simultaneously attended four junior colleges in the fall of 1977 to gain admission to USC for 1978." The disclosures made in the university's report led to penalties from the PAC 10 conference and the NCAA, including prohibiting USC from competing in the 1981 Rose Bowl. USC's president described the situation as symptomatic of a "system gone awry" and announced proposed reforms. The USC faculty committee noted that "big-time athletics has taken on an existence of its own and threatens to undermine the integrity of higher education." The next day the *Los Angeles Times*'s editorial stated that big-time college sports had become "a beast that needs taming" and concluded that the university's report and correctives provided hope that the abuses of college sports could be contained.

This was the kind of article that signaled how in the 1980s the themes of shame and scandals would literally move intercollegiate athletics from the sports page to the front page. It was also a good example of the life cycle of reform in which a combination of journalism and institutional investigation led to penalties for violations. Over the next decade, newspapers and magazines published numerous stories that echoed the 1980 USC case as the national press covered serious abuses in the athletic programs at major universities, including Tulane, Virginia Tech, Kentucky, Maryland, Oklahoma, Oklahoma State, Illinois, Minnesota, Southern Methodist, Georgia, Florida, Texas Christian, Clemson, and the University of San Francisco.[2] Articles were followed by books: *Major Violation: The Unbalanced Priorities in Athletics and Academics; Sports For Sale: Television, Money, and the Fans; The Hundred Yard Lie: The Corruption of College Football and What We Can Do to Stop It; Down and Dirty: The Life and Crimes of Oklahoma Football; Win at Any Cost: The Sell Out of College Athletics; A Payroll to Meet: A Story of Greed, Corruption, and Football at SMU; Personal Fouls: The Broken Promises and Shattered Dreams of Big Money Basketball at Jim Valvano's North Carolina State;* and others.[3]

What did the exposés accomplish? Were they an impetus to lasting reform? At best, they promised to realize an optimistic American ideal, actualized through muckraking, whereby revelations about abuses in government or business led to an informed, outraged citizenry, who in turn demanded institutional reform. On closer inspection, the 1980 USC case showed that despite inordinate press coverage the resulting changes were relatively minor: resignation of the athletic department's academic coordinator, a one-year ban on participating in bowl games, and a pledge to create a counseling position were a small price to pay for a decade of violations. There was no mention of accountability by the athletic director or an academic dean, nor was there mention of changes in governance at high levels of the athletic program. Even the president's proposed reforms were contradictory: he announced creation of a new position dedicated to monitoring the academic progress of athletes while shortly thereafter the committee recommended "abolition of special arrangements for athletes."

Nor did the reforms offer much assurance that comparable abuses would not reoccur. A decade later, a similar problem surfaced when a former testing coordinator at USC told *Washington Post* reporters that he had been ordered by university administrators to "discontinue a study of academically at-risk USC student athletes" because "administrators didn't want outsiders to learn that athletes were being admitted to USC with serious reading deficiencies."[4]

At best, exposés illustrated the limits of reform because the essential structures of NCAA Division I sports were left intact. University presidents may have learned that big-time sports had the potential to generate publicity unfavorable to institutional reputations. At the same time, academic leaders and university boards were spared the obligation to make profound changes because there was no evidence that any athletic scandal had jeopardized a university's regional accreditation.

A steady succession of articles about scandals did alter public opinion. According to a 1989 Associated Press–Media General Survey, "Americans widely doubt the integrity of the nation's top sports colleges, believing they commonly give secret payments and inflated grades to student athletes." Americans "also suspected athletic booster clubs of making secret payments to players. And two-thirds of those surveyed said the colleges overemphasize sports and neglect academic standards for athletes."[5]

Advocates of muckraking as a reform strategy had overlooked the prospect of saturation: readers became immune to sensational exposés so that what had been a shocking story in 1980 became standard athletic procedure in 1985. From time to time, a scandal elicited a new level of disgust and even severe penalties from the NCAA; for example, accounts of the systematic pay-off of athletes at Southern Methodist University and the involvement of the governor of Texas and the university's board led to the NCAA's so-called death penalty, which closed down the SMU football program for two years.[6] Another example of infamy made headlines in 1986, when University of Maryland basketball star Len Bias died of a drug overdose in a dormitory room while celebrating being drafted by the professional Boston Celtics. But the public's reaction to these two stories was highly exceptional, and most stories of corruption elicited little response. The cumulative exposés between 1980 and 1990 altered American attitudes but made virtually no enduring contribution to reforming college sports. Only when public opinion was directly tied to a mechanism of public policy, such as legislation or litigation, did revelations of corruption matter to reform.

The Booster College and Resistance to Institutional Reform

The construct of "national concern" about cheating was an ineffective tool for changing an athletic program at a specific campus. When the NCAA charged a university with violations, alumni and boosters often denied the charges, then accused the NCAA of harassment and "selective enforcement." Exposés in the national press often served to increase solidarity within the besieged university and its state or local culture. According to two reporters who won Pulitzer Prizes for their studies of college sports, a favored strategy for a university with a championship tradition was to dare arrogantly "to play above the rules."[7] And, when a university's program was hit with sanctions, the usual pledge was to return when probation was over with an even stronger team. If there was "shame" from scandals, it often was embarrassment at having been caught. At one university, athletic officials and varsity boosters were outraged when their president avoided the NCAA death penalty by cooperating with an NCAA investigation. To the boosters he was a traitor who had sold out.[8]

Another ploy for defusing athletic reform was the itinerant coach. Charged with abuse, the coach could leave one campus amid controversy (often with a generous settlement of his contract) and be welcomed elsewhere as savior for a losing program.[9] This ploy had an added benefit for an institution placed on NCAA probation: it could explain away its conduct by attributing it to a "rotten apple": a former coach whose behavior was not endemic to the university's program. A good example was the University of Oklahoma, whose football program was placed on three years' probation by the NCAA after it violated numerous major rules over several years; in addition, five players were arrested for serious crimes. After the head coach was forced to resign, the new coach was charged to "just clean up the Sooners' image of a street gang in shoulder pads while keeping the season victory total in double digits." According to university officials, the violations and crimes were "isolated incidents." In an attempt to vindicate the system, the new coach explained that "five guys tarnished a great program."[10] Reform was cosmetic because the disgrace of scandals coexisted with popular enthusiasm for commercialized college sports. It was not unusual for a newspaper to run a headline celebrating a big victory and an article by the same writer deploring the excesses of college sports.[11]

The Student-Athlete

A good example of how a legal strategy outstripped reliance on "popular opinion" as a vehicle for reforming colleges and universities was a 1981 case at the University of Minnesota, whose transcripts closed the gap between fictional image and institutional reality of the "student-athlete." From time to time, a landmark court case documents foul play in the institutional treatment of student-athletes. In 1982, a federal judge found that officials at the University of Minnesota allowed a student to play varsity basketball for three seasons yet would not admit that same student to a degree program. As the judge noted in his decision:

> The court is not saying that athletes are incapable of scholarship; however, they are given little incentive to be scholars and few persons care how the student athlete performs academically, including many of the athletes themselves. The exceptionally talented student athlete is led to perceive the basketball, football, and other athletic programs as farm teams and proving grounds for professional sports leagues. It may well be true that a good academic program for the athlete is made virtually impossible by the demands of their sport at the college level. If this situation causes harm to the University, it is because they have fostered it, and the institution rather than the individual should suffer the consequence.[12]

The court decision accomplished two things: first, it required the University of Minnesota to rectify its negligence by admitting the student-athlete to a degree program; second, the decision set a precedent beyond the specifics of a single case and served notice to university academic and athletic officials that henceforth they had legal responsibilities to student-athletes. It also pointed out that the NCAA was either unwilling or unable to police such systemic abuses. What had been a matter of institutional preference and public relations now was a matter of law.

Another example of the courts as an agent of change in the education of student-athletes came in the case of Jan Kemp, an instructor at the University of Georgia who apparently was harassed when she questioned the propriety of special courses intended to keep athletes with marginal academic records eligible for varsity competition. Her lawsuit against the University of Georgia brought attention to irregularities in the "developmental studies" program for student-athletes.[13]

College Sports' Fiscal Fitness?

The exposé articles were sometimes counterproductive because their preoccupation with the scandals obscured a fundamental problem: intercollegiate athletic programs, especially at the Division I level of the NCAA, showed signs of precarious fiscal fitness. The media's dominant image of big-time college sports as a lucrative enterprise was accurate in the aggregate, since the NCAA hit a bonanza with its television contract for the NCAA basketball tournament. Big-time programs, however, had begun to encounter rising costs and flat revenues.[14]

A profile of the 1979 University of Missouri athletic department revealed how athletic success was often combined with fiscal distress. The sports program at Missouri appeared to be easy to market: it had the only Division I football program in the state and traditionally was among the top ten in the nation in annual attendance. Its stadium seated sixty-five thousand, and the university competed in a major conference. Despite such good fortune, the Missouri athletic program was barely breaking even. It had pushed ticket prices, booster donations, and parking fees to their limits. Its only remaining income source was television, but without championship seasons the football games held little appeal for national networks. Missouri's program provided a baseline for problems that big-time athletic programs would face in the coming decade when campuses would have to explain themselves in court and to Congress.[15]

The finances of intercollegiate athletics were reshaped in 1984 when the U.S. Supreme Court ruled in favor of the universities of Georgia and Oklahoma in their suit against the NCAA, a decision that ended the NCAA's monopoly over television broadcasts and restored self-determination to institutions and their conferences. The initial impact of this decision was to increase college football revenues, but these were unevenly distributed because there was no NCAA revenue-sharing arrangement. Eventually football games started to saturate the television market, driving down the fees colleges could command.[16]

Over the next decade, a number of flagship programs ran deficits. A good example of this well-kept secret was the University of Maryland: even its football program was running in the red as early as 1978, when it started to show an annual deficit of over $300,000. By 1987, the Maryland athletic program had a deficit exceeding $1 million. Gradually the public learned just how overextended programs everywhere were. Lotteries in Oregon failed to bail out multimillion-dollar short-falls for athletic programs at Oregon, Oregon State, and Portland State universities. Even Big Ten universities' athletic programs were in financial trouble: the University of Wisconsin announced a deficit of over $2.5 million. If universities were balancing their athletic budgets, it was through a practice that received little press coverage: by dropping selected varsity sports. By the early 1980s, one finds that the University of Colorado had eliminated baseball, swimming, wrestling, and tennis; the University of Washington had dropped gymnastics and wrestling; LSU and Tennessee had eliminated their nationally ranked wrestling teams. This strategy attracted headlines only in the 1990s, although it had been going on for a decade.[17]

Cleavages between "have" and "have-not" athletic programs continued to grow. Each year a few more institutions reported athletic deficits. One short-term adjustment was for athletic associations to increase private fundraising, often by requiring season ticket holders to donate a large amount (e.g., ten thousand dollars) for the right to renew their tickets. Indicative of shifting loyalty was the College Football Association (CFA). The CFA was formed in 1981 as a special interest group whose original membership was sixty-two universities with large-scale football programs. It did not include those universities who belonged to the PAC 10 and the Big Ten conferences. The CFA's major purpose was to exert pressure within the NCAA to give priority and protection to members' football programs; at times there was talk that the CFA was considering seceding from the NCAA. This prospect prompted the NCAA to create the distinction between IA and IAA football programs, based on such criteria as stadium size and average game attendance. The CFA also became an agent for negotiating a lucrative group package television deal with major networks—an arrangement whose consequence was to increase the cleavage between wealthy and financially strained programs among large universities. In 1990, when Notre Dame bolted from CFA ranks to negotiate its own television deal, CFA officials charged Notre Dame with avarice. This indictment was hard to countenance considering that the same dynamic had led to the creation of the CFA, meaning that its members had distanced themselves from the less powerful and less lucrative university football programs.[18]

Institutions gambled on the payoff of a bowl game or an NCAA basketball berth. Even this was found to be risky; one estimate was that a university received three million dollars for playing in a major New Year's Day football bowl game, but immediately spent one million on travel and entertainment. Contrary to the claim that a winning team helped overall university fundraising, bowl game monies usually stayed within the athletic department.[19] Most troubling was a short wire service item in September 1988 reporting that the University of Michigan athletic department had projected a budget deficit of about $2.5 million for fiscal year 1989, increasing to $5.2 million by 1993. The assistant athletic director reported that expenses "were likely to increase by almost 25 percent, while revenues are expected to increase by only 15 percent over the next five years." The Michigan situation was traumatic because Michigan was one of the best run, most prosperous programs: its annual features included sellout crowds of over 100,000 for home football games, several television appearances, major bowl games, and NCAA championship teams in basketball. Despite such resources, it showed an annual budget of $21.1 million in expenses and $18.5 in revenues. Only later would reporters outside the sports department develop the story, heeding a point about the economics of college sports which historians and economists had made years earlier.[20]

Research and Scholarship

Scholars, more so than journalists, critically analyzed the finances of intercollegiate athletics in the 1980s.[21] Economists found that the so-called revenue-producing sports were also inordinate revenue consumers—a fact not usually mentioned by athletic directors. The research made football coaches uncomfortable because for years they had been complaining about the "non-revenue sports" that had relied on football for support. Scholarly studies prompted a conceptual revision: even though athletic directors claimed that they ran their programs like a business, the deficits and subsidies profiled by economists indicated that a business could not long survive if it were run like a big-time college athletic program.

Scholarship from a variety of disciplines converged to show reasonable doubt about many benefits attributed to college sports. For example, it was not clear that college sports "built character"—or, that they did so any more than many campus activities. Sociologists and psychologists even found some evidence of dysfunction associated with being a college athlete. A work that captured the frustration of concerned faculty was Murray Sperber's *College Sports, Inc.*, which pointed out that an athletic department was apart from, and at odds with, the university.[22] Sperber relied on public statements made by coaches and athletic directors to describe "College Sports, Inc.," and then responded with his own analysis to question facile claims made about college sports.

Economists and political scientists studied college sports as an industry, and the NCAA as a cartel, asking the following questions: Did winning teams stimulate and enhance fund raising for the entire university? How exactly did a big-time athletic program contribute to a university's reputation? Their research tested conventional wisdom and pointed out a void in the NCAA and in athletic departments at its member institutions: how could such programs have so much statistical data on items they chose to monitor (including field goal percentages, average yards rushing, and so forth), yet so little on items that would subject the same programs to educational and financial scrutiny? For example, NCAA sports information directors often constructed "academic all-star teams" to demonstrate their commitment to education. If they were able to do this, how explain either their reluctance or their inability to answer questions about graduation rates for all athletes?

Faculty Involvement

The view that faculty were ineffective in reforming athletic policy warrants examination.[23] Their record in governance was admittedly weak; as noted in Chapter 6, at some universities faculty senates abdicated the responsibility to view athletic policy as connected to academic affairs. Elsewhere, faculty were either burned out or left out of athletic policy matters. Faculty also were justifiably wary of being co-opted by presidents and athletic departments. For NCAA member institutions, a typical arrangement was to have a faculty athletic representative (a FAR), who was usually appointed by the university president and cast in a difficult role. Despite alleged autonomy, the FAR was subject to pressure from the athletic director, the coaches, and the president. In sum, it was unreasonable to expect the FAR either to represent faculty or to be influential in the NCAA forum.

Another explanation for weak faculty involvement in athletic policy was the structure of the American university. Boards of trustees and presidents were under no obligation to listen to faculty. When, for example, faculty objected to the president's and board's decision to hire a coach who had gained notoriety at another campus, they were ignored. A president could then conveniently claim that faculty silence was faculty consent, which was not the case. Nationally, professors constituted a loosely linked profession that did not have lobbying groups such as the American Medical Association or even the National Education Association.

Lack of power in governance did not, however, mean lack of concern or interest. Why should a faculty member devote primary attention to governance of athletics if the role was advisory or superficial? Furthermore, the structure of athletic programs, often with a separately incorporated athletic association, precluded faculty oversight. As the preceding section suggested, concerned faculty were aware of issues and contributed to the national debates through their systematic research on questions that had been avoided both by athletic department officials and by university presidents. In marked contrast to the 1929 Carnegie Foundation study, the 1990 Knight Foundation Commission relied heavily on the body of research which various faculty members had published on aspects of college sports.

Faculty members contributed to policy debates between 1980 and 1990 through the American Association of University Professors (AAUP). Indicative of AAUP concern was the July–August 1987 issue of *Academe*, entitled "The Commercialization of College Sports." Following that issue, it kept the topic alive with frequent book reviews and commentaries. To show the staying power of the subject, the January–February 1991 issue was entitled "Reforming College Sports: How? When? Ever?" An example of a collective effort to participate in policy making was an AAUP document, *The Role of Faculty in the Governance of College Athletics: A Report of the Special Committee on Athletics*, published in *Academe* in January 1990.[24] It was a thoughtful, forceful statement that showed that faculty as a group were aware of issues and abuses. The AAUP report also showed that no mechanism existed that could enter a decentralized national organization such as the AAUP into campus governance. The upshot was that while some advocates of college sports reform asked, Where are the faculty? the faculty in turn were also right to ask, Where are the presidents? This was precisely the question that guided the Knight Foundation Commission from 1989 to 1991.

Presidential Involvement and the Knight Foundation Commission

Faulting faculty for their lack of collective power needed to be tempered with the historical fact that presidents, too, had experienced disappointment when they tried to control athletic programs.[25] The decade 1980 to 1990 was simultaneously a time characterized by abuses and one promising sign of reform. For years, the NCAA convention had by default been controlled by athletic directors and coaches. In 1985, however, presidents of member institutions started to regain control. Despite some gains, the presidents were outmaneuvered and their reform measures were gutted. The reform-minded presidents regrouped, and by 1988 the President's Commission of the NCAA started to assert influence.

The difficulty in reclaiming presidential authority was illustrated by an episode at Michigan State University, where the president, John DiBiaggio, was thwarted by his own board when he attempted to take responsibility for approving appointments of athletic department personnel. The university became involved in a bidding war for its head football coach; to counter an NFL team's attempt to hire him away, the board offered the incumbent coach a dual appointment as coach and athletic director. The board overruled DiBiaggio's objection to the contract. Although President DiBiaggio lost the battle, subsequent press coverage, along with his own record of supporting a responsible athletic and educational policy, enhanced his reputation as a principled leader. At the same time, the episode provided a reminder that presidents who devoted themselves to the job of college sports reform faced criticism and burnout.

This constituency of university presidents (and their apparent loss of influence in athletics) brought about a national reform effort initiated by a private foundation. In October 1989, the trustees of the Knight Foundation created a Commission on Intercollegiate Athletics, expressing their concern that "abuses in athletics had reached proportions threatening the very integrity of higher education." The leader was Creed C. Black, ex officio member of the commission and foundation president, who was not an academic. As editor of the Lexington (Kentucky) *Herald* newspaper, he had authorized some of the most substantive inquiries about intercollegiate athletic programs; his interest now moved the public forum to a new setting.

The heart of the Knight Foundation's report, released in March 1991 as *Keeping Faith with the Student-Athlete*, was a "new model for intercollegiate athletics," the so-called One-Plus-Three plan in which the principle of presidential control was to be directed toward three interlocking dimensions: academic integrity, financial integrity, and the independent certification of intercollegiate athletic programs.[26] The report was the product of two years' work by a blue ribbon commission whose membership included William C. Friday (former president of the University of North Carolina); Father Theodore Hesburgh, president emeritus of Notre Dame; several college and university presidents and athletic officials; representatives from government; and a former Heisman Trophy winner, Princeton alumnus Richard Kazmaier. Whereas the Carnegie Foundation worked secretly, the Knight Commission enlisted key figures in higher education and athletics and held open hearings.

The report's reminder to campus trustees was that ultimate authority had to be vested in presidents if presidents were to be leaders. A concurrent obligation facing presidents was that they, not athletic directors or alumni, were to be in charge of conferences and the NCAA. Meaningful reform would take place only if, for example, presidents showed commitment to gender equity, or if presidents were keenly aware of television contracts. The increasing financial problems of college sports demanded university-wide attention to athletic program costs and awareness of the lean economic environment facing American higher education. The foremost structural challenge was to curb independence of athletic booster clubs and athletic foundations. Presidents also had to be aware of the phenomenon of the "power coach," making certain to review and retain the right to approve coaches' outside income from endorsing products such as athletic shoes. For the commonwealth of college sports, the report urged attention to revenue sharing from television. Avoiding the win-at-all-costs syndrome probably meant consideration of long-term contracts for coaches. Finally, universities of the 1990s were prompted to consider making institutional support available for athletic programs to reduce emphasis on pressure to bring in revenue.

According to the Knight Foundation Commission, to restore academic integrity to intercollegiate athletics, college and university presidents were going to have to renew their attention to the admission, academic progress, and graduation rates of student-athletes. Practices and policies ought to turn away from the convenient arrangements of disproportionate "special admits" and low graduation rates, which had made a travesty of educational standards.

The report devoted a separate section to mechanisms for certifying and auditing athletic programs. The commission report was not explicit about which external agency ought to be in charge. It could be the NCAA, which in 1981 had published informational guidelines on auditing athletic programs and by the late 1980s was working on a pilot program of certification for member institutions. To empower the NCAA with that role, however, risked credibility: the NCAA was not part of the educational and academic world. Also, as Tom McMillen, Congressman from Maryland's Fourth District and a former All-American basketball player and Rhodes Scholar, cautioned, the Knight Commission had not "addressed an area of intercollegiate athletics in dire need of investigation: the enforcement process. It behooves forces outside of athletics circles, including government entities, to ensure that the NCAA and other intercollegiate athletics associations do not haphazardly enforce their own concept of justice without appropriate consideration of the due process rights of individuals and institutions."[27]

This concern brings to mind Murray Sperber's faculty perspective that to place the NCAA in charge of program review was like having the "fox guard the henhouse."[28] Reviving George Hanford's 1974 proposal to involve regional accreditation associations probably was a more appropriate plan, if the aim was academic credibility. There were some promising innovations from the Southern Association of Colleges and Schools that provided models. But any external reviews, whether from the NCAA or regional accreditation associations, would be only as effective as presidents and academic leaders demanded. Review could be evaded or complied with on paper. One problem was that most universities, despite their commitment to certification and reform, resisted measures that would require them to publish the financial records of their athletic programs.[29]

Resisting Reform

The primary contribution of the Knight Foundation Commission's report was to bring together college presidents to face serious issues involving intercollegiate athletics. The commission included NCAA leadership but was independent from that organization. It was hard to disagree with the report's findings, although the allegedly timid faculty used reviews published in *Academe* to turn the tables on presidents by asking why reform was going to be slow and uncertain.

The first difficulty the Knight Foundation Commission faced was that overt opposition to sports reform was unlikely because no group wanted to be seen as "against" good things. A second deterrent was the inertia of custom. Presidents, even when they assumed a leadership role in college sports, could be avoided by alliances of alumni booster clubs and athletic department officials. Football coaches from the big-time programs usually resisted reform proposals such as a shift from athletic grants-in-aid to need-based financial aid or a reduced number of allowable grants for football. As one major football coach told reporters, proposals to reduce the maximum number of football grants-in-aid at a Division I program below ninety-five per year constituted a "threat to the integrity of the game." National reform campaigns and academic leaders usually underestimated the lobbying power of coaches—hence, as John DiBiaggio, president of Michigan State University, warned, the temptation was to opt for cosmetic changes.[30]

The politics of member institutions within the NCAA was marked by infighting: Division IA programs cared little about the financial plight of institutions who belonged to divisions IAA, II, or III. Football coaches cared little that other sports were eliminated if the football budget was spared. When big-time programs were faced with a financial crunch, their tendency was to retain resources for football and men's basketball while reducing or eliminating nonrevenue sports.[31] National reform faced another impediment: athletic directors and coaches habitually complained about overregulation, symbolized by the thick NCAA manual. What they failed to mention was that they and their own colleagues caused this proliferation of precise rules. Most attempts to draft a general code resulted in coaches themselves evading the spirit of the law.

Legislation and Litigation

A major structural revolution in American life since 1900 has been the persistent attention to institutional compliance with regulation. Colleges and universities, including their athletic programs, had long been spared the regulations businesses faced, but this started to change after 1980. Perhaps the major miscalculation that the athletic establishment made was to allow sports programs to drift from being part of the educational mission of a university. Creating a distinct intercollegiate athletic department (as distinguished from, e.g., physical education), separation from Student Affairs, incorporation as an athletic association, and the subsequent chartering of "athletic educational foundations" and booster clubs were typical decisions that legally changed the identity of college sports. It was codified by 1989 when the NCAA officially defined a Division I program as one that "strives for regional and national excellence and prominence," whose program "serves both [the] college community and [the] general public," and that was expected "to finance its athletic program with revenues of the program itself."[32]

Although that separation served athletic programs well for years, it also started to move athletic programs from under the protective umbrella that state and federal agencies had customarily afforded educational and nonprofit activities. The partnership of legislation and litigation as an increasingly consequential force is well illustrated by the issue of gender equity in college sports. In the early 1970s, the NCAA staff and membership strongly objected to inclusion of intercollegiate athletics under the rubric of Title IX. Despite strong lobbying, the NCAA did not win this campaign; it then countered with a request for special exemptions. Only then did the NCAA abruptly shift to embrace, and essentially take over, women's varsity sports—a move that undermined the existing Association of Intercollegiate Athletics for Women (AIAW). This NCAA "victory" of sorts had a belated consequence, because by 1989–90, Title IX had become the legislation that the NCAA could not ignore. The NCAA and its member institutions could no longer blame some outside force for obligation to provide women's sports, for it was the NCAA membership that approved adding women's championships. The short-run solution of 1980–81 became the long-term obligation to fund and administer women's sports in the 1990s. As of 1991, only one major coeducational university with a Division I program—Washington State University—had come close to compliance. The issue was no longer one of public relations or popular opinion; it mattered less what alumni and boosters might think, but whether the athletic program passed legal tests established by courts and federal agencies.[33]

This legal environment shaped athletic program cost-cutting strategies in the 1990s. For example, an athletic director facing a budget deficit who was tempted to cut women's sports faced double resistance: first, the NCAA made eligibility for Division I status contingent upon offering a certain number of women's sports; second, any attempt to reduce women's sports was subject to a class action suit under Title IX. The result was that cost cutting tended to be in minor men's sports. Ironically, cost cutting would be of relatively little help because it focused on low-budget sports.

The Campus in a Period of Commercialism and Compliance

By 1990, higher education was at a crossroads in both the popular conception and the legal definition of its major intercollegiate athletic programs.[34] Division I intercollegiate athletics were in a position where an institution's financial practices interacted directly with such external bodies as municipal governments, state and federal agencies, legislatures, and the courts. These had become the pressure points where athletic departments were free to behave as they wished but where external agencies also were justified in modifying how they in turn viewed universities that hosted big-time intercollegiate athletic programs. In short, if a sports department claimed to be run like a business, it would be regulated like a business. The period 1980 to 1990 was characterized by a shift from privilege to scrutiny. Nowhere was this more evident than in congressional hearings and proposed legislation that would require intercollegiate athletic programs to publish their annual financial records and student-athlete graduation rates.[35]

Historically, colleges and universities enjoyed status as privileged institutions, provided they fulfilled certain criteria. State and federal governments granted tax exemptions, and for the most part government-academic relations had been cordial. But athletic programs' aggressive shift toward entertainment and business altered government attitudes toward colleges and universities. In 1979, sociologist Nathan Glazer argued that corporations and colleges have switched positions since 1900 vis-à-vis the federal government.[36] While antitrust legislation at the turn of the century sought to control business practices, public policy tended to exempt colleges from external restraints. In the 1980s, federal policy increasingly sought to stimulate corporate enterprise by deregulation, while colleges and universities were increasingly expected to comply with federal regulations and to be accountable for their internal practices.

This was evident in personnel matters, including affirmative action, environmental safety, hazard insurance, and social security taxes. Compliance has led to concern by university officials who warned that federal policies from numerous agencies could jeopardize what Harvard president Derek Bok called in 1980 the classic freedoms of "what shall be taught, who shall be taught, and who shall teach."[37] To invoke academic freedom became less compelling as a university increasingly chose to behave like a business. An interesting aside was that in 1991 a group called Nevada Citizens for Academic Freedom was formed to protest the forced resignation of the basketball coach at the University of Nevada at Las Vegas. One wonders whether state citizens would have formed a comparable group to protect a faculty member. The populist event demonstrated how susceptible the university was to having its essential rights and missions trivialized, an indulgence it could no longer afford.

The upshot was that between 1980 and 1990 universities could expect little sympathy when they tried to depict themselves as small, struggling institutions. Universities were large, complex organizations—often the largest employer in a city or even a state. As a campus took on the features of an industry, so it would increasingly be treated like one—possibly losing some of its customary privileges and exemptions. This started to take place in local town and gown relations where city governments, facing declining revenues, started to consider whether university-sponsored spectator events held at a campus facility were subject to property taxes. Such "university" cities as New Haven, Connecticut; Syracuse, New York; and Evanston, Illinois reviewed the extraordinary burdens that university activities placed on municipal services.[38] Municipal taxation thus far had been confined to commercial events on campus, excluding intercollegiate athletics. But when college sports programs defined themselves as "commercial" and "entertainment," they were subject to the same obligations as when a college hosted a rock concert. A test was whether revenues from the varsity sports contest went primarily to support educational activities. University sports were increasingly hard pressed to fulfill the exemption criterion. A comparable development under federal law dealt with athletic associations' incorporation as tax-exempt nonprofit educational organizations. The Internal Revenue Service was starting to question whether a separate athletic association for a Division I NCAA program was truly an educational activity.[39]

If large-scale college sports had a vulnerable point, it was in the commercialism of bowl games and television broadcasts. In May 1990, the Internal Revenue Service audited the 1988–89 tax returns for the Cotton Bowl Classic football game. Traditionally the Cotton Bowl's status was as a not-for-profit activity; however, since the game now was sponsored by the Mobil Corporation, the IRS argued that revenues from the game's advertising should be taxable as "unrelated business income." If this ruling prevailed, a university would lose about one-third of its expected bowl game revenues.[40] Another legacy of the decade was that in September 1990 the Federal Trade Commission charged the College Football Association and ABC, Inc., with violating federal antitrust law in its broadcast package.[41] Whether or not the FTC prevailed in this case, it was clear that big-time college sports were encountering an increasingly critical public policy environment. The added jeopardy was that the strategies big-time sports used to maximize revenues (television broadcasts, bowl games, booster club donations) were also the activities most likely to be taxed.

One legacy of the period 1980 to 1990, then, was that university presidents no longer could assume that maintenance of a large-scale athletic program was an institutional asset because the increasingly commercial character of Division I sports cast universities and their athletic programs into an environment of business risks and government regulation. Some of the most significant contests involving varsity sports were taking place, not in the stadium or field house, but in the offices of the Internal Revenue Service and the Federal Trade Commission, at television network headquarters, in corporate board rooms, in courtrooms, and at congressional hearings. By 1990, newspaper coverage of college sports had changed once again, so that to follow the games colleges play, along with the sports page and front page, one now had to read the business page.

• • • • • • • • • • • • • • •

An American Dilemma

Balancing Academics and Athletics

Four national reports—the 1929 Carnegie Foundation study, the 1952 Presidents' Report for the American Council on Education, George Hanford's 1974 study for the American Council on Education, and the 1991 Knight Foundation Commission study—are significant events in attempts to reform intercollegiate athletics over the past six decades. The four reports displayed remarkable similarities of theme and vocabulary: commitment to the idea of the student-athlete; acknowledgment that varsity athletics were important to the college experience; and praise for the role of the coach as teacher. All four emphasized that college and university presidents must be centrally involved if athletic programs were to be an appropriate, accountable part of higher education. They warned against commercialization of college sports and its imbalanced dependence on media and constituencies outside the campus. Finally, the reports portrayed the excesses of recruitment, athletic scholarships, and special privileges as corruptions of the student-athlete ideal.

This liturgy suggests that college sports have achieved continuity in twentieth-century American life as a distinctive part of both higher education and popular culture, an activity whose importance has also made it a source of perennial problems. The recurrence of the same language and motifs in the national studies every two decades or so leaves a perplexing question: if the reform reports were consequential, why have the same problems persisted without solutions over more than a half century? What reforms have taken root?

One explanation is that invocation of the same themes and words by each generation of sports reformers has tended to obscure an unfortunate drift. The vocabulary has remained the same, but the expectations have changed almost beyond recognition. For example, in both 1930 and 1990 one could talk about the "student-athlete" while overlooking the social fact that the meanings were markedly different. To read the four reports without attention to the specific conditions at the time each was published reinforces the impression that amateurism and academic control endured as the "right thing" for colleges to pursue. When one looks at the debates and proposals that followed publication of each report, it also becomes evident that an equally durable legacy has been the capacity of athletic departments and their supporters to defer publicly to the rhetoric of reform while simultaneously diluting the intent of the new policies and proposals. "Reform" all too often took the form of capitulation to and accommodation of professionalism. To argue that this has been a pragmatic and realistic adaptation to America's commercial and competitive culture conveniently explains away the right and the obligation of a college or university to offer a distinctive experience, including that of the genuine student-athlete.

Certainly there have been substantial changes in the organization and control of college sports since 1929. Intercollegiate athletics, once a chaotic, unregulated activity, have become one of the most sophisticated and codified enterprises in American life. However, the gestures toward codification and control have often represented the ironies of reform; that is, they have perfected and perpetuated some of the very practices they were intended to correct. The student-athlete came to be the athlete-student. The organizational revolution has been the ascent of the incorporated athletic association, a structure that has allowed athletic directors and boosters to create, basically on their own terms, a privileged entity attached to the university. The ability of the NCAA to organize, promote, and control college sports has been an equally awesome success story. Such accomplishments have not necessarily involved sound educational reforms.

Another interesting legacy of the four reform reports is that in each episode organized intercollegiate athletics has tended to resist systematic analysis, often because many of the favorable characteristics attributed to high-powered college sports programs have been either untestable or exaggerated. This siege mentality has perpetuated the erroneous stereotype that those who have studied the condition and character of college sports were by definition a lunatic fringe intent on abolishing varsity sports. It is important to keep in mind that, historically, most charges of corruption have been family feuds within the ranks of major conferences in which one coach or athletic official has made accusations about another. An interesting variation on this theme occurred in August 1991, when the football coach at Vanderbilt University offered the following commentary to place his football program and university within the context of their league, the Southeastern Conference: "At Vanderbilt, we have everything it takes to win, but at Vanderbilt, our system is academically sound while the football program is corrupt. Most schools in the Southeastern Conference are academically corrupt and athletically sound."[1] The coach was publicly reprimanded by the Southeastern Conference's commissioner for having violated the league's Code of Ethics. The penalty was for candor and speaking out of turn. The intriguing research question was whether the reprimanded coach was accurate in his depiction.

A watchword of the four reform reports has been to balance, not abolish, intercollegiate athletics. To advocate that college sports ought to be fused with scholarly programs has left the historical puzzle that in each era it was not clear how that fusion should take place. Once in a while, the two spheres of high-powered academics and athletics have coincided, but even this has not always been a panacea. For example, in September 1991 an article in the *Washington Post* reported that the University of Michigan used federal research grant money to cover entertainment expenses for the Rose Bowl game, an incident that led to an investigation by a House of Representatives subcommittee.[2] So, although the university had achieved a "balance" and an "integration" of sorts, it had not convincingly fulfilled the more subtle task of maintaining a proper balance of academics and athletics. It also was a reminder that academic leaders, not only athletic officials, have often been involved in the activities of college sports that lead to the dubious games colleges play.

New Heroes for College Sports

The conventional wisdom is that the college sports heroes are the athletes who receive the Heisman Trophy or the coach who leads a team to the NCAA championship. Looking at the history of college sports from the perspective of policy debates suggests belated recognition of another group: the reform advocates, including Howard Savage of the Carnegie Foundation for the Advancement of Teaching; Victor O.

Schmidt, commissioner of the Pacific Coast Conference after World War II; George Hanford, of the College Entrance Examination Board; Robert Atwell, of the American Council on Education during the 1980s; and Creed Black, of the Knight Foundation. They were tough-minded idealists who combined skills of analysis, argument, and leadership. They were articulate and prompted healthy debate while demonstrating the courage to take principled, informed stands on the controversial educational issues of their day, even when this led to unpopularity.

Their leadership by example was highlighted by some remarkable turning points in the course of intercollegiate athletic policies. For example, the period immediately after World War II probably was the closest that organized college sports came to a collapse of safeguards and standards. One can argue that the 1920s were characterized by comparable abuses, but there were fewer structures in place or rules to break in 1928 than in 1948. The period 1946–53 showed how belief that the system of regulation would work was misplaced confidence. One of the most interesting cases was the Pacific Coast Conference because it showed that the evolution of intercollegiate athletics toward commercialism was not inevitable and could be renegotiated if presidents and faculty wished to do so. The fact that a conference commissioner, Victor O. Schmidt, and faculty athletic representatives from PCC member institutions were seriously committed to drafting and enforcing a code committed to the concepts of the student-athlete and of faculty governance in college sports at major universities was exciting, even if it fell short.

There are few university presidents in this pantheon of college sports reformers. The memoirs and biographies of university presidents repeatedly emphasize their regret about accommodation and compromise when dealing with alumni and other constituencies. So, it is understandable and unfortunate that the role of university president since 1930 has usually precluded a strong, principled stand that has allowed an institution to achieve that elusive balance of excellence in academics and athletics.

Research and Reasonable Doubt about the Student-Athlete Ideal

Research on college sports reform has been characterized by the juxtaposition of diverse, often conflicting, data. For example, while analyzing official documents, minutes, transcripts, and memorandums on Pacific Coast Conference disputes and national athletic scandals after World War II, I rediscovered Jackie Jensen's 1970 memoir about his undergraduate days at the University of California, Berkeley, circa 1946 to 1949, published in an anthology along with recollections by such fellow alumni as economist John Kenneth Galbraith and Nobel Prize-winning chemist Glenn T. Seaborg. Jensen epitomized an American phenomenon of the post–World War II period: the college athlete who enjoyed a rewarding career as professional athlete. As an outfielder for the Boston Red Sox, his achievements included being named Most Valuable Player in the American League. Later, he served as varsity baseball coach at his alma mater.

At precisely the time of the Pacific Coast Conference controversies, Jensen was an All-American halfback at Berkeley who starred in the Rose Bowl. Jensen had been an outstanding player on the Berkeley varsity baseball team that defeated Yale (whose first baseman was George Bush) for the NCAA championship in 1947. As an undergraduate, Jensen initially was a bright but uninspired student whose decision to leave college at the end of his junior year to sign a professional baseball contract symbolized all that was suspect about an American culture that promoted athletics at the expense of academics.

Jensen's memoir about his undergraduate days at Berkeley had an unusual twist: even though athletics had dominated his campus achievements and shaped his professional life, he devoted most of his essay to paying tribute to those professors who had refused to allow him to slide into the role of the "dumb athlete." They had pushed him to see himself as a student, as an educated person who was articulate and informed about politics, art, and history. Jensen recalled with pride how he changed his major and eventually returned to complete his degree. Apart from that formal accomplishment, he enjoyed his studies, and he remembered his teachers.[3]

Such a case brings a measure of doubt to the cynicism one acquires after reading about the extensive corruption and abuse of college athletes, circa 1930 to 1990. On balance, however, Jensen and others with comparable experiences were not representative of the intercollegiate athletic system. They were exceptions, and for the study of athletic programs, these exceptions do not make the rule. Jensen's heartening example cannot displace the overwhelming data on low graduation rates, abuses of special admission, and other patterns of exploitation.

For student-athletes, college sports of 1990 represented a world turned upside down since 1930. Accommodation to the professionalization of intercollegiate athletics was suggested by the following item: in December 1991, a reporter from the *Chicago Tribune* documented the attention that colleges give to a highly recruited high school athlete. One Chicago high school basketball star received 2,184 pieces of correspondence from 135 colleges and universities over a three-year period. One university sent the student 255 pieces of mail; the student-athlete ultimately signed with a university whose coach had sent him 207 letters, including six in a single day. All this was in accordance with NCAA and conference rules.[4]

Financial problems have been a stronger force for rethinking and reforming priorities in intercollegiate athletics than has moral outrage. A sad footnote that underscores the importance of financial crisis as a vehicle for reform is that now even the Ivy League institutions are trying to reduce their athletic expenses by dropping selected varsity sports.

Even though the highly publicized scandals have been conspicuous events in college sports history, they were not the most significant historical development. The paradox of college sports reform from 1930 to 1990 has not been the corruption but, rather, what colleges and universities and the American public have come to accept as approved practices. The initial impulse in each era was to deplore the illegal and unethical activities in college sports, then to proceed to make them legal. If there is an epitaph for the demise of educationally sound athletic programs on the American campus, it will read, "The rules were unenforceable."

This study started with the observation that Howard Savage's 1929 Carnegie Foundation study was important because it became the canon that was rediscovered and invoked by reform advocates in each of the later studies. The temptation, then, is to close by citing a perceptive observation that Howard Savage made about sixty years ago, with the implication that it is still pertinent to presidents, deans, students, faculty, coaches, and athletic directors today. An intriguing alternative is to acknowledge the legacy of reform by showing that the present also has something to tell the past and the future: in 1992, a university president involved in trying to restore integrity to an intercollegiate athletic program gone awry observed, "This is a struggle for the soul of this institution. The question that will be answered here is essentially this: What is our mission? Why do we exist? Are we here to teach and learn or are we here to house big-time athletics?"[5]

Whether or not reformers have found solutions to the problems of college sports, this was the right question for members of the American college and university community to ask in 1930 as well as 1990. And it is surely the right question for the foreseeable future—until university administrations and faculties demonstrate the will and the capacity to force intercollegiate athletics to reform.

Preface

1. Exemplary articles in national periodicals include a cover story, "The Shame of College Sports," *Newsweek*, Sept. 22, 1980, pp. 54–59, and Alvin P. Sanoff, "Behind Scandals in College Sports," *U.S. News and World Report*, Feb. 11, 1980, pp. 61–63. A representative example of detailed investigation is John Underwood, "Special Report—Student-Athletes: The Sham, The Shame," *Sports Illustrated*, May 19, 1980, pp. 36–74.

2. Examples of extended analysis of college sports problems in the news section of metropolitan newspapers include Al Moss, "College Football Has a Case of the Shorts," *San Francisco Chronicle*, Mar. 18, 1981; Pete Alfano, "Big-Time Football: Colorado Pays the Price in Its Quest to Win," *Los Angeles Times*, June 21, 1979; Bob Monahan, "Tightening Belts: Like Nearly Everybody, Colleges Are Feeling the Pinch of Inflation," *Los Angeles Times*, June 26, 1980. See also Douglas S. Looney, "There Ain't No More Gold in Them Thar Hills," *Sports Illustrated*, Oct. 6, 1980, pp. 30–37.

3. Early indications of sustained concern from national higher education groups was expressed by the American Council on Education and the College Entrance Examination Board. The cover story for the fall 1978 issue of the *College Board Review* was titled, "The Future of College Athletics." The fall 1979 issue of the American Council on Education journal, *Educational Record*, was devoted entirely to the topic "On College Sports." A year later, its cover and theme were "The Athletics Predicament." The American Council on Education further demonstrated its concern about the commercialization of intercollegiate athletics with its 1980 publication of an innovative, perceptive study, *The Money Game: Financing Collegiate Athletics*, by Robert H. Atwell, Bruce Grimes, and Donna A. Lopiano. Later, the July–August 1987 issue of *Academe* was organized around the theme, "The Commercialization of College Sports."

4. James Michener, "Colleges and Universities," in *Sports in America* (New York: Random House, 1976), chap. 7; Allen Guttmann, *From Ritual to Record: The Nature of Modern Sports* (New York: Columbia University Press, 1978); Michael Novak, *The Joy of Sports* (New York: Basic Books, 1976). See also

Guttmann's later work, *A Whole New Ball Game: An Interpretation of American Sports* (Chapel Hill: University of North Carolina Press, 1988).

5. Jeffrey Marx and Michael York, "Playing above the Rules," *Lexington [Ky.] Herald-Leader*, Oct. 27 and 28, 1985; see also Marx and York, "NCAA Can't Agree on How to Clean Up College Sports," *Lexington Herald-Leader*, Dec. 22, 1985.

6. The athletic director's quote is from Charles Thompson and Allan Sonnenschein, *Down and Dirty: The Life and Crimes of Oklahoma Football* (New York: Carroll and Graf, 1990), p. 285.

7. See, for example, John R. Thelin and Lawrence Wiseman, *The Old College Try: Balancing Academics and Athletics in Higher Education* (Washington, D.C.: George Washington University and the Association for the Study of Higher Education, 1989).

8. Alexander W. Astin, "VMI Case Dramatizes Basic Issues in the Use of Educational Research," *Chronicle of Higher Education*, July 24, 1991, p. A36.

9. Edwin E. Slosson, *Great American Universities* (New York: Macmillan, 1910); Clark Kerr, *The Uses of the University* (Cambridge: Harvard University Press, 1964); Laurence R. Veysey, *The Emergence of the American University* (Chicago: University of Chicago Press, 1965); Christopher Jencks and David Riesman, *The Academic Revolution* (Garden City, N.Y.: Doubleday, 1968); Burton R. Clark, *The Distinctive College* (Chicago: Aldine, 1970); David O. Levine, *The American College and the Culture of Aspiration, 1915 to 1940* (Ithaca: Cornell University Press, 1986).

10. Frederick Rudolph, *Curriculum: A History of the American Undergraduate Course of Study Since 1636* (San Francisco: Jossey-Bass, 1977), p. 1.

11. Frederick Rudolph, "The Rise of Football," in *The American College and University: A History* (New York: Knopf, 1962), pp. 373–93; Daniel J. Boorstin, "Culture with Many Capitals: The Booster College," in *The Americans: The National Experience* (New York: Random House, 1965), pp. 152–61; Warren I. Susman, *Culture as History: The Transformation of American Society in the Twentieth Century* (New York: Pantheon, 1984), esp. pp. 122–49. See also David Riesman and Reuel Denny, "Football in America: A Study in Culture Diffusion," *American Quarterly* 3 (1953): 309–25.

12. For example, Allison Danzig, *The History of American Football: Its Great Teams, Players, and Coaches* (Englewood Cliffs, N.J.: Prentice-Hall, 1956).

13. John F. Rooney, Jr., *The Recruiting Game: Toward a New System of Intercollegiate Sport*, 2d ed. (Lincoln: University of Nebraska Press, 1987); James Frey, ed., *The Governance of Intercollegiate Athletics* (West Point, N.Y.: Leisure Press, 1982); Nand Hart-Nibbrig and Clement Cottingham, *The Political Economy of College Sports* (Lexington, Mass.: D. C. Heath, Lexington Books, 1986); Donald Chu, *The Character of American Higher Education and Intercollegiate Sport* (Albany: State University of New York Press, 1989). See also Judith Andre and David N. James, eds., *Rethinking College Athletics* (Philadelphia: Temple University Press, 1991).

14. Historical studies that have been especially important are Ronald A. Smith's *Sports and Freedom: The Rise of Big-Time College Athletics* (New York: Oxford University Press, 1988); Patrick Bryant Miller, "Athletes in Aca-

deme: College Sports and American Culture, 1850–1920" (Ph.D. diss., University of California, Berkeley, 1987); John S. Watterson, "Inventing Modern Football," *American Heritage* 39 (Sept.–Oct. 1988): 103–11; and Paul R. Lawrence, *Unsportsmanlike Conduct: The National Collegiate Athletic Association and the Business of College Football* (New York: Praeger, 1987).

Introduction. American Higher Education's "Peculiar Institution"

1. Arthur Padilla and Janice L. Boucher, "On the Economics of Intercollegiate Athletics Programs," *Journal of Sport and Social Issues* 11, nos. 1, 2 (1987–88): 61–73.

2. John R. Thelin and Lawrence L. Wiseman, "The Numbers Game: The Statistical Heritage in Intercollegiate Athletics," in *Monitoring the Intercollegiate Athletics Enterprise*, ed. Bruce I. Mallette and Richard D. Howard, New Directions in Institutional Research, no. 74, pp. 5–12 (San Francisco: Jossey-Bass, 1992).

3. Mark Asher, "Coaches: NCAA Can Handle Its Own Problems: Congressional Support Welcome, But Not Role in Rule Making," *Washington Post*, June 20, 1991, pp. C1, C8.

4. An important recent exception to the tendency for university presidents and board members to avoid asking serious questions about the character and condition of college sports is L. Jay Oliva's *What Trustees Should Know about Intercollegiate Athletics* (Washington, D.C.: Association of Governing Boards of Universities and Colleges, 1989).

5. See, for example, Committee on Education and Labor, *Hearings on the Role of Athletics in College Life: Hearings before the Subcommittee on Postsecondary Education of the Committee on Education and Labor* (Washington, D.C.: Government Printing Office, 1989); John R. Thelin and Lawrence L. Wiseman, "The Future of Big-Time Intercollegiate Athletics," *Planning for Higher Education* 19 (Winter 1990–91): 18–26; U.S. Department of Education, Office of Educational Research and Improvement, *Revenues and Expenditures in Intercollegiate Athletics: The Feasibility of Collecting National Data by Sport* (Washington, D.C.: Department of Education, 1992). For renewed interest in legislation for data collection, see "Collins Introduces Bill Requiring Release of Athletic Expenses," *Higher Education & National Affairs* (American Council on Education), Feb. 22, 1993, pp. 1, 4.

6. Jim Luther, "IRS Blitzes Bowl Games' Corporate Donors: Agency Rules Contributions Are Really Payments for Advertising," *Washington Post*, Dec. 5, 1991, pp. B11, B14; Ed Sherman, "IRS Coming to Collect on College Profits: Proposed Taxes, Antitrust Decision Could Crush Athletic Departments," *Lexington [Ky.] Herald-Leader*, July 10, 1991, pp. C1, C14. See also Douglas Lederman, "IRS Signals It Still Plans to Tax Donations for College Sports Programs, Bowl Games—But New Guidelines Also Indicate Agency Has No Intention to Tax Other Gifts to Universities," *Chronicle of Higher Education*, Jan. 29, 1992, pp. A36–A37.

7. For examples of the eulogies and obituaries about Red Grange, see Paul Greenberg, "'Galloping Ghost' Captured the Essence of a Singular Era," *Richmond [Va.] News Leader*, Feb. 4, 1991, p. 11. Earlier accounts from the perspec-

tive of sportswriters and sports historians include Allison Danzig, "A Ghost Gallops at Illinois," in *The History of American Football: Its Great Teams, Players, and Coaches* (Englewood Cliffs, N.J.: Prentice-Hall, 1956), pp. 259–262, and Maury White, "Land of the Giants: The Midwest," in *The College Game* (Indianapolis: Bobbs-Merrill, 1974), p. 129.

8. Gerald Eskenazi, "Red Grange, 1903–1991," and Ira Berkow, "A Conversation with the Ghost," in *The New York Times Book of Sports Legends*, ed. Joseph J. Vecchione (New York: Random House, 1991), pp. 83–87. See also Melissa Larson, "The Galloping Ghost: Red Grange" and "Poets in the Press Box," in *The Pictorial History of College Football* (New York: Gallery Books, 1989), pp. 60–63, 70–71.

9. John Davies, *The Legend of Hobey Baker* (Boston: Little, Brown, 1966).

10. Sue E. Inderhees, "One Scientist's Remarkable Legacy," *Washington Post*, Feb. 8, 1991, p. A18.

11. George Lynn Cross, *Presidents Can't Punt: The OU Football Tradition* (Norman: University of Oklahoma Press, 1977), pp. 145–46.

12. Ellen Condliffe Lagemann, *Private Power for the Public Good: A History of the Carnegie Foundation for the Advancement of Teaching* (Middletown, Conn.: Wesleyan University Press, 1983).

13. Howard J. Savage, with Harold W. Bentley, John T. McGovern, and Dean F. Smiley, M.D., *American College Athletics*, Bulletin Number Twenty-three (New York: Carnegie Foundation for the Advancement of Teaching, 1929); *Report of the Special Committee on Athletic Policy* (Washington, D.C.: American Council on Education, 1952); George H. Hanford, *An Inquiry into the Need for and Feasibility of a National Study of Intercollegiate Athletics* (Washington, D.C.: American Council on Education, 1974); Commission on Intercollegiate Athletics, *Keeping Faith with the Student-Athlete: A New Model for Intercollegiate Athletics* (Charlotte, N.C.: Knight Foundation, 1991).

Chapter One. The Reform Canon

1. Howard J. Savage, with Harold W. Bentley, John T. McGovern, and Dean F. Smiley, M.D., *American College Athletics*, Bulletin Number Twenty-three (New York: Carnegie Foundation for the Advancement of Teaching, 1929).

2. Abraham Flexner, *Medical Education in the United States and Canada*, Bulletin Number Four (New York: Carnegie Foundation for the Advancement of Teaching, 1910).

3. Even the straightforward, nondescript title of "Bulletin Number Twenty-three" was a source of confusion and misquotation. For example, both John R. Tunis's 1934 article in *Harper's Magazine* and Hardy and Berryman's subsequent excellent historical analysis incorrectly call it "Bulletin Number Twenty-nine"—probably because it was published in 1929. Cf. Jack Berryman and Stephen H. Hardy, "The College Sports Scene," in *Sports in Modern America*, ed. William J. Baker and John M. Carroll (Saint Louis: River City Publishers, 1983), pp. 63–76.

4. Henry F. Pritchett, "Preface," in Savage et al., *American College Athletics*, p. vii.

5. Howard J. Savage, *Fruit of an Impulse: Forty-Five Years of the Carnegie*

Foundation, 1905–1950 (New York: Harcourt, Brace, 1953), pp. 155–60; see esp. p. 158. An example of the fondness that contemporary higher education reform advocates have for resurrecting and invoking Savage's 1929 report is the foreword by Ernest L. Boyer, president of the Carnegie Foundation for the Advancement of Teaching, to Richard E. Lapchick and John B. Slaughter's anthology, *The Rules of the Game: Ethics in College Sports* (New York: Macmillan, 1989), pp. ix–xv.

6. Frederick Rudolph, "The Rise of Football," in *The American College and University: A History* (New York: Knopf, 1962), chap. 18; John S. Watterson, "Inventing Modern Football," *American Heritage* 39 (Sept.–Oct. 1988): 103–13; Jack Falla, *NCAA: The Voice of College Sports: A Diamond Anniversary History, 1906–1981* (Mission, Kans.: National Collegiate Athletic Association, 1981), chaps. 2–5.

7. Ronald Smith, *Sports and Freedom: The Rise of Big-Time College Athletics* (New York: Oxford University Press, 1988), esp. pp. 138, 179.

8. John R. Thelin, *The Cultivation of Ivy: A Saga of the College in America* (Cambridge, Mass.: Schenkman, 1976), pp. 13–19.

9. Accounts of the "Yale Spirit" and "Yale's Democracy" include Edwin E. Slosson, "Yale University," in *Great American Universities* (New York: Macmillan, 1910), pp. 34–74; George Santayana, "A Glimpse of Yale," *Harvard Monthly* (Dec. 1892): 89–97. The strong tradition of Yale football is chronicled in *The Blue Football Book* (New Haven: Yale Banner, 1970). For an analysis of the popular image of Yale projected by the "Frank Merriwell at Yale" series, see James Cain, "The Man Merriwell," *Saturday Evening Post,* June 11, 1927, p. 129, and Richard O'Donnell, "America's Most Popular Character," *National Retired Teachers Association Journal* (Nov.–Dec. 1969): 61.

10. Parke H. Davis, in the 1925 *Football Guide,* quoted in Allison Danzig, *The History of American Football* (Englewood Cliffs, N.J.: Prentice-Hall, 1956), pp. 125–27.

11. Walter Camp, "Introduction," *Walter Camp's Book of College Sports* (New York: Century, 1893), pp. 2–4.

12. Patrick Bryant Miller, "Athletes in Academe: College Sports and American Culture, 1850–1920" (Ph.D. diss., University of California, Berkeley, 1987), pp. 430, 467.

13. Robert A. Caro, *The Power Broker: Robert Moses and the Fall of New York* (New York: Knopf, 1974), p. 42; see also pp. 1–4, 38–47.

14. Ibid., p. 42.

15. Smith, *Sports and Freedom,* p. 198.

16. Miller, "Athletes in Academe." See also John R. Thelin and Lawrence Wiseman, "The Numbers Game: The Statistical Heritage in Intercollegiate Athletics," in *Monitoring the Intercollegiate Athletics Enterprise,* ed. Bruce I. Mallette and Richard D. Howard, New Directions in Institutional Research, no. 74, pp. 5–12 (San Francisco: Jossey-Bass, 1992).

17. Smith, *Sports and Freedom,* p. 206.

18. Paul R. Lawrence, "The Association's Formation and Its Early Years," in *Unsportsmanlike Conduct: The National Collegiate Athletic Association and the Business of College Football* (New York: Praeger, 1987), pp. 1–37.

19. Savage, *Fruit of an Impulse,* p. 155.

20. Ellen Condliffe Lagemann, "Henry Smith Pritchett and the Gospel of Efficiency," in *Private Power for the Public Good: A History of the Carnegie Foundation for the Advancement of Teaching* (Middletown, Conn.: Wesleyan University Press, 1983), chap. 2.

21. Savage et al., *American College Athletics*, p. 3.

22. Pritchett, "Preface," in ibid., p. xxi.

23. Savage et al., *American College Athletics*, p. 310.

24. Ibid., p. 277.

25. "Report Attacked at Brown," *New York Times*, Oct. 24, 1929, p. 23; "Brown Takes Stand on Carnegie Report," *New York Times*, Jan. 24, 1930, p. 31. Examples of the extended press coverage and sample articles from the *New York Times* are found in "Tarnished Ideals: The Business of Amateur Sports," in *Sports and Society: The Great Contemporary Issues*, ed. Gene Brown and Robert Lipsyte (New York: New York Times/Arno Press, 1980), pp. 17–24.

26. "Defends Big Ten Policies: F. L. Griffith Says Carnegie Report Gives an Unfair Picture," *New York Times*, Oct. 24, 1924, p. 23; see also Mervin D. Hyman and Gordon S. White, Jr., "The Big Ten's Dirty Linen," in *Big Ten Football: Its Life and Times, Great Coaches, Players, and Games* (New York: Macmillan, 1977), chap. 4.

27. "Defends Michigan on Its Athletics," *New York Times*, Jan. 21, 1930, p. 12.

28. Howard J. Savage, quoted in Arthur J. Daley, "NCAA Endorses Carnegie Report," *New York Times*, Jan. 2, 1930, p. 20.

29. Quoted in *New York Times*, Oct. 25, 1929, p. 17.

30. C. W. Mendell, "Athletics and the College: Review of The Carnegie Foundation for the Advancement of Teaching Bulletin Number Twenty-three," *Saturday Review of Literature*, Feb. 15, 1930, p. 735.

31. Savage et al., *American College Athletics*, pp. 80–83; for a summary of the discussion and differences between Henry S. Pritchett and Howard Savage on the interpretation of the college athletics study, see Savage, *Fruit of an Impulse.*

32. Savage et al., *American College Athletics*, p. 296.

33. Mendell, "Athletics and the College," p. 735.

34. Savage et al., *American College Athletics*, p. 207.

35. Pritchett, "Preface," in Savage et al., *American College Athletics*, p. xxi.

36. Laurence R. Veysey, "The Gulf between Students and Faculty," in *The Emergence of the American University* (Chicago: University of Chicago Press, 1965), pp. 294–302.

37. Henry Seidel Canby, *Alma Mater: The Gothic Age of the American College* (New York: Farrar and Rinehart, 1936), pp. 26–27.

38. Smith, *Sports and Freedom*; Miller, "Athletes in Academe"; Watterson, "Inventing Modern Football."

39. Paul Starr, *The Social Transformation of American Medicine: The Rise of a Sovereign Profession and the Making of a Vast Industry* (New York: Basic Books, 1982), pp. 117–27; see also Lagemann, *Private Power for the Public Good*, pp. 61–71.

40. John Young Brown, Sr. *The Legend of the Praying Colonels* (Louisville:

J. Marvin Gray, 1976). See also Danzig, *History of American Football*, pp. 235–36.

Chapter Two. Responses to Reform, 1930 to 1946

1. Howard J. Savage, John T. McGovern, and Harold W. Bentley, *Current Developments in American College Sport*, Bulletin Number Twenty-six (New York: Carnegie Foundation for the Advancement of Teaching, 1931). Cf. Howard J. Savage, with Harold W. Bentley, John T. McGovern, and Dean F. Smiley, M.D., *American College Athletics*, Bulletin Number Twenty-three (New York: Carnegie Foundation for the Advancement of Teaching, 1929).

2. Henry Suzzallo, "Preface," in Savage et al., *Current Developments*, p. v. See also Howard J. Savage, *Fruit of an Impulse: Forty-Five Years of the Carnegie Foundation, 1905–1950* (New York: Harcourt, Brace, 1953), pp. 155–60.

3. Savage et al., *Current Developments*, p. 46.

4. Ibid., p. 52.

5. Ibid., p. 53.

6. Robert F. Kelley, "Football Reforms Urged By Dr. Angell," *New York Times*, Jan. 1, 1931, p. 57.

7. Abraham Flexner, *Medical Education in the United States and Canada*, Bulletin Number Four (New York: Carnegie Foundation for the Advancement of Teaching, 1910).

8. Abraham Flexner, *Universities: American, English, German* (New York: Oxford University Press, 1930), pp. 64–66; see also p. 206 for Flexner's comments on the relatively high salaries of football coaches compared to faculty pay.

9. Ibid., p. 66.

10. Robert Hutchins, *The New College Plan* (Chicago: University of Chicago Press, 1931), p. 16; see also Hutchins, *The Higher Learning in America* (New Haven: Yale University Press, 1936).

11. "Chicago Abandons Intercollegiate Football in Surprise Move by Trustees," *New York Times*, Dec. 22, 1939.

12. Henry S. Pritchett, "Preface," in Savage et al., *American College Athletics*, p. xxi.

13. "Sports Heads Split on Carnegie Report," *New York Times*, Jan. 11, 1931, sec. 10, p. 4.

14. "Carnegie Report Called Fruitless," *New York Times*, Jan. 14, 1931. Cf. "Coach Rockne Finds Football Not Commercialized Enough," *New York Times*, Dec. 17, 1930, and "Envy of Football's Popularity Is Cited by Stuhldreher as Reason for Criticism," *New York Times*, Feb. 28, 1931.

15. Associated Press, "Federal Report Says Loss of Amateur Status Is 'Most Serious Evil' Confronting Football," *New York Times*, Jan. 1, 1931, p. 57.

16. Associated Press, "Football Viewed as Facing Crisis," *New York Times*, Jan. 3, 1931, p. 13. Estimates of football attendance and revenues for the 1929 and 1930 seasons are drawn from Jack Berryman and Stephen H. Hardy, "The College Sports Scene," in *Sports in Modern America*, ed. William J. Baker and John M. Carroll (Saint Louis: River City Publishers, 1983), pp. 63–76; see esp. pp. 64–65.

17. "Less Recruiting Seen by Officials: Subsidization Also Diminished, Survey by Associated Press in Middle West Shows," *New York Times*, Jan. 6, 1931, p. 31.

18. "No Curtailments Planned on Coast: Colleges to Continue Normal Athletic Programs, Survey by Associated Press Indicates," *New York Times*, Jan. 8, 1931, p. 26.

19. "Old Big Three Seen as Reform Leaders: Harvard, Yale, and Princeton Retain Influence," *New York Times*, Jan. 7, 1931, p. 35; see also "Yale Journal Hits Dr. Butler's Plan," and "Football Viewed as Facing Crisis," *New York Times*, Jan. 3, 1931, p. 13.

20. "Nation's Colleges Face Sports Crisis," *New York Times*, Jan. 15, 1933, pp. S1, S3.

21. "Football Costly to Small Colleges: Survey of 22 Schools Reveals Game Conducted at a Loss," *New York Times*, Mar. 23, 1938, p. 29.

22. For an analysis of Henry Pritchett's vision for the Carnegie Foundation for the Advancement of Teaching and the reform of American education, see esp. Ellen Condliffe Lagemann, "Henry Smith Pritchett and the Gospel of Efficiency," in *Private Power for the Public Good: A History of the Carnegie Foundation for the Advancement of Teaching* (Middletown, Conn.: Wesleyan University Press, 1983), pp. 21–36.

23. "Reports Football Wanes in Colleges: Carnegie Board, Which Scored 'Overemphasis' 3 Years Ago, Finds Sport in 'Lean Days,'" *New York Times*, June 15, 1931, p. 12.

24. Foster Rhea Dulles, "Drawing the Big Crowds," in *America Learns to Play* (New York: Appleton-Century, 1940), pp. 258–60.

25. Ibid.

26. George Orwell, *The Road to Wigan Pier* (originally published 1937; New York: Harcourt Brace Jovanovich, 1985).

27. Mary Martha Hosford Thomas, *Southern Methodist University: Founding and Early Years* (Dallas: Southern Methodist University Press, 1974); see also John R. Thelin, "Looking for the Lone Star Legacy: Higher Education in Texas," *History of Education Quarterly* (Summer 1977): 221–28.

28. Mervin D. Hyman and Gordon S. White, Jr., "The Big Ten's Dirty Linen," in *Big Ten Football: Its Life and Times, Great Coaches, Players, and Games* (New York: Macmillan, 1977), chap. 4; see esp. pp. 30–31. See also Melissa Larson, "Giants of the Midwest," in *The Pictorial History of College Football* (New York: Gallery Books, 1989), pp. 72–75.

29. John Gerald Tobin, "The Pacific Coast Conference Football Scandal and the Los Angeles Press" (Master's thesis, UCLA, 1959), pp. 19–27.

30. "Ban on Recruiting Is Voted in South," *New York Times*, Dec. 20, 1931, p. S2.

31. Bert Randolph Sugar, ed., *The SEC: A Pictorial History of Southeastern Conference Football* (Indianapolis: Bobbs-Merrill, 1979), pp. 121–27.

32. John R. Thelin, "Broken Triangle: The Harvard-Princeton Feud, 1926 to 1934," in *The Cultivation of Ivy: A Saga of the College in America* (Cambridge, Mass.: Schenkman, 1976), pp. 25–27.

33. "The Time Is Now," joint editorial appearing in *Columbia Spectator, Cornell Daily Sun, Harvard Crimson, Daily Pennsylvanian, The Dartmouth,*

Daily Princetonian, and *Yale Daily News*, Dec. 3, 1936. See also John R. Thelin, "The Ivy League Proposal of 1936," in *The Cultivation of Ivy*, pp. 27–30.

34. John R. Thelin, "Presidents' Agreements, 1939 to 1945," in *The Cultivation of Ivy*, pp. 30–32.

35. Hyman and White, "The Big Ten's Dirty Linen."

36. "Sees Training Table Step toward Paying Players," *New York Times*, Oct. 11, 1933, p. 29.

37. Hyman and White, "The Big Ten's Dirty Linen."

38. "South Relaxes Rules on Help to Athletes: Ban Unenforceable, Problem Is Left to Individual Colleges," *New York Times*, Dec. 19, 1938, p. 28.

39. "All-Out Aid to Recruit Athletes Given to Coaches by Southeastern Conference," *New York Times*, Feb. 18, 1941, p. 28.

40. "Proselytizing Ban Lifted by Big Six," *New York Times*, Dec. 10, 1944, p. 28.

41. Paul R. Lawrence, *Unsportsmanlike Conduct: The National Collegiate Athletic Association and the Business of College Football* (New York: Praeger, 1987), pp. 27–31.

42. See, for example, "Colleges Upheld on Radio Question," *New York Times*, Dec. 29, 1936, p. 24. For popular discussion of the emerging impact of radio broadcasts on college football, see H. I. Phillips, "Hold 'Em, Mike!" *Saturday Evening Post*, Oct. 17, 1936, pp. 25, 95.

43. Berryman and Hardy, "The College Sports Scene," pp. 63–76; see esp. pp. 64–65.

44. Melissa Larson, "Orange, Sugar, Cotton: New Bowl Games," in *The Pictorial History of College Football*, pp. 76–81.

45. James Thurber, "University Days," *New Yorker*, Sept. 23, 1933, pp. 15–17.

46. Prof. William Phelps of Yale, quoted in John McCallum, *Ivy League Football since 1872: The Games, Rituals, Storied Players and Coaches, Team and Conference Records* (New York: Stein and Day, 1977), p. 144.

47. John R. Thelin and Barbara K. Townsend, "Fiction to Fact: College Novels and the Study of Higher Education," in *Higher Education: Handbook of Theory and Research*, vol. 4, ed. John C. Smart (New York: Agathon Press, 1988), pp. 183–211.

48. Max Shulman, *Barefoot Boy with Cheek* (Garden City, N.Y.: Doubleday, 1943), p. 42.

49. James Farrell, *My Days of Anger* (New York: Vanguard, 1943), p. 382.

50. Thelin and Townsend, "Fiction to Fact," p. 192.

51. Henry S. Pritchett, "A Substitute for Football," *Atlantic Monthly* 150 (Oct. 1932): 446–48.

52. Associated Press, "Carnegie Report Assails Colleges," *New York Times*, Feb. 19, 1934, p. 21.

53. Associated Press, "Notre Dame Head Defends Policy," *New York Times*, Feb. 20, 1934, p. 28.

54. Lagemann, "Pritchett and the Gospel of Efficiency," pp. 21–36.

55. "Topics of the Times: A Report of Progress," *New York Times*, June 15, 1931, p. 18; see also Savage et al., *Current Developments*, p. 5.

56. Oliver Jensen, *A College Album* (New York: McGraw-Hill for American

214 • Notes to Pages 66–70

Heritage, 1974), p. 61; see also John R. Thelin, *Higher Education and Its Useful Past* (Cambridge, Mass.: Schenkman, 1982), p. 131.

57. Paul R. Lawrence, "The NCAA during World War II," in *Unsportsmanlike Conduct*, pp. 31–34.

58. "Colleges Allot 25 Million for Sports Construction," *New York Times*, Dec. 21, 1945, p. 18; see also David O. Levine, "The Middle Class Culture on Campus," in *The American College and the Culture of Aspiration, 1915–1940* (Ithaca: Cornell University Press, 1986), pp. 113–35.

Chapter Three. Regional Pride and Institutional Prestige

1. David O. Levine, *The American College and the Culture of Aspiration, 1915 to 1940* (Ithaca: Cornell University Press, 1986); Charles J. Andersen et al., *1989–90 Fact Book on Higher Education* (New York: Macmillan for the American Council on Education, 1989); Frederick Rudolph, *The American College and University: A History* (New York: Knopf, 1962).

2. Edwin E. Slosson, *Great American Universities* (New York: Macmillan, 1910). For data on 1940 university enrollments, see College of William and Mary, *Report of Self-Study* (Williamsburg, Va., 1974).

3. Martin Trow, "Reflections on the Transition from Mass to Universal Higher Education," *Daedalus* 99, no. 1 (1970): 1–42.

4. Anonymous, "The Class of 1937," *Life* 2, no. 23, June 7, 1937.

5. See Levine, "The Middle Class Culture on Campus," in *The American College and the Culture of Aspiration*, pp. 113–35; see also Helen Lefkowitz Horowitz, "The Organized," in *Campus Life: Undergraduate Cultures from the End of the Eighteenth Century to the Present* (New York: Knopf, 1987), pp. 118–50, and Laurence R. Veysey, "Stability and Experiment in the American Undergraduate Curriculum," in *Content and Context: Essays on College Education*, ed. Carl Kaysen (New York: McGraw-Hill for the Carnegie Commission on Higher Education, 1973), pp. 1–64.

6. Daniel J. Boorstin, "Culture with Many Capitals: The Booster College," in *The Americans: the National Experience* (New York: Vintage Books, 1970), pp. 152–61; see also Burton R. Clark, "Belief and Loyalty in College Organization," *Journal of Higher Education* 42 no. 6 (1971): 499–515.

7. Merle Borrowman, "The False Dawn of the State University," *History of Education Quarterly* 1, no. 1 (1961): 6–20; see also John R. Thelin, "Campus and Community: College Building in California," *Pacific Historian* 25, no. 4 (1981): 32–38.

8. For a historical analysis of the incorporation of such professions as agriculture, forestry, business, and engineering into the university curriculum during this period, see Earl F. Cheit, *The Useful Arts and the Liberal Tradition* (New York: McGraw-Hill for the Carnegie Commission on Higher Education, 1975). For a representative account of the accommodation of intense scholarship and graduate programs at the margin of campus life and of the organizational culture of the large state university, see John Kenneth Galbraith's memoir of his graduate school years at Berkeley, in *There Was Light: Autobiography of a University, Berkeley, 1868 to 1968*, ed. Irving Stone (Garden City, N.Y.: Doubleday, 1970), pp. 19–32.

9. "Sports Records Move West," *Life* 2, no. 23, June 7, 1937, pp. 72–73; see also John F. Rooney, Jr., "Geography of Sports," in *Encyclopedia of Southern Culture*, ed. Charles Reagan Wilson and William Ferris (Chapel Hill: University of North Carolina Press, 1989), pp. 564–65.

10. J. Steven Picou and Duane Gill, "Football"; see also Benjamin K. Hunnicutt, "Sports," and Tom Rankin, "Basketball," all in *Encyclopedia of Southern Culture*, pp. 1221–24, 1239–40, 1212–14.

11. Alan Brinkley, "Huey P. Long," in *Encyclopedia of Southern Culture*, pp. 1191–92.

12. Ruth Laney, "Huey's LSU: The Campus and the Kingfish," *LSU Magazine*, n.d. [1990?], pp. 16–20; see also Jack Fiser, "Louisiana State University," in *Encyclopedia of Southern Culture*, p. 292.

13. William E. Davis (LSU Chancellor), "Higher Education in Louisiana: What Became of the Dream?" *LSU Magazine*, n.d. [1991?], pp. 4–6.

14. Paul Manasseh, "Louisiana State University," in *The SEC: A Pictorial History of Southeastern Conference Football*, ed. Bert Randolph Sugar (Indianapolis: Bobbs-Merrill, 1979), pp. 117–44, esp. 121–27.

15. Ibid., pp. 121–27.

16. Laney, "Huey's LSU." For an architect's historical appraisal of the enduring significance of Louisiana State University's campus plan from the Long era, see Thomas A. Gaines, *The Campus as a Work of Art* (New York: Praeger, 1991), pp. 146–50.

17. Hugh Hawkins, "The University Builders Observe the Colleges," *History of Education Quarterly* 11, no. 4 (1971): 362.

18. D. Wharton, "Scribner's Examines Louisiana State University," *Scribner's Magazine*, Sept. 1937, pp. 71–78; see also John Callahan, "The Kingfish and L.S.U." (paper, 1991).

19. Major sources for this profile of the University of Georgia circa 1930 to 1946 include the following: Thomas G. Dyer, *The University of Georgia: A Bicentennial History, 1785–1985* (Athens: University of Georgia Press, 1985), pp. 246–50, 285–90; Karen M. McDearman, "University of Georgia," in *Encyclopedia of Southern Culture*, pp. 285–86; John F. Stegeman, "University of Georgia," in *The SEC*, pp. 79–94; and F. N. Boney, *A Pictorial History of the University of Georgia* (Athens: University of Georgia Press, 1984).

20. Dyer, "Retrenchment and Reform," in *University of Georgia*, pp. 200–221; F. N. Boney, *Pictorial History of the University of Georgia*.

21. Dyer, *University of Georgia*, p. 285.

22. Ibid., pp. 246–47.

23. Ibid.

24. Boney, *Pictorial History of the University of Georgia*, pp. 158–59; Dyer, "In Search of Radicals," in *University of Georgia*, pp. 222–40.

25. Boney, *Pictorial History of the University of Georgia*, pp. 158–59; Dyer, "In Search of Radicals," in *University of Georgia*, pp. 222–40.

26. Dyer, *University of Georgia*, pp. 245–46.

27. Ibid., p. 250.

28. John R. Thelin, "California and the Colleges," pt. 1, *California Historical Quarterly* 56, no. 2 (1977): 140–63; pt. 2, 56, no. 3 (1977): 230–49.

29. The commissioned institutional history is Manuel P. Servin and Iris

Higbie Wilson, *Southern California and Its University: A History of USC, 1880–1964* (Los Angeles: Ward Ritchie Press, 1969), pp. 166–83. A good example of a critical analysis of the University of Southern California as part of the region's social and cultural history is Kevin Starr, "USC, Electricity, Music, and Cops: The Emergence of Institutional Los Angeles," in *Material Dreams: Southern California through the 1920s* (New York: Oxford University Press, 1990), chap. 7, pp. 151–79.

30. Richard Whittingham, "The Big Game: Notre Dame–USC," in *Saturday Afternoon: College Football and the Men Who Made the Day* (New York: Workman, 1985), pp. 138–42.

31. Servin and Wilson's history and Starr's chapter both report 123,000, which would have been a national record; however, Notre Dame publications report 112,912. See Michael R. Steele, "Appendix A: Notre Dame's Football Record, 1910–1930," in *Knute Rockne: A Bio-bibliography* (Westport, Conn.: Greenwood Press, 1983), pp. 267–70.

32. Servin and Wilson, *Southern California and Its University*, pp. 174–75; Starr, *Material Dreams*, pp. 154–55. A narrative account of the University of Southern California's football program circa 1920 to 1940 is provided by Al Moss, "Howard Jones and the Thundering Herd," in *PAC-10 Football* (Greenwich, Conn.: Crescent Books, 1987), pp. 46–53.

33. Starr, *Material Dreams*, p. 153.

34. Earl C. Gottschalk, Jr., "The Day Is at Hand for Legal Break-Ins on Cal Tech Campus," *Wall Street Journal*, May 13, 1986, pp. 1, 27; see also Thelin, "California and the Colleges," pt. 2, p. 245.

35. *Life* 2, no. 23, June 7, 1937, p. 45.

36. John J. Powers, "The Time between the Wars," *Notre Dame Magazine*, Sesquicentennial edition, Summer 1991, pp. 22–24. Information on records and the history of football at Notre Dame was drawn from Gene Schoor, *100 Years of Notre Dame Football: A Centenary Celebration of the Fighting Irish Tradition* (New York: Morrow, 1987).

37. Powers, "Time between the Wars"; see also John Monczunski, "Bright Ideas," *Notre Dame Magazine*, Sesquicentennial edition, Summer 1991, pp. 27–32.

38. Powers, "Time between the Wars," pp. 27–32.

39. Christopher Jencks and David Riesman, *The Academic Revolution* (Garden City, N.Y.: Doubleday, 1968), pp. 316–20; see also Ralph McInerny, "A Civilizing Force," *Notre Dame Magazine*, Sesquicentennial edition, Summer 1991, pp. 36–39.

40. David Riesman and Reuel Denney, "Football in America: A Study in Culture Diffusion," *American Quarterly* 3, no. 4 (1951): 309–25.

41. Associated Press, "Carnegie Report Assails Colleges," *New York Times*, Feb. 19, 1934, p. 21.

42. Associated Press, "Notre Dame Head Defends Policy," *New York Times*, Feb. 20, 1934, p. 28.

43. Powers, "Time between the Wars," 22–24; Ian Thomsen, "The Grandfather Clause: Knute Rockne III Grapples With History," *Sports Illustrated*, 1988, n.d., n.p.

44. Michael D. Koehler, "College Football: America's Great Division I Football Coach: Knute Rockne," in *America's Greatest Coaches* (Champaign, Ill.:

Leisure Press, 1990), pp. 67–68; Jack Clary, "Knute Rockne," in *Great College Football Coaches* (New York: Gallery Books, 1990), pp. 125–32; Robert F. Kelley, "Knute Rockne, 1889–1931," in *New York Times Book of Sports Legends*, ed. Joseph J. Vecchione (New York: Random House, Times Books, 1991), pp. 272–77.

45. David Anderson, "Rockne's Twenty-five Commandments," in *New York Times Book of Sports Legends*, pp. 278–79.

46. Steele, *Knute Rockne*; Robert Quakenbush and Mike Bynum, *Knute Rockne: His Life and Legend* (Chicago: October Football, 1988).

47. Warren I. Susman, "Culture Heroes: Ford, Barton, Ruth," in *Culture as History: The Transformation of American Society in the Twentieth Century* (New York: Pantheon, 1984), pp. 123–49.

48. "Sidelines: The Gipper Will Return. . .," *Chronicle of Higher Education*, Feb. 24, 1988, p. A45. In contrast to the stereotypical images the movie projected for student-athlete George Gipp, see James A. Cox, "Was 'the Gipper' Really for Real? You Can Bet He Was!" *Smithsonian*, Dec. 1985, pp. 130–50.

49. Scriptwriter for the movie *Knute Rockne, All-American* was Robert Buckner (1940: Warner Brothers). Reviews from national publications when the movie was first released include the following: "Movies—Saga of Gridiron Genius: O'Brien Portrays Knute Rockne in Screen Story of Coach," *Newsweek*, Oct. 14, 1940, p. 73; "Knute Rockne—All American," *Time*, Oct. 21, 1940, n.p.; Bosley Crowther, "The Screen: 'Knute Rockne—All American,' a Thrilling Biography of the Great Coach, at the Strand," *New York Times*, Oct. 19, 1940, p. 21. For an analysis of the historical accuracy of the movie biography, see Steele, "Images of Rockne," in *Knute Rockne*, pp. 147–204.

50. Schoor, *100 Years of Notre Dame Football*, p. 70.

51. Clary, "Knute Rockne," in *Great College Football Coaches*, pp. 125–32; see esp. p. 132.

52. "Coach Rockne Finds Football Not Commercial Enough," *New York Times*, Dec. 17, 1930, n.p.

Chapter Four. Schools for Scandal, 1946 to 1960

1. Jack W. Berryman and Stephen Hardy, "The College Sports Scene," in *Sports in Modern America*, ed. William J. Baker and John M. Carroll (Saint Louis: River City Publishers, 1981), pp. 63–76, esp. pp. 72–75.

2. Arthur A. Fleisher III, Brian L. Goff, and Robert D. Tollison, *The National Collegiate Athletic Association: A Study in Cartel Behavior* (Chicago: University of Chicago Press, 1992), p. 43.

3. Melissa Larson, "The Golden Decade: The 1950s," in *The Pictorial History of College Football* (New York: Gallery Books, 1989), pp. 98–109.

4. Larry Fox, "The Giants Arrive," in *Illustrated History of Basketball* (New York: Grosset and Dunlap, 1974), pp. 74–95; see also Neil D. Isaacs, *All The Moves: A History of College Basketball* (Philadelphia: Lippincott, 1975).

5. Virginius Dabney, *Mister Jefferson's University: A History* (Charlottesville: University Press of Virginia, 1981), pp. 202–3.

6. Mickey Herskowitz, *The Legend of Bear Bryant* (New York: McGraw-Hill, 1987), pp. 48–49.

7. Quoted in "Colleges Adopt the 'Sanity Code' to Govern Sports: NCAA Bans Scholarships in Which Athletic Ability Is the Major Factor," *New York Times*, Jan. 11, 1948, p. S1.

8. For press coverage, see ibid. Secondary sources dealing with the "Sanity Code" include the following: Jack Falla, "The Sanity Code," in *NCAA: The Voice of College Sports: A Diamond Anniversary History, 1906–1981* (Mission, Kans.: National Collegiate Athletic Association, 1981), pp. 132–35; George Gipe, "The De-Emphasis of 1951," in *The Great American Sports Book* (Garden City, N.Y.: Doubleday, 1978), pp. 403–4, 482–83; Paul R. Lawrence, "Controlling Competition and Enforcing the Rules," in *Unsportsmanlike Conduct: The National Collegiate Athletic Association and the Business of College Football* (New York: Praeger, 1987), pp. 38–64.

9. "Schools to Decide Need of Athletes: NCAA Sanity Code Must Be Interpreted by Individual Colleges and Leagues," *New York Times*, Apr. 17, 1948, p. 18.

10. "NCAA Drops Sanity Code Control of Financial Aid to Athletes, Amendment Wins by 3-Vote Margin," *New York Times*, Jan. 13, 1951.

11. Lawrence, "Controlling Competition and Enforcing the Rules," pp. 38–63.

12. Alfred Clark, "Sollazzo Is Jailed with Five Players in Basketball Fix," *New York Times*, Nov. 20, 1951, p. 1. Articles and sources on 1951 scandals include: Charles Rosen, *Scandals of '51: How Gamblers Almost Killed College Basketball* (New York: Holt, Rinehart and Winston, 1978); Randy Roberts and James Olson, "Scandal Time," in *Winning Is the Only Thing: Sports in America since 1945* (Baltimore: Johns Hopkins University Press, 1989), pp. 73–94; Isaacs, "The Serpent in the Garden," in *All the Moves*, pp. 102–8; Robert Stern, "Scandal and Expansion, 1951–1952," in *They Were Number One: A History of the NCAA Basketball Tournament* (New York: Leisure Press, 1983), pp. 63–68; Fox, "Scandal," in *Illustrated History of Basketball*, pp. 110; Gipe, "Fixes," in *The Great American Sports Book*, pp. 16–38—see esp. "The Basketball Scandals," pp. 27–29.

13. "J. E. Hoover Scores Colleges on 'Fixes,'" *New York Times*, Apr. 10, 1951, p. 18; Louis Effrat, "Cinch Courses Hit as Root of Trouble," *New York Times*, Nov. 27, 1951, p. 39; "College Scandals Laid to Teaching," *New York Times*, Nov. 23, 1951, p. 31; "'Czar' Is Demanded in College Sports," *New York Times*, Mar. 29, 1951, p. 35.

14. John Y. Brown, *The Legend of the Praying Colonels* (Louisville: J. Marvin Gray, 1974), pp. 23–25.

15. James A. Cox, "Was 'the Gipper' Really for Real? You Can Bet He Was!" *Smithsonian*, Dec. 1985, pp. 130–50.

16. Ibid., p. 138.

17. William H. Beezley, "The 1961 Scandal at North Carolina State and the End of the Dixie Classic," in *Sport and Higher Education*, ed. Donald Chu, Jeffrey O. Segrave, and Beverly J. Becker (Champaign, Ill.: Human Kinetics Press, 1985), pp. 81–99.

18. Nicholas Pileggi, *Wiseguy: Life in a Mafia Family* (New York: Simon and Schuster, 1985), p. 170.

19. Henry Hill, quoted in Pileggi, *Wiseguy*, p. 174.

20. "Excerpts from Judge Streit's Comments," *New York Times*, Nov. 20, 1951, p. 26.

21. Adolph Rupp, quoted in Russell Rice, *The Wildcat Legacy* (Virginia Beach, Va.: JCP, 1982), p. 85.

22. "Two Coaches Quit Posts at W & M," *New York Times*, Aug. 12, 1951, p. 5; "William and Mary Inquiry On," *New York Times*, Aug. 16, 1951, p. 21; "College Found Lax in Athletic Inquiry," *New York Times*, Sept. 9, 1951, p. 72; "President Pomfret of William and Mary Resigns Following Scandal in Athletics at Virginia College," *New York Times*, Sept. 14, 1951, p. 27; "Big-time Sports Corrupt College, William and Mary Faculty Asserts," *New York Times*, Sept. 20, 1951, p. 51; "B.A. in Athletics," *New York Times*, Sept. 21, 1951, p. 22; "Athletic Change Backed," *New York Times*, Sept. 25, 1951, p. 27.

23. "Academies Urged to Ban Football," *New York Times*, Aug. 5, 1951, p. 1.

24. Charles Grutzner's articles in the *New York Times* include the following: "College Emphasis on Sports Found to Victimize Students," Mar. 18, 1951, p. 1; "School Athletes Face Many Lures," Mar. 19, 1951, p. 29; "Athletic Problem Handicaps Schools," Mar. 20, 1951, p. 31; "Educators Defend Athletic Courses," Mar. 21, 1951, p. 35; "Colleges Concede Evils in Athletics," Mar. 23, 1951, pp. 23, 26, 27.

25. "Coast Conference Considers Withdrawal from Rose Bowl Football Contest," *New York Times*, Jan. 5, 1951, p. 38; "Conference Bans Video," *New York Times*, Jan. 6, 1951, p. 12.

26. Arthur S. Adams, Letter to President Raymond B. Allen, University of Washington, Oct. 17, 1951 [ACE Archives]; also, "Presidents of 10 Colleges Named to Consider Ethics of Athletics," *New York Times*, Nov. 10, 1951, p. 1; and the related editorial, "Ethics and Athletics," *New York Times*, Nov. 11, 1951, p. 11.

27. "College Presidents Ready to Hurl Flying Block at Football Scandals," *New York Times*, Nov. 14, 1951, p. 39; "College Heads Open Inquiry Today on 'Ethical Lapses' in Athletics," *New York Times*, Nov. 19, 1951, p. 30; "Colleges' Inquiry on Athletics Opens," *New York Times*, Nov. 20, 1951, p. 27; "Athletics Inquiry Reports Progress," *New York Times*, Nov. 21, 1951, p. 17; Benjamin Fine, "College Officials Favor De-emphasis of Sports as a Result of the Basketball Scandals," *New York Times*, Nov. 25, 1951, sec. 4, p. 9.

28. Saul S. Streit, judge of the Court of General Sessions, Letter to Arthur S. Adams, American Council on Education, Dec. 6, 1951 [ACE Archives].

29. Special Committee on Athletic Policy of the American Council on Education, Minutes of the Second Meeting, Dec. 12 and 13, 1951, Washington, D.C. [ACE Archives].

30. Committee on Athletic Problems, *Intercollegiate Athletics and the North Central Association of Colleges and Secondary Schools: A Statement*, 1952 [ACE Archives].

31. American Council on Education, "Note to Editors," Press Release, Feb. 12, 1952; *Report of the Special Committee on Athletic Policy*, Feb. 16, 1952.

32. Milton S. Eisenhower, president, Pennsylvania State College, Letter to Arthur S. Adams, American Council on Education, Feb. 25, 1952 [ACE Archives].

33. Eisenhower, Letter to Arthur S. Adams, American Council on Education, Feb. 29, 1952 [ACE Archives].

34. "Biggie" Munn, quoted in Don Pieper, "Husker Horizons: Daddy's Ball Player," *Daily Nebraskan*, Dec. 8, 1951; see also R. G. Gustavson, chancellor, University of Nebraska, Letter to Arthur S. Adams, American Council on Education, Dec. 14, 1951 [ACE Archives].

35. Blair Cherry, "Pressures on the Coach," excerpts from article in *Saturday Evening Post*, Oct. 1951 [ACE Archives].

36. Ernest L. Wilkinson, president, Brigham Young University, Letter to Arthur S. Adams, May 8, 1952; see also Albert Ray Olpin, president, University of Utah, Letter to Arthur S. Adams, May 15, 1952 [ACE Archives].

37. Louis T. Benezet, president, Allegheny College, Letter to Prof. Hugh C. Willett, University of Southern California and president of the National Collegiate Athletic Association, Nov. 17, 1952. See also Arthur S. Adams's reply to Benezet, Letter of Nov. 24, 1952 [ACE Archives].

38. John A. Hannah, president, Michigan State College, Letter to Prof. Hugh Willett, University of Southern California, and president, National Collegiate Athletic Association, Jan. 14, 1952. For examples of the NCAA's early involvement with the ACE committee, see Raymond F. Howes, American Council on Education, Letter to Walter Byers, executive director, National Collegiate Athletic Association, Feb. 8, 1952 [ACE Archives].

39. Raymond F. Howes, ACE staff, Letter to Ted Smits, sports editor, Associated Press, Sept. 2, 1952 [ACE Archives].

40. W. Henry Johnston, director of Sports Information, Harvard Athletic Association, Letter to Arthur S. Adams, American Council on Education, Oct. 17, 1952 [ACE Archives].

41. Mill Marsh, "MSC's Dr. Hannah Tells Writers Sports De-Emphasis Sure to Come," *Ann Arbor News*, Oct. 15, 1952.

42. Raymond F. Howes, staff associate, American Council on Education, Letter to W. Henry Johnston, Harvard Athletic Association, Apr. 3, 1952 [ACE Archives].

43. Gayle Talbot, Associated Press Sports Round Up, News Release, Nov. 12, 1952 [ACE Archives].

44. Mervin D. Hyman and Gordon S. White, Jr., *Big Ten Football: Its Life and Times, Great Coaches, Players, and Games* (New York: Macmillan, 1977), pp. 35–36.

45. Arthur S. Adams, Letter to J. D. Williams, chancellor, University of Mississippi, Dec. 3, 1952 [ACE Archives].

46. Umphrey Lee, president, Southern Methodist University, Letter to Arthur S. Adams, Jan. 2, 1952 [ACE Archives]. For data on athletic scholarships at Southern Methodist University, see Charles Grutzner, "Colleges Concede Evils in Athletics: But Their Opinions on How to Clean Up Vary Widely," *New York Times*, Mar. 23, 1951, pp. 23, 27.

47. Arthur S. Adams, Letter to John A. Hannah, Jan. 16, 1952 [ACE Archives].

48. James P. Cornette to Arthur S. Adams; see also Adams's reply letter of Apr. 11, 1952 [ACE Archives].

49. George Lynn Cross, *Presidents Can't Punt: The OU Football Tradition* (Norman: University of Oklahoma Press, 1977), pp. 145–46.

50. "Excerpts from Judge Streit's Comments," *New York Times*, Nov. 20, 1951, p. 26. The Kentucky rebuttal is presented in *Preliminary Statement of the Joint Meeting of the Executive Committee of the Board of Trustees, the Board of Directors of the Athletic Association, and the Executive Committee of the Alumni Association of the University of Kentucky* (1952, Mimeographed, 5 pp.) [UK Archives].

51. Thomas D. Clark, *A History of Kentucky* (Lexington, Ky.: John Bradford Press, 1960), pp. 371–76, 474–75; Charles Gano Talbert, "The Postwar Years," in *The University of Kentucky: The Maturing Years* (Lexington: University of Kentucky Press, 1965), pp. 160–81.

52. Key works on Coach Rupp and basketball at the University of Kentucky, circa 1930 to 1960, include the following: Dan Chandler and Vernon Hatton, *Rupp: From Both Ends of the Bench* (Lexington, Ky., n.p., 1972); Tev Laudeman, *The Rupp Years: The University of Kentucky's Golden Era of Basketball* (Louisville: Courier-Journal/Louisville Times, 1972); *The Glory Road: Adolph Rupp and Kentucky Basketball, 1930–1972* (Lexington, Ky.: Kentucky Gifts Video, 1991); Burt Nelli, *The Winning Tradition: A History of Kentucky Wildcat Basketball* (Lexington: University Press of Kentucky, 1984).

53. For historical background on University of Kentucky football, see Russell Rice, "University of Kentucky," in *The SEC: A Pictorial History of Southeastern Conference Football*, ed. Bert Randolph Sugar (Indianapolis: Bobbs-Merrill, 1979), pp. 95–116, and Russell Rice, *The Wildcats: A Story of Kentucky Football* (Huntsville, Ala.: Strode Publishers, 1975).

54. Herman Lee Donovan, "The Athletics Program of the University," in *Keeping the University Free and Growing* (Lexington: University of Kentucky Press, 1959), pp. 102–16—see esp. pp. 104–7; Talbert, "The Postwar Years."

55. Articles of Incorporation of the University of Kentucky Athletic Association, Nov. 17, 1945; and Agreement between the Board of Trustees of the University of Kentucky and the University of Kentucky Athletic Association, Nov. 20, 1945. The official version of the University of Kentucky Athletic Association's founding and related fundraising is "Organization and Administration of Athletics at the University," in Minutes of the Board of Trustees, University of Kentucky, Dec. 18, 1951, pp. 14–18 [UK Archives].

56. James C. Klotter, ed., *The Public Papers of Governor Simeon Willis, 1943–1947* (Lexington: University Press of Kentucky, 1988), esp. pp. 4, 157; Governor Simeon Willis, Letter to Dr. H. L. Donovan, president, University of Kentucky, July 17, 1946 [UK Archives].

57. Griffenhagen and Associates, Division of Education Studies, *Report No. 7: University of Kentucky*, 2 vols. (Commonwealth of Kentucky, Apr. 2, 1947) [UK Archives].

58. Griffenhagen and Associates, "Summary Recommendation Number 116," in *Report No. 7: University of Kentucky*, p. 13.

59. Griffenhagen and Associates, "Intercollegiate Athletics," in *Report No. 7: University of Kentucky*, pp. 172–75.

60. Minutes of the Board of Trustees meeting, University of Kentucky, Sept. 27, 1947, pp. 51–53, and attachment, "An Analysis of the Griffenhagen and Associates Study of Education in Kentucky as It Applies to the University of Kentucky" (Mimeographed, 27 pp.) [UK Archives]; *You Cannot Have a Great*

State . . . Without a Great University (Lexington: University of Kentucky, 1947) [UK Archives].

61. University of Kentucky Athletic Association, *Audit Report* (June 30, 1955, Mimeographed, 22 pp.; see esp. p. 4) [UK Archives].

62. H. C. Robinson and Marguerite McLaughlin, Executive Committee of the Alumni Association, University of Kentucky, Letter to Alumni, 1946. See also Cover Letter, Helen G. King to Mr. Earle C. Clements, House of Representatives, Feb. 23, 1946 [UK Archives].

63. Talbert, "The Postwar Years," p. 170.

64. Donovan, "The Athletics Program of the University," pp. 110–11.

65. Ibid., p. 113.

66. "A Genuine University Atmosphere," in University of Kentucky, *Ten Year Self-Study Re-Accreditation Reports* (1960), pp. 241–53 [UK Archives].

67. John R. Thelin, "The Ivy League Saga, 1910 to 1960," in *The Cultivation of Ivy* (Cambridge, Mass.: Schenkman, 1976), pp. 21–50; John McCallum, "Football in the Early Fifties" and "De-Emphasis in Earnest," *Ivy League Football since 1872* (New York: Stein and Day, 1977), pp. 160–94.

68. "Something For the Boys," *Newsweek*, Aug. 21, 1950, p. 82.

69. David L. Goldberg, "What Price Victory? What Price Honor? Pennsylvania and the Formation of the Ivy League, 1950–1952," *Pennsylvania Magazine of History and Biography* 92, no. 2 (1988): 248.

70. "Ivy League De-Emphasizes Football; Bars Spring Drill, Post-Season Play," *New York Times*, Feb. 19, 1952, pp. 1, 32; "Three Colleges Assail Athletic Subsidy," *New York Times*, Oct. 29, 1951, p. 17; Charles Grutzner, "Pennsylvania Ban by Ivy League Seen," *New York Times*, Mar. 22, 1951, p. 33; Leo Riordan, "The Football Blues Hit Penn," *Saturday Evening Post*, Nov. 7, 1953, pp. 95–98; Arthur C. Pariente, "Penn, 1953: The Tragedy of Over-Emphasis," *Ivy*, Nov. 1956, p. 36.

71. Paul R. Lawrence, "Controlling Television and Postseason Bowl Games, 1945–1960," in *Unsportsmanlike Conduct*, pp. 65–93.

72. Goldberg, "What Price Victory?" p. 248.

73. R. K. Gooch, A. K. Davis, Jr., and J. W. Beams, *Report of the Athletic Committee of the Academic Faculty of the University of Virginia Appointed March 28, 1951* (Oct. 10, 1951, Mimeographed, 43 pp.) [UVA Archives]; "Sport without Aid Urged at Virginia," *New York Times*, Oct. 12, 1951, p. 39; Dabney, *Mister Jefferson's University*, pp. 318–20.

Chapter Five. Faculty Control and the Irony of Reform

1. Al Moss, *Pac-10 Football* (Greenwich, Conn.: Crescent Books, 1987); Jack Murphy, "More Than Fitting Hosts: The West," in *The College Game* (Indianapolis: Bobbs-Merrill, Rutledge Books, 1974), pp. 210–37; Richard Whittingham, "Pac-10 Conference," in *Saturday Afternoon: College Football and the Men Who Made the Day* (New York: Workman, 1985), pp. 62–65.

2. Examples of immediate national newspaper coverage include the following: "UCLA Probation to Cost It $95,000," *New York Times*, May 20, 1956, pp. S1, S5; "Coast Approves New Code on Aid," *New York Times*, Jan. 5, 1957, p. K13. See also John Gerald Tobin, "The Pacific Coast Conference Football Scan-

dal and the Los Angeles Press" (Master's Thesis, UCLA, June 1959—N.B., one of the committee members for Tobin's thesis was Wilbur Johns, athletic director at UCLA during the PCC controversies); Al Stump, "Football's Biggest Stink," *True*, Sept. 1956 [?], pp. 41–42, 95–100; Tim Cohane, "Inside the West Coast Football Scandal," *Look*, Aug. 7, 1956, pp. 72–80; Victor O. Schmidt, "The Facts about the Pacific Coast Conference Controversy: An Examination of the Ethical and Educational Aspects" (Address before the Commonwealth Club of San Francisco, Aug. 10, 1956) [University of Oregon Archives, PCC Box 597, File 10].

3. Faculty Athletic Committee, *The Athletic Situation at the University of Southern California: A Report from the Faculty Athletic Committee to the Board of Trustees Concerning the Discontinuance of Athletic Relations with Stanford University and the University of California*, Information Bulletin No. 1 (Los Angeles: University of Southern California, Nov. 1924), 35 pp. [USC Archives]; J. A. Butler, "General Report of Athletic Conditions within the Pacific Coast Intercollegiate Athletic Conference: With Comments and Recommendations," Dec. 11, 1932, 48 pp. [USC Archives].

4. Paul R. Lawrence, *Unsportsmanlike Conduct: The National Collegiate Athletic Association and the Business of College Football* (New York: Praeger, 1987), pp. 45, 63.

5. Commissioner's Report, June 13–15, 1949, p. 23 [University of Oregon Archives, PCC Box 571, File 8, 12-B-11].

6. Minutes of PCC, Commissioner's Report of June 1950, p. 1 [University of Oregon Archives, PCC Box 571, File 6, No. 12-B-13].

7. See Mickey Herskowitz, *The Golden Age of Pro Football* (Dallas: Taylor Publishing, 1974), p. 115; Dick Rockne, "The King and the Arm," in *Bow Down to Washington: A Story of Husky Football* (Huntsville, Ala.: Strode Publishers, 1975), pp. 114–30.

8. Report of the Commissioner, PCC, "Proposal of the Commissioner for a Modified Conference Program," Appendix B in Minutes, June 11, 1951, p. 1 [University of Oregon Archives, PCC Box 582, File 2].

9. Victor O. Schmidt, "Rules Enforcement," Report of the Commissioner, PCC, June 1951, p. 1 [University of Oregon Archives, PCC Box 571, File 3, 12-B-16].

10. Charles Grutzner, "Colleges Concede Evils in Athletics," *New York Times*, Mar. 23, 1951, pp. 23, 26, 27.

11. H. Eames Bishop, president, PCC Athletic Alumni Committees, Letter to Victor Schmidt, PCC Commissioner, Dec. 5, 1951 [University of Oregon Archives, PCC Box 569, File 12]; Victor Schmidt, Letter to H. Eames Bishop, PCC Athletic Alumni Committees, Jan. 24, 1952 [UCLA Archives, Box 258, Folder 5, 1952]. See also Pacific Coast Intercollegiate Athletic Conference, "Report of the Committee on Regulation of Organized Recruiting" (May 23, 1952), 28 pp. [University of Oregon Archives, PCC Box 573, File 4].

12. See Schmidt, Letter to presidents, May 22, 1953 [UCLA Archives, Box 268, File 7, 1953].

13. Schmidt, Commissioner's Report, PCC, Dec. 1953 [University of Oregon Archives, PCC Box 572, File 7, 12-B-21].

14. Jan. 1953 conference minutes; see also Claude Jones, Memo to Allen, Apr. 20, 1953 [UCLA Archives, Box 268, File 7, 1953].

15. "Coast Conference Considers Withdrawal from Rose Bowl Football Contest," *New York Times*, Jan. 5, 1951, p. 38; "Conference Bans Video," *New York Times*, Jan. 6, 1951, p. 12; "Colleges Exhorted to Reform Sports," *New York Times*, July 24, 1951, p. 25; "Sport De-emphasis Urged on Colleges," *New York Times*, Apr. 15, 1951, p. 32. See also Al Stump, "Football's Private Eyes," *This Week Magazine*, 1951 [n.d.], pp. 7, 35–36; Report on Special Conference Meeting, San Francisco, Nov. 23–24, 1952 [UCLA Archives, Box 258, Folder 5, 1952].

16. Resolution of June 6, 1954, as quoted by Victor O. Schmidt in Memorandum to the Presidents and Chancellors of All Member Institutions of the Pacific Coast Conference, July 1, 1954 [UCLA Archives, Box 281, Folder 1, 1954 (Jan.–June)].

17. Robert Sproul, Memorandum to Chancellors Allen and Kerr, Dec. 7, 1954 [UCLA Archives, Box 282, File 2, 1954 (Dec.)].

18. Minutes of the Meeting of the Presidents of the Pacific Coast Conference, Jan. 3, 1955 [UCLA Archives, Box 294, Folder 4, 1955 (Jan.–May)].

19. Minutes of the Meeting of the Presidents of the Pacific Coast Conference, May 10, 1955, p. 20 [UCLA Archives, Box 294, Folder 5, 1955 (May–July)].

20. Joseph Kaplan, Memorandum to Raymond Allen, June 4, 1955 [UCLA Archives, Box 294, Folder 5, 1955].

21. PCC, Report of the Commissioner, Minutes of Winter Meeting, Dec. 2–4, 1955 [University of Oregon Archives, PCC Box 572, File 1, 12-B-27].

22. Victor Schmidt, Memorandum to PCC Presidents [UCLA Archives, Box 294, Folder 6, 1955 (Aug.–Dec.)]; see also PCC, Report of the Commissioner, Winter Meeting, December 1956 [University of Oregon Archives, PCC Box 594, File 14].

23. Victor O. Schmidt and Bernard Hammerback, *1956 Action on Major Rules Violations* (Los Angeles: Pacific Coast Intercollegiate Athletic Conference, 1956), 40 pp. [USC Archives].

24. Stub Nelson, "Aid Fund Disclosed," *Seattle Post-Intelligencer*, Feb. 8, 1956 [University of Oregon Archives, PCC Box 596, File 19]; Rockne, *Bow Down to Washington* (Huntsville, Ala.: Strode Publishers, 1975), pp. 141–63; Vice-President's Letter to Conference about his ignorance of the "Washington Advertising Fund": H. P. Everest, Letter to V. O. Schmidt, RE: Roscoe Torrance Fund, with attached statement, Mar. 7, 1956; D. Wollett, Letter to members of PCC, RE: comments from U. of Washington to the Report of the Commissioner on Rules Enforcement, Apr. 27, 1956 [both in UCLA Archives, Box 310, File 4, 1956 (Jan.–Apr.)].

25. See also "Report of the Commissioner on the Case of the Greater Washington Advertising Fund," 1956, 39 pp. [UCLA Archives, Box 311, File 4, 1956]; P. Cartwright, Letter to President Schmitz, University of Washington, RE: Faculty Committee on Intercollegiate Athletics meeting and suggestions, Nov. 28, 1956; P. Cartwright, Letter to President Schmitz, University of Washington, RE: Faculty Committee on Intercollegiate Athletics views concerning proposals from Council of Presidents, Dec. 20, 1956 [USC Archives].

26. *Confidential Report to the Committee on Infractions of the National Collegiate Athletic Association*, University of Southern California, Oct. 2, 1956 [USC Archives]; Walter Byers, executive director of the NCAA, Letter to Chan-

cellor Raymond Allen, UCLA, Report by the NCAA Committee on Infractions: Results of Inquiry, Aug. 10, 1956 [UCLA Archives, Box 311, File 2, 1956 (July–Aug.)].

27. "Presidents' Council In Re: Pacific Coast Conference," St. Francis Hotel, San Francisco, Room 211, July 17, 1956, Jean Rodger, C.S.R., Official Court Reporter, Court House, Oakland, Calif., Transcript, 134 pp. [UCLA Archives, Box 311, Series 359, 246-5].

28. Edwin Pauley, Letters to Robert Sproul [May 23, 1956, June 13, 1956] [USC Archives].

29. John Vaughn, Letter to Edwin Pauley, June 11, 1956 [USC Archives].

30. Donald H. McLaughlin, Letter to Edwin Pauley, Sept. 4, 1956; see also Minutes of UC Regents Meeting, Aug. 24, 1956 [UCLA Archives, Box 311, File 3, 1956 (Aug.–Nov.)].

31. "Wide End Run by Regents Threatens UC Standards," *San Francisco Chronicle*, May 28, 1957, p. 18 [University of Oregon Archives, PCC Box 596, File 19].

32. See, for example, Bradford Booth, UCLA FAR, Letter to UCLA Chancellor Raymond Allen RE: Regents' Five Point Program, Dec. 9, 1957 [UCLA Archives, Box 325, File 3, 1957 (Oct.–Dec.)].

33. George A. Petit, "Alumni and Intercollegiate Athletics," in *Twenty-eight Years in the Life of a University President* (Berkeley: University of California Press, 1966), pp. 133–75; see also Verne A. Stadtman, "Robert Gordon Sproul's One University," in *The University of California, 1868–1968* (New York: McGraw-Hill, 1970), pp. 257–80, esp. p. 427 for Stadtman's brief account of Sproul and the Pacific Coast Conference controversies.

34. A. L. Strand, Letter to Robert Gordon Sproul, Dec. 17, 1957 [USC Archives]. See Bolton, Cover Memo to Asa Call, Dec. 29, 1957: "In my judgement this is one of the most remarkable letters ever written by the President of a College to the President of a University."

35. See also [D. Theophilus], president, University of Idaho, Letter to A. L. Strand, president, Oregon State, June 13, 1956 [Oregon State University Archives, Office of the President: Research Group 13, Roll no. 6, S64, Series 2].

36. Andrew Hamilton and John B. Jackson, *UCLA on the Move during Fifty Golden Years, 1919–1969* (Los Angeles: Ward Ritchie Press, 1969).

37. John R. Thelin, "California and the Colleges," pt. 1, *California Historical Quarterly* 56, no. 22 (1977): 140–63.

38. See, for example, the following memorandums from George Taylor, director of Business Affairs, to Chancellor Raymond Allen, concerning "employment for students, especially athletes": Nov. 14, 1952; July 1, 1953; July 2, 1953; July 19, 1954 [UCLA Archives, Box 258, File 5, 1952; Box 268, File 7, 1953; Box 281, File 4, 1954].

39. Schmidt and Hammerback, *1956 Action on Major Rules Violations*, p. 23.

40. Tim Cohane, "College Football's Greatest Folly: The Curious Case of Ronnie Knox, UCLA Halfback," *Look*, Nov. 15, 1955, pp. 141–47; Harvey Knox, "Why Ronnie Knox Quit California," *Sports Illustrated*, Sept. 6, 1954, pp. 32–33 [University of Oregon Archives, PCC Box 595, File 1 (Knox File)]; Ronnie Knox with Melvin Durslag, "College Football Is Pro Football: It's All Business, Says

the Big Name in the West Coast Furor; Only the Salary Is 'Peanuts,'" *Collier's*, Oct. 12, 1956, pp. 34–37 [USC Archives].

41. "City Council Asks for Probe of Entire PCC," *Los Angeles Examiner*, May 26, 1956.

42. Ed Schoenfield, "UCLA Head Attacks PCC as Unfair," *Oakland Tribune*, July 11, 1956 [University of Oregon Archives, PCC Box 596, File 17].

43. "PCC Suicide Near: UCLA Chancellor Sees New Set Up," *San Francisco Examiner*, June 9, 1956; Hamilton and Jackson, "The PCC Hassle," pp. 130–32, also "Athens of Athletics," pp. 169–86, in *UCLA on the Move*. See also J. Vaughn, Letter to Edwin Pauley, June 11, 1956, concerning UCLA alumni opinions—it makes a strong case for an independent UCLA apart from UC Berkeley [USC Archives]; and "Pacific Coast Conference," *UCLA Alumni Magazine*, July 15, 1957, pp. 7–10 [University of Oregon Archives, PCC Box 594, File 4].

44. "Governor Enters UCLA Grid Problem," news clipping, circa June 1956 [UCLA Archives, Box 310, File 5, 1956 (Apr.–June)].

45. Hendrik Van Leuven, *Touchdown UCLA: The Complete Account of Bruin Football* (Tomball, Tex.: Strode Publishers, 1988), pp. 77–139—see esp. p. 119 for the quoted passage as a good example of popular appraisal of Coach Sanders in Los Angeles. See also Steve Springer and Michael Arkush, *Sixty Years of USC-UCLA Football* (Stamford, Conn.: Longmeadow Press, 1991), p. 104. The circumstances of Sanders's death were a source of public relations concern, as suggested by the following excerpt from page 104 of Springer and Arkush, which was highly favorable in its depiction of Sanders:

> Sanders had gone to visit William T. (Pop) Grimes, a retired commercial hotel owner who lived at the Lafayette Hotel. Sanders then complained about the heat, and shed his coat and shirt. When Grimes left the room to get cool soft drinks, Sanders collapsed.
>
> After Grimes departed, Sanders, according to newspaper accounts, began talking about football to Ernestine Drake, a woman in the hotel room.
>
> "He kept talking football and asked me if I'd seen many games," Drake said. "I said I hadn't." Suddenly Sanders clutched his chest and fell to the floor. He was dead when medical help arrived.

46. Thomas J. Cunningham, general counsel, University of California Regents, to Chancellor Allen, RE: Sanders Problem, June 11, 1957; see also R. B. Allen and Wilbur Johns, Letter to Mr. Henry R. Sanders, cc to President Sproul, Thomas Cunningham, and Paul Hutchinson, July 29, 1957 [UCLA Archives, Box 325, File 2, 1957 (June–Dec.)].

47. Tobin, "Pacific Coast Conference Football Scandal," p. 209.

48. Hamilton and Jackson, *UCLA on the Move*, pp. 131–32.

49. R. B. Allen, Letter to Wallace Sterling, Apr. 9, 1958 [UCLA Archives, Box 341, File 5, 1958 (Jan.–June)].

50. Wilbur Johns, Memorandum to Bradford A. Booth, FAR, UCLA, June 10, 1958 [UCLA Archives, Box 341, File 5, 1958 (Jan.–June)].

51. Minutes of conversation of Kerr, Sterling, and Topping, Mar. 9, 1960 [USC Archives].

52. Gaylord Harnwell, University of Pennsylvania, Letter to President Norman D. Topping, May 12, 1960 [USC Archives]. For the University of Houston's

proposal that USC join Houston, Pittsburgh, Miami, and UCLA to form an urban university group, see Clanton D. Williams, Letter to Norman Topping, Sept. 13, 1957 [USC Archives].

53. Chancellor's Ad Hoc Committee on IAAC Report, sec. 3, "Accountability, Organization, and Financing of Athletics," UCLA, July 1, 1959 [UCLA Archives, Box 360, File 5, 1959 (May–July and Sept.)]. For student response, see Mort Salzman, "UC Group Proposes Big Switch in Athletic Policy," *Daily Bruin*, Nov. 4, 1959 [UCLA Archives, Box 360, File 6, 1959].

54. Creed C. Black, "Reforming College Sports: Myth or Reality?" quoted in *Academe*, July–Aug. 1991, p. 7.

55. Victor O. Schmidt, *Pacific Coast Conference Report of the Commissioner*, Winter Meeting, Dec. 1956, p. 1 [University of Oregon Archives, PCC Box 574, File 14].

Chapter Six. Critics and Controversies, 1960 to 1980

1. Paul R. Lawrence, "Television and the Reorganization of the NCAA," in *Unsportsmanlike Conduct: The National Collegiate Athletic Association and the Business of College Football* (New York: Praeger, 1987), pp. 94–98. See also Nand Hart-Nibbrig and Clement Cottingham, "The Media and the Transformation of College Sports," in *The Political Economy of College Sports* (Lexington, Mass.: D. C. Heath, Lexington Books, 1986), pp. 33–53.

2. Lawrence, *Unsportsmanlike Conduct*, p. 96. See also Jack Falla, "The Electronic Free Ticket," in *NCAA: The Voice of College Sports* (Mission, Kans.: National Collegiate Athletic Association, 1981), pp. 97–123, 243.

3. Christopher Jencks and David Riesman, *The Academic Revolution* (Garden City, N.Y.: Doubleday, 1968).

4. Andrew Hamilton and John B. Jackson, "Athens of Athletics," in *UCLA on the Move during Fifty Golden Years, 1919–1969* (Los Angeles: Ward Ritchie Press, 1969), pp. 169–86.

5. Manuel P. Servin and Iris Higbie Wilson, "Athletics: Excellence in Nonprofit Sports," in *Southern California and Its University: A History of USC, 1880–1964* (Los Angeles: Ward Ritchie Press, 1969), pp. 144–63.

6. Sporadic complaints about commercialism are exemplified in Howard M. Tuckner, "All-America Stalwarts Still Love Football, But Many Feel They Are Part of a Business," *New York Times*, Dec. 11, 1960. A summary of the feud between the NCAA and the AAU is in Joseph M. Sheehan, "Power Fight: Peril to Amateur Sports: An Analysis of the N.C.A.A.'s Struggle to Capture Control from the A.A.U.," *New York Times*, Jan. 21, 1963.

7. Frank Graham, Jr., "The Story of a College Football Fix," *Saturday Evening Post*, Mar. 23, 1963, pp. 80–83.

8. James Kirby, *Fumble: Bear Bryant, Wally Butts, and the Great College Football Scandal* (San Diego: Harcourt Brace Jovanovich, 1986).

9. Quoted in Kirby, *Fumble*, pp. 146–47.

10. Paul W. Bryant and John Underwood, *Bear: The Hard Life and Good Times of Alabama's Coach Bryant* (Boston: Little, Brown, 1975), pp. 242–46. See also Mickey Herskowitz, "The Trial," in *The Legend of Bear Bryant* (New York: McGraw-Hill, 1987), pp. 129–42.

11. "Three Illinois Coaches Resign Positions: Their Dismissal Ordered by Big Ten for Role in Fund," *New York Times*, Mar. 20, 1967, p. 36; Mervin D. Hyman and Gordon S. White, Jr., "The Big Ten's Dirty Linen," in *Big Ten Football: Its Life and Times, Great Coaches, Players, and Games* (New York: Macmillan, 1977), pp. 35–45.

12. Duffy Daugherty, quoted in Hyman and White, *Big Ten Football*, p. 140.

13. James A. Michener, "Coaches," in *Sports in America* (New York: Random House, 1976), pp. 317–33.

14. Bryant and Underwood, *Bear*, pp. 325–26.

15. The anecdote is paraphrased from Herskowitz, *Legend of Bear Bryant*, p. 72.

16. The anecdote is paraphrased from Tony Kornheiser, "The Baron of the Blue Grass," in *The New York Times Book of Sports Legends*, ed. Joseph J. Vecchione (New York: New York Times, 1991), pp. 285–87.

17. Darrell Royal with Blackie Sherrod, "Public Relations: The Faculty," in *Darrell Royal Talks Football* (Englewood Cliffs, N.J.: Prentice-Hall, 1963), p. 207.

18. Royal and Sherrod, "The Scholastic Look," in ibid., pp. 190–99.

19. John Majors, quoted in Dan Hruby, "Football Degree May Be Next," *San Jose [Calif.] Mercury-News*, June 25, 1978.

20. Michener, "Colleges and Universities," in *Sports in America*, pp. 219–80.

21. Jack Scott, ed., *The Athletic Revolution* (New York: Free Press, 1971); Dave Meggyesy, *Out of Their League* (Berkeley: Ramparts Press, 1970); Gary Shaw, *Meat on the Hoof* (New York: St. Martin's Press, 1972).

22. Harry Edwards, *The Revolt of the Black Athlete* (New York: Free Press, 1969).

23. "Faculty and Students Protesting Carolina Stadium's Top Priority," *New York Times*, Dec. 21, 1969, p. 44; Steven V. Roberts, "Students Questioning Role and Cost of College Athletics; Interest in Sports Declines," *New York Times*, Jan. 3, 1971, p. 55; Leonard Koppett, "Colleges Question Old Views on Sports," *New York Times*, Jan. 11, 1971, p. 70; Ivar Peterson, "The Football Phenomenon and Its Place on Campus," *New York Times*, Jan. 16, 1974, p. 91; Joseph Durso, "Athletic Recruiting: A Campus Crisis," *New York Times*, Mar. 10, 1974, pp. 1, 52; Steve Cady, "Costly Business of Sports Recruiting Escalates toward a Public Scandal," *New York Times*, Mar. 11, 1974, pp. 1, 38; Joseph Durso and the *New York Times* Sports Department, *The Sports Factory: An Investigation into College Sports* (New York: New York Times, Quadrangle Books, 1975).

24. Michener, *Sports in America*, p. 320. For analysis of sports metaphors in American political life of the early 1970s, see Ike Balbus, "Politics as Sports: The Political Ascendancy of the Sports Metaphor in America," *Monthly Review* (Mar. 1975): 27–39.

25. Earl F. Cheit, *The New Depression in Higher Education* (New York: McGraw-Hill, 1971); Howard R. Bowen, *Investment in Learning: The Individual and Social Value of American Higher Education* (San Francisco: Jossey-Bass, 1977). See also Howard R. Bowen, *The Costs of Higher Education* (San Francisco: Jossey-Bass, 1980).

26. Carnegie Commission on Higher Education, *Sponsored Research of the Carnegie Commission on Higher Education* (New York: McGraw-Hill, 1975); Carnegie Council on Policy Studies in Higher Education, *The Carnegie Council on Policy Studies in Higher Education: A Summary of Reports and Recommendations* (San Francisco: Jossey-Bass, 1980); Carnegie Council on Policy Studies in Higher Education, *Three Thousand Futures: The Next Twenty Years for Higher Education* (San Francisco: Jossey-Bass, 1980). Examples of campus planning guides that pay little attention to college sports include Richard I. Miller, *The Assessment of College Performance: A Handbook of Techniques and Measures for Institutional Self-Evaluation* (San Francisco: Jossey-Bass, 1979), and Lewis B. Mayhew, *Surviving the Eighties: Strategies and Procedures for Solving Fiscal and Enrollment Problems* (San Francisco: Jossey-Bass, 1980).

27. George H. Hanford, *An Inquiry into the Need for and Feasibility of a National Study of Intercollegiate Athletics* (Washington, D.C.: American Council on Education, 1974).

28. Ibid., p. 9.

29. Ibid., pp. 21–22.

30. Ibid., p. 31.

31. Ibid., p. 65.

32. Ibid., pp. 102–9; see also Robert H. Atwell, "Financial Problems of Intercollegiate Athletics," Appendix B in Hanford, *Inquiry*.

33. Ibid., p. 49. See also Mary McKeown, "Women in Intercollegiate Athletics," Appendix H in Hanford, *Inquiry*. A related, later article is Nancy Brocklehurst, "Are Sports Changing?" *College Board Review*, no. 109 (Fall 1978): 14–16. Implications of gender and equity issues for litigation are discussed in Carlos Alvarez, "Current Litigation Involving Intercollegiate Athletics: Analysis and Implications for Intercollegiate Sports," Appendix A in Hanford, *Inquiry*.

34. Hanford, *Inquiry*, pp. 91–92.

35. Ibid., p. 85.

36. Michener, "Colleges and Universities," in *Sports in America*, pp. 219–80; see esp. pp. 244–47.

37. *The Commission on Collegiate Athletics* (Washington, D.C.: American Council on Education, Mar. 1978); Ewald B. Nyquist, James R. Spence, and Harry A. Marmion, *Final Report: The Commission on Collegiate Athletics* (Washington, D.C.: American Council on Education, Nov. 5, 1979) [ACE Archives]. See also Ewald B. Nyquist, "The Future of Collegiate Athletics," *College Board Review*, no. 109 (Fall 1978): 10–13, 17.

38. Mitchell H. Raiborn, *Revenues and Expenses of Intercollegiate Athletic Programs: Analysis of Financial Trends and Relationships* (Shawnee Mission, Kans.: National Collegiate Athletic Association, 1978).

39. Harry A. Marmion, guest editor, "On Collegiate Athletics" issue, *Educational Record* 60, no. 4 (1979).

40. A good example of early economic analysis of intercollegiate athletics programs is Robert H. Atwell, "Some Reflections on Collegiate Athletics," *Educational Record* 60 (Fall 1979): 367–73. A more developed presentation of Atwell's ideas is found in Robert Atwell, Bruce Grimes, and Donna Lopiano, *The Money Game: Financing Collegiate Athletics* (Washington, D.C.: American Council on Education, 1980).

41. Gordon S. White, Jr., "Freshmen Given Varsity Status in Major Sports," *New York Times*, Jan. 9, 1972, pp. S1, S9. See also "Ungovernable Monster," Editorial, *New York Times*, Jan. 12, 1972; "College Athletes Permitted Pro Status in Different Sports," *New York Times*, Jan. 9, 1974, p. 27.

42. Hanford, *Inquiry*, p. 76.

43. "Comes the Revolution: Joining the Game at Last, Women Are Transforming American Athletics," *Time*, June 26, 1978, pp. 54–60; see also Michener, "Women and Sports," in *Sports in America*, pp. 155–82.

44. Hanford, *Inquiry*, pp. 46–48, 139; see also Roscoe C. Brown, Jr., "Race, Sport, and Academe: Report of the Task Force on the Black Athlete," Appendix D in Hanford, *Inquiry*; Michener, "Sports and Upward Escalation," in *Sports in America*, pp. 183–217; Richard Pennington, *Breaking the Ice: The Racial Integration of Southwest Conference Football* (Jefferson, N.C.: McFarland, 1987).

45. Raiborn, *Revenues and Expenses*.

46. Mark Asher, "Play and Not Pay? Maryland's Kehoe Blasts Title IX, Says Women Can't Produce Income," syndicated *Washington Post* article appearing in *Louisville Courier-Journal*, June 10, 1975. See also John R. Thelin, "Higher Education and Athletics: Probing an American Ethos," *Journal of Educational Thought* 12, no. 3 (1978): 176–83.

47. "Curci Concerned over Recruiting," *Lexington [Ky.] Leader*, Nov. 15, 1975.

48. Hanford, *Inquiry*, p. 34.

49. Figures and quotes from "A Majors Success," *Time*, Dec. 2, 1974, p. 84.

50. Resolution by Professor James Marsden, Minutes of University Senate, University of Kentucky, Mar. 2, 1976; Recommendation of Senate Council, Minutes of University Senate, University of Kentucky, Apr. 12, 1976.

51. Gordon S. White, Jr., "Transient Coaches Trouble Colleges," *New York Times*, Jan. 23, 1978, p. C3; Gordon S. White, Jr., "N.C.A.A. Is Accused of Professional Tactics," *New York Times*, Apr. 18, 1978, p. 48; Neil Amdur, "Will Commercialism Be a Threat to Amateur Sports?" *New York Times*, June 5, 1979, p. B14.

52. For discussion of government concern over intercollegiate athletics problems, see Joseph Froomkin, "Sports and the Post-Secondary Sector," Appendix E in Hanford, *Inquiry*.

Chapter Seven. From Sports Page to Front Page, 1980 to 1990

1. George Reasons, "USC Says Athletic Department Bypassed Admissions Office," *Los Angeles Times*, Oct. 14, 1980, pt. 1, pp. 1, 24; see also Editorial, "A Beast That Needs Taming," *Los Angeles Times*, Oct. 15, 1980, pt. 2, p. 12.

2. John R. Thelin and Lawrence L. Wiseman, "Intercollegiate Athletics: The Perils of Publicity," in *The Old College Try: Balancing Academics and Athletics in Higher Education* (Washington, D.C.: George Washington University and the Association for the Study of Higher Education, 1989), pp. 1–11. Examples of articles in periodicals with a national circulation include the cover story, "The Shame of College Sports," *Newsweek*, Sept. 22, 1980, pp. 54–59, and Alvin P. Sanoff, "Behind Scandals in College Sports," *U.S. News and World Report*,

Feb. 11, 1980, pp. 61–63. A representative example of detailed investigation is John Underwood, "Special Report—Student-Athletes: The Sham, The Shame," *Sports Illustrated*, May 19, 1980, pp. 36–74.

3. Gary D. Funk, *Major Violation: The Unbalanced Priorities in Athletics and Academics* (Champaign, Ill.: Leisure Press, 1991); David A. Klatell and Norman Marcus, *Sports for Sale: Television, Money, and the Fans* (New York: Oxford University Press, 1988); Rick Telander, *The Hundred Yard Lie: The Corruption of College Football and What We Can Do to Stop It* (New York: Simon and Schuster, 1990); Charles Thompson and Allan Sonnenschein, *Down and Dirty: The Life and Crimes of Oklahoma Football* (New York: Carroll and Graf, 1990); Francis X. Dealy, Jr., *Win at Any Cost: The Sell Out of College Athletics* (New York: Carol Publishing, 1990); David Whitford, *A Payroll to Meet: A Story of Greed, Corruption, and Football at SMU* (New York: Macmillan, 1989); and Peter Golenbock, *Personal Fouls: The Broken Promises and Shattered Dreams of Big Money Basketball at Jim Valvano's North Carolina State* (New York: Signet, 1990).

4. Bill Brubaker, "Ex-USC Official: Study of Athletes, Academics Halted," *Washington Post*, Oct. 1, 1991, pp. C1, C8.

5. Associated Press, "College Sports Crooked, Nation Says in Survey," *Newport News [Va.] Daily Press*, Apr. 13, 1989, pp. C1, C6.

6. Leroy T. Howe, "Academics and Athletics at SMU: A View from a Swaying Bridge," *Academe*, vol. 73, July–Aug. 1987, pp. 18–24; see also Whitford, *A Payroll to Meet*.

7. Jeffrey Marx and Michael York, "Playing above the Rules," *Lexington [Ky.] Herald-Leader*, Oct. 27 and 28, 1985; see also Marx and York, "NCAA Can't Agree on How to Clean Up College Sports," *Lexington Herald-Leader*, Dec. 22, 1985.

8. Steve Wieberg, "College Presidents Get on Ball: Kentucky President Took Grief For Righting Wrongs," *USA Today*, Aug. 3, 1989, p. 1C; Jerry Tipton, " 'We Could Have Been Shut Down': NCAA Hands UK Tough Sanctions, Spares Program," *Lexington Herald-Leader*, May 20, 1989, pp. A1, A11. See "Kentucky's Shame," cover story, and Curry Kirkpatrick, "Dodging a Bullet," *Sports Illustrated*, May 29, 1989, pp. 24–34.

9. See, for example, William F. Reed, "What Price Glory? Lusting for Football Success, Mississippi State Hired Jackie Sherrill," *Sports Illustrated*, Dec. 24, 1990, pp. 34–38.

10. Dave Johnson, "Oklahoma Cleans Up Its Act—Changes Made to Improve Image: Sooners Are OK Again," *Newport News [Va.] Daily Press*, Sept. 26, 1991, pp. B1, B6.

11. Robert H. Atwell, "Putting College Sports in Perspective: Solutions for the Long Term," *AAHE Bulletin*, Jan. 1988, pp. 7–10.

12. Austin C. Wehrwein, "Court Orders University of Minnesota to Admit Athlete to Degree Program," *Chronicle of Higher Education*, Jan. 13, 1982, p. 5, which quotes Judge Miles W. Lord; see also *Mark D. Hall v. University of Minnesota*, 530 Fed. Supp., Case 104, 1982, U.S. District Court, District of Minnesota, pp. 104–11. For an example of connection with public policy, see Mark Asher, "NCAA Hears Senate's Wrath on Graduation Rates," *Washington Post*, Sept. 13, 1989, pp. C1, C3.

13. Diane K. Roberts, "The Jan Kemp Controversy: An Index to Media Coverage" (Athens: University of Georgia Libraries, University Archives, Sept. 1987), 130 pp.

14. Examples of early warnings about financial problems of college sports published in the news section of metropolitan newspapers include: Al Moss, "College Football Has a Case of the Shorts," *San Francisco Chronicle*, Mar. 18, 1981; Pete Alfano, "Big-Time Football: Colorado Pays the Price in Its Quest to Win," *Los Angeles Times*, June 21, 1979; Bob Monahan, "Tightening Belts: Like Nearly Everybody, Colleges Are Feeling the Pinch of Inflation," *Los Angeles Times*, June 26, 1980; see also Douglas S. Looney, "There Ain't No More Gold in Them Thar Hills," *Sports Illustrated*, Oct. 6, 1980, pp. 30–37. After several years of neglect, the topic was rediscovered with articles such as Malcolm Moran, "Saturday Afternoon in Crisis: Colleges Fight to Pay for a U.S. Tradition," *New York Times*, Aug. 13, 1989, pp. 1, 9; Barbara R. Bergmann, "Do Sports Really Make Money for the University?" *Academe*, vol. 77, Jan.–Feb. 1991, pp. 28–31.

15. Gil Gilbert, "Hold That Tiger: Big Game at Mizzou," *Sports Illustrated*, Sept. 24, 1980, pp. 70–86.

16. Paul R. Lawrence, "Division within the Intercollegiate Athletic Cartel, 1960–1985," in *Unsportsmanlike Conduct: The National Collegiate Athletic Association and the Business of College Football* (New York: Praeger, 1987), pp. 104–20. See also Nand Hart-Nibbrig and Clement Cottingham, "The Media and the Transformation of College Sports," in *The Political Economy of College Sports* (Lexington, Mass.: D. C. Heath, Lexington Books), pp. 33–54; Arthur A. Fleisher III, Brian L. Goff, and Robert D. Tollison, *The National Collegiate Athletic Association: A Study in Cartel Behavior* (Chicago: University of Chicago Press, 1992).

17. Thelin and Wiseman, *The Old College Try*, pp. 18–20; Peter Monaghan, "Olympic Sports Losing Out on U.S. Campuses? Budget Cuts and NCAA Rules Said to Threaten Sports Programs That Nurture Olympic Talent," *Chronicle of Higher Education*, Aug. 5, 1992, pp. A1, A29, A30.

18. Malcolm Moran, "Colleges Fight to Pay for a U.S. Tradition," *New York Times*, Aug. 13, 1989, pp. 1, 9; John R. Thelin and Lawrence L. Wiseman, "Fiscal Fitness: The Peculiar Economics of Intercollegiate Athletics," *Capital Ideas* 4, no. 4 (1990): 1–12; see also Ben Brown, "Old College Try Not Enough for Some: Probes Driven by Skeptics of Movement," *USA Today*, July 10, 1991, p. 6C. Coverage of the controversial television pacts includes the following: Douglas Lederman, "Notre Dame's New Football TV Contract: A Blemish on the Squeaky-Clean Image of the Fighting Irish?" *Chronicle of Higher Education*, Mar. 7, 1990, pp. A1, A40; Associated Press, "CFA Rips Notre Dame for TV Greed, Wildcatting," *Newport News [Va.] Daily Press*, Feb. 8, 1990, p. B8.

19. Linda Robertson, "The Economics of Going to a Bowl," *Lexington [Ky.] Herald-Leader*, Dec. 24, 1989, p. C9.

20. Associated Press, "University of Michigan Athletic Department Deficits," *Washington Post*, Sept. 11, 1988; see also Alvin P. Sanoff with Joannie M. Schrof, "The Price of Victory: College Sports vs. Education," *U.S. News and World Report*, Jan. 8, 1990, p. 52; Thelin and Wiseman, "Fiscal Fitness."

21. For a synthesis of scholarship from several disciplines on intercollegiate

athletics, see John R. Thelin, "Athletics in Higher Education," in Marvin C. Alkin, ed., *Encyclopedia of Educational Research*, 6th ed. (New York: Macmillan for the American Educational Research Association, 1992), pp. 96–99. See also John F. Rooney, Jr., *The Recruiting Game: Toward a New System of Intercollegiate Sport* (Lincoln: University of Nebraska Press, 1980); James Frey, ed., *The Governance of Intercollegiate Athletics* (West Point, N.Y.: Leisure Press, 1982); Hart-Nibbrig and Cottingham, *The Political Economy of College Sports*; Donald Chu, *The Character of American Higher Education and Intercollegiate Sport* (Albany: State University of New York Press, 1989); Allen Guttmann, *A Whole New Ball Game: An Interpretation of American Sports* (Chapel Hill: University of North Carolina Press, 1988); and Judith Andre and David N. James, eds., *Rethinking College Athletics* (Philadelphia: Temple University Press, 1991).

22. Murray Sperber, *College Sports, Inc.: The Athletic Department vs. the University* (New York: Henry Holt, 1990).

23. John C. Weistart, "College Sports Reform: Where Are the Faculty?" *Academe*, vol. 73, July–Aug. 1987, pp. 12–17; for a sequel, see Robert H. Atwell, "Sports Reform: Where Is the Faculty?" *Academe*, vol. 77, Jan.–Feb. 1991, pp. 10–12. See also Douglas Lederman, "U. of North Carolina Faculty Council Pushes for Sports Reforms: Effort Could Set National Standard for Involvement of Professors," *Chronicle of Higher Education*, Jan. 31, 1990, pp. A37–A38.

24. American Association of University Professors, "The Role of Faculty in the Governance of College Athletics: A Report of the Special Committee on Athletics," *Academe*, vol. 76, Jan.–Feb. 1990, pp. 43–47.

25. "Michigan State Trustees Name Coach to Be Athletic Director," *Chronicle of Higher Education*, Jan. 31, 1990, pp. A36–A37; John Brooks Slaughter, "Where Was the President? Presidents' Responsibility for Change in Intercollegiate Athletics," in Richard E. Lapchick and John B. Slaughter, eds., *The Rules of the Game: Ethics in College Sport* (New York: Macmillan and American Council on Education, 1989), pp. 179–92; Thelin and Wiseman, "Presidential Leadership: Who's in Charge?" in *The Old College Try*, pp. 63–83.

26. Commission on Intercollegiate Athletics, *Keeping Faith with the Student-Athlete: A New Model for Intercollegiate Athletics* (Charlotte, N.C.: Knight Foundation, Mar. 1991); see also Minutes of the Knight Foundation Commission on Intercollegiate Athletics, Washington, D.C., June 28–29, 1990.

27. Congressman McMillen, quoted in Commission on Intercollegiate Athletics, *Keeping Faith with the Student-Athlete*, p. 30.

28. Sperber, "The NCAA: The Fox in the Henhouse," in *College Sports, Inc.*, pp. 309–44; see also Sperber, "Why the NCAA Can't—and Won't—Reform College Athletics," *Academe*, vol. 77, Jan.–Feb. 1991, pp. 13–20.

29. George H. Hanford, "1990 Proposal to Review Athletics as Part of Accreditation Echoes a 1974 Report," *Chronicle of Higher Education*, Nov. 28, 1990; see also Douglas Lederman, "Southern Accrediting Association Adopts Criteria to Evaluate Athletics Programs," *Chronicle of Higher Education*, Dec. 18, 1991, p. A35.

30. John DiBiaggio, "Cosmetic Change versus Real Reform," *Academe*, vol. 77, Jan.–Feb. 1991, pp. 21–23.

31. For an account of arguments over limits on scholarships and coaches, see

"Bill Calls for Reforms at NCAA Institutions," *Higher Education and National Affairs* (American Council on Education), Aug. 12, 1991, pp. 1–4; Robert Fachet, "Colleges May Be Regaining Control of Sports Programs," *Washington Post*, Mar. 18, 1992, pp. D1, D3; Douglas Lederman, "Knight Panel Praises Sports-Reform Movement but Sees 'a Long and Hazardous Road' Ahead," *Chronicle of Higher Education*, Mar. 25, 1992, pp. A33, A34.

32. NCAA, *1989–90 Manual of the National Collegiate Athletic Association: Constitution, Bylaws, Rules of Order, Executive Regulations, Recommended Policies, Enforcement Procedure, Administration Case Book* (Mission, Kans.: NCAA, 1989).

33. G. Ann Uhlir, "Athletics and the University: The Post-Woman's Era," *Academe*, vol. 73, July–Aug. 1987, pp. 25–29; Steve Wieberg, "NCAA: Women's Sports Still on Short End," *USA Today*, Mar. 12, 1991, pp. 1C, 7C. See also a special report by David Teel, "Title IX Revisited: Colleges Alerted—Women's Sports Need Fair Share," *Newport News [Va.] Daily Press*, July 26, 1992, pp. C1, C4; Linda Jean Carpenter and Vivian Acosta, "Back to the Future: Reform with a Woman's Voice," *Academe*, vol. 77, Jan.–Feb. 1991, pp. 23–27; Douglas Lederman, "Advocates of Women's Sports Vow to Keep Equity Issue at Center Stage," *Chronicle of Higher Education*, Mar. 25, 1992, pp. A33, A34; Donna A. Lopiano and Connee Zotos, "Equity and Policy Problems in Women's Intercollegiate Athletics," in Lapchick and Slaughter, *Rules of the Game*, pp. 31–54.

34. This section draws from John R. Thelin and Lawrence L. Wiseman, "The Future of Big-Time Intercollegiate Athletics," *Planning for Higher Education* 19 (Winter 1990–91): 18–27.

35. House Committee on Education and Labor, Subcommittee on Postsecondary Education, *Hearings on the Role of Athletics in College Life*, 101st Cong., 1st sess. May 18 and 24, 1989, pp. 1–207. See also Debbie Becker, "'Right to Know' Bill Attracts Support," *USA Today*, Sept. 13, 1989; "Bill Calls for Reforms at NCAA Institutions," *Higher Education and National Affairs* (American Council on Education), Aug. 12, 1991, pp. 1, 4. An example of one congressman's sustained interest in government regulation of college sports is Tom McMillen, *Out of Bounds: How the American Sports Establishment Is Being Driven by Greed and Hypocrisy—And What Needs to Be Done about It* (New York: Simon and Schuster, 1992). Cf. McMillen's comments as a member of the Knight Foundation Commission, in *Keeping Faith with the Student-Athlete*, p. 30.

36. Nathan Glazer, "Regulating Business and the Universities: One Problem or Two?" *Public Interest* 56 (Summer 1979): 43–65.

37. Derek Bok, "The Federal Government and the University," *Public Interest* 57 (Winter 1980): 80–101.

38. Goldie Blumenstyk, "Town-Gown Battles Escalate as Beleaguered Cities Assail College Tax Exemptions," *Chronicle of Higher Education*, June 29, 1988; Lois Therrien, "Getting Joe College to Pay for City Services," *Business Week*, July 16, 1990, p. 37; Donald Kirby, "The Carrier Dome Controversy: Re-Writing the Town-Gown Relationship," *Change*, Mar.–Apr. 1988, pp. 42–49.

39. D'Vera Cohn, "IRS Eyes Universities' Tax-Deductible Services," *Washington Post*, May 5, 1985, pp. B1, B5; Scott Jaschik, "Three More States Adopt

Measures to Restrict Campus-run Businesses," *Chronicle of Higher Education,* Sept. 7, 1988, p. A1; Liz McMillen, "Reports of Misuse Prompt Widespread Investigations of Public Colleges' Private Fund Raising," *Chronicle of Higher Education,* Sept. 14, 1988, p. A33.

40. Michael Hiestand, "Cotton Bowl Audit Could Affect Many Tax-Exempt Organizations," *USA Today,* May 15, 1990, p. 9C; Albert B. Crenshaw, "IRS Looks at Where Charity Ends and Ads Begin," *Washington Post,* July 21, 1992, pp. C1, C5; see also "NCAA's Income from Advertisements in Program Is Taxable, Court Rules," *Chronicle of Higher Education,* Mar. 8, 1989.

41. Ivan Maisel, "CFA Television Pact Threatened: Illegal Cartel's Future Uncertain," *Newport News [Va.] Daily Press,* Aug. 4, 1990, pp. B1, B3; Douglas Lederman, "College Football Association's Pacts with TV Networks Violate Antitrust Law, Trade Commission Charges," *Chronicle of Higher Education,* Sept. 12, 1990, pp. A35–36.

Epilogue

1. Vanderbilt University Coach Gerry DiNardo, quoted in "Colleges," *Washington Post,* Aug. 18, 1991, p. D2.

2. Kenneth J. Cooper, "Rose Bowl Expenses Billed as Research Costs: University of Michigan Charges Questioned," *Washington Post,* Sept. 11, 1991, p. A21.

3. Jackie Jensen, *There Was Light: Autobiography of a University, Berkeley, 1868–1968,* ed. Irving Stone (Garden City, N.Y.: Doubleday, 1970), pp. 165–70.

4. Data culled from "Junk Mail Plagues Recruit," *Newport News [Va.] Daily Press,* Dec. 16, 1991, p. D2.

5. Robert C. Maxson, president, University of Nevada at Las Vegas, quoted in *Chronicle of Higher Education,* Mar. 4, 1992, p. A1.

A Note on Sources

The chapter notes provide complete citations for my references to primary sources, newspaper and periodical articles, archival documents, correspondence, and minutes of meetings, as well as to secondary sources and articles in scholarly journals. In tracking newspaper coverage of developments in college sports, I relied heavily on what may be termed the "national press": namely, the *New York Times* from 1920 to 1990, Associated Press releases since 1929, and the *Washington Post* and the *Los Angeles Times* since 1970. An excellent reference work that provides a chronological survey of the *New York Times*'s coverage of the social and political developments in college sports is the anthology of reprinted articles edited by Gene Brown, *Sports and Society* (New York: Arno Press, 1980). To balance the regional and metropolitan bias of the national press and major newspapers, I have attempted to assemble pertinent clippings from newspapers within the immediate campus community whenever I was analyzing a specific campus episode. This has, for example, included analysis of articles published in such newspapers as the *Lexington [Ky.] Herald* when discussing the University of Kentucky athletic program and from the *Los Angeles Times* for Southern California response to the Pacific Coast Conference issues during the years 1930 to 1960.

My research based on primary sources included analysis of the four major reports and selected campus controversies. When I was conducting research, the files for the Carnegie Foundation for the Advancement of Teaching were being transferred from the foundation's offices in Princeton and New York City; these are now catalogued and housed in the Special Collections Library of Columbia University's Teachers College. There has been relatively little primary source research dealing with the Pacific Coast Conference disputes, because when the conference was dissolved in 1958, its files were sealed until 1964. To study the Pacific Coast Conference controversies and historical developments at member institutions, circa 1920 to 1959, the following archives were rich in research materials: the University of Oregon's Knight Library, which is the official repository for the complete records of the Pacific Coast Conference; the University of Southern California, for holdings on both USC and the conference; the chancellor's files in the archives of the University of California, Los Angeles, for documents dealing with both the history of athletics at UCLA and its membership in the Pacific Coast Conference; correspondence and minutes pertaining to the conference in the microfilm holdings of the university presidents' files at the Oregon State University library and special collections. Other campus archives that provided crucial documents included the University of Virginia, for its 1953 faculty report on intercollegiate athletics; the College of William and Mary, for materials dealing with college football abuses after World War II; and the University of Kentucky, for historical records on state development and the university, circa 1930 to 1990. The American Council on Education's archives in Washington, D.C., were an excellent source for minutes, files, drafts, and correspondence related to the 1952 ACE special report, George Hanford's 1974 feasibility study, and the 1978–79 Commission on Collegiate Athletics.

The bibliographic entries presented below are confined to reasonably accessible books and secondary sources, organized under the following categories: general works on American history, culture, and public policy; American higher education; commission reports and official studies; college sports scandals and controversies; scholarly analysis of intercollegiate athletics; and histories of college sports teams and coaches.

General Works on American History, Culture, and Public Policy

Bissinger, H. G. *Friday Night Lights: A Town, a Team, and a Dream.* New York: Harper Perennial, 1990.

Boorstin, Daniel. "Culture with Many Capitals: The Booster College." In *The Americans: The National Experience,* pp. 152–61. New York: Random House, Vintage Books, 1970.

Caro, Robert. *The Power Broker: Robert Moses and the Fall of New York.* New York: Knopf, 1974.

Dulles, Foster Rhea. *America Learns to Play.* New York: Appleton-Century, 1940.

Glazer, Nathan. "Regulating Business and the Universities: One Problem or Two?" *Public Interest* 56 (Summer 1979): 43–65.

Lagemann, Ellen Condliffe. *Private Power for the Public Good: A History of the Carnegie Foundation for the Advancement of Teaching.* Middletown, Conn.: Wesleyan University Press, 1983.

Laney, Ruth. "Huey's LSU: The Campus and the Kingfish." *LSU Magazine* [n.d.], 1990, pp. 16–20.

Michener, James. *Sports in America.* New York: Random House, 1976.

Savage, Howard. *Fruit of an Impulse: Forty-Five Years of the Carnegie Foundation, 1905–1950.* New York: Harcourt, Brace, 1953.

Starr, Kevin. "USC, Electricity, Music, and Cops: The Emergence of Institutional Los Angeles." In *Material Dreams: Southern California through the 1920s,* pp. 151–79. New York: Oxford University Press, 1990.

Starr, Paul. *The Social Transformation of American Medicine: The Rise of a Sovereign Profession and the Making of a Vast Industry.* New York: Basic Books, 1982.

Susman, Warren I. *Culture as History: The Transformation of American Society in the Twentieth Century.* New York: Pantheon, 1984.

Thurber, James. "University Days." *New Yorker,* Sept. 23, 1933, pp. 15–17.

Wilson, Charles Reagan, and William Ferris, eds. *The Encyclopedia of Southern Culture.* Chapel Hill: University of North Carolina Press, 1989.

American Higher Education

Birnbaum, Robert. *How Colleges Work: The Cybernetics of Academic Organization and Leadership.* San Francisco: Jossey-Bass, 1988.

Bok, Derek C. "The Federal Government and the University." *Public Interest* 57 (Winter 1980): 80–101.

Bowen, Howard R. *Investment in Learning: The Individual and Social Value of American Higher Education.* San Francisco: Jossey-Bass, 1977.

———. *The Costs of Higher Education.* San Francisco: Jossey-Bass, 1980.

Canby, Henry Seidel. *Alma Mater: The Gothic Age of the American College.* New York: Farrar and Rinehart, 1936.

Carnegie Commission on Higher Education. *Sponsored Research of the Carnegie Commission on Higher Education.* New York: McGraw-Hill, 1975.

Carnegie Council on Policy Studies in Higher Education. *A Summary of Reports and Recommendations.* San Francisco: Jossey-Bass, 1980.

———. *Three Thousand Futures: The Next Twenty Years for Higher Education.* San Francisco: Jossey-Bass, 1980.

Cheit, Earl F. *The Useful Arts and the Liberal Tradition.* New York: McGraw-Hill for the Carnegie Commission on Higher Education, 1975.

Clark, Burton R. *The Distinctive College.* Chicago: Aldine, 1970.

Dyer, Thomas G. *The University of Georgia: A Bicentennial History, 1785–1985.* Athens: University of Georgia Press, 1985.

Flexner, Abraham. *Universities: American, English, German.* New York: Oxford University Press, 1930.

Hamilton, Andrew, and John B. Jackson. *UCLA on the Move during Fifty Golden Years, 1919–1969.* Los Angeles: Ward Ritchie Press, 1969.

Horowitz, Helen Lefkowitz. *Campus Life: Undergraduate Cultures from the End of the Eighteenth Century to the Present.* New York: Knopf, 1987.

Hutchins, Robert. *The New College Plan.* Chicago: University of Chicago Press, 1931.

Jencks, Christopher, and David Riesman. *The Academic Revolution.* Garden City, N.Y.: Doubleday, 1968.

Jensen, Oliver. *A College Album.* New York: McGraw-Hill for American Heritage, 1974.

Kerr, Clark. *The Uses of the University.* Cambridge: Harvard University Press, 1964.

Levine, David O. *The American College and the Culture of Aspiration, 1915 to 1940.* Ithaca: Cornell University Press, 1986.

Mayhew, Lewis B. *Surviving the Eighties: Strategies and Procedures for Solving Fiscal and Enrollment Problems.* San Francisco: Jossey-Bass, 1980.

Petit, George A. *Twenty-eight Years in the Life of a University President.* Berkeley: University of California Press, 1966.

Rudolph, Frederick. *The American College and University: A History*. New York: Knopf, 1962.

———. *Curriculum: A History of the American Undergraduate Course of Study since 1636*. San Francisco: Jossey-Bass, 1977.

Servin, Manuel P., and Iris Higbie Wilson. *Southern California and Its University: A History of USC, 1880–1964*. Los Angeles: Ward Ritchie Press, 1969.

Slosson, Edwin E. *Great American Universities*. New York: Macmillan, 1910.

Spectorsky, A. C., ed. *The College Years*. New York: Hawthorn, 1958.

Stadtman, Verne A. *The University of California, 1868–1968*. New York: McGraw-Hill, 1968.

Stone, Irving, ed. *There Was Light . . . : Autobiography of a University: Berkeley, 1868 to 1968*. Garden City, N.Y.: Doubleday, 1970.

Talbert, Charles Gano. *The University of Kentucky: The Maturing Years*. Lexington: University of Kentucky Press, 1965.

Thelin, John R. *The Cultivation of Ivy: A Saga of the College in America*. Cambridge, Mass.: Schenkman, 1976.

———. *Higher Education and Its Useful Past*. Cambridge, Mass.: Schenkman, 1982.

Thelin, John R., and Barbara K. Townsend. "Fiction to Fact: College Novels and the Study of Higher Education." In *Higher Education: Handbook of Theory and Research*, vol. 4, ed. John C. Smart, pp. 183-211. New York: Agathon Press, 1988.

Thomas, Mary Martha Hosford. *Southern Methodist University: Founding and Early Years*. Dallas: Southern Methodist University Press, 1974.

Trow, Martin. "Reflections on the Transition from Mass to Universal Higher Education." *Daedalus* 99, no. 1 (1970): 1–42.

Veysey, Laurence R. *The Emergence of the American University*. Chicago: University of Chicago Press, 1965.

Commission Reports and Official Studies

American Association of University Professors. "The Role of the Faculty in the Governance of College Athletics: A Report of the Special Committee." *Academe*, vol. 76, Jan.–Feb. 1990, pp. 43–47.

American Council on Education. *Report of the Special Committee on Athletic Policy*. Washington, D.C.: American Council on Education, Feb. 16, 1952.

Carnegie Foundation for the Advancement of Teaching. *The Control of the Campus: A Report on the Governance of Higher Education*. Washington, D.C.: Carnegie Foundation for the Advancement of Teaching, 1982.

Flexner, Abraham. *Medical Education in the United States and Canada* (Bulletin Number Four). New York: Carnegie Foundation for the Advancement of Teaching, 1910.

Hanford, George H. *An Inquiry into the Need for and Feasibility of a National Study of Intercollegiate Athletics*. Washington, D.C.: American Council on Education, 1974.

Knight Foundation. *Keeping Faith with the Student-Athlete: A New Model for Intercollegiate Athletics*. Charlotte, N.C.: Knight Foundation Commission on Intercollegiate Athletics, Mar. 1991.

———. Minutes of the Commission on Intercollegiate Athletics. Washington, D.C., June 28–29, 1990.

National Collegiate Athletic Association. *1981 NCAA Football Television Committee Report*. Shawnee Mission, Kans., 1982.

Nyquist, Ewald B., James R. Spence, and Harry A. Marmion. *Final Report: The Commission on Collegiate Athletics*. Washington, D.C.: American Council on Education, 1979.

Oliva, L. Jay. *What Trustees Should Know about Intercollegiate Athletics: AGB Special Report*. Washington, D.C.: Association of Governing Boards of Universities and Colleges, 1989.

Raiborn, Mitchell. *Financial Reporting and Control for Intercollegiate Athletics*. Shawnee Mission, Kans.: National Collegiate Athletic Association, 1974.

Savage, Howard J., with Harold W. Bentley, John T. McGovern, and Dean F. Smiley, M.D. *American College Athletics* (Bulletin Number Twenty-three). New York: Carnegie Foundation for the Advancement of Teaching, 1929.

Savage, Howard J., with John T. McGovern and Harold W. Bentley. *Current Developments in American College Sport* (Bulletin Number Twenty-six). New York: Carnegie Foundation for the Advancement of Teaching, 1931.

U.S. Congress. House. Committee on Education and Labor. *Hearings on the Role of Athletics in College: Hearings before the Subcommittee on Postsecondary Education of the Committee on Education and Labor*. 101st Cong., 1st sess. Serial 101–22. 208 pp. Washington, D.C.: U.S. Government Printing Office, 1989.

U.S. Department of Education. *Revenues and Expenditures in Intercollegiate Athletics: The Feasibility of Collecting National Data by Sport*. Washington, D.C.: Office of Educational Research and Improvement, USDOE, Oct. 1992.

Waldorf, John. *NCAA Football Rules Committee Chronology of One Hundred Years, 1876 to 1976*. Shawnee Mission, Kans.: National Collegiate Athletic Association, 1975.

College Sports Scandals and Controversies

Dealy, Francis X., Jr. *Win At Any Cost: The Sell Out of College Athletics*. New York: Birch Lane, 1990.

Durso, Joseph. *The Sports Factory: An Investigation into College Sports*. New York: New York Times, 1975.

Funk, Gary D. *Major Violation: The Unbalanced Priorities in Athletics and Academics*. Champaign, Ill.: Leisure Press, 1991.

Golenbock, Peter. *Personal Fouls: The Broken Promises and Shattered Dreams of Big Money Basketball at Jim Valvano's North Carolina State*. New York: Penguin Books, 1989.

Kirby, James. *Fumble: Bear Bryant, Wally Butts, and the Great College Football Scandal*. San Diego: Harcourt Brace Jovanovich, 1986.

Klatell, David, and Norman Marcus. *Sports for Sale: Television, Money, and the Fans*. New York: Oxford University Press, 1988.

McMillen, Tom, with Paul Coggins. *Out of Bounds: How the American Sports*

Establishment Is Being Driven by Greed and Hypocrisy—and What Needs to Be Done about It. New York: Simon and Schuster, 1992.

Meggyesy, Dave. *Out of Their League.* Berkeley: Ramparts Press, 1970.

Rosen, Charles. *Scandals of 1951: How Gamblers Almost Killed College Basketball.* New York: Holt, Rinehart and Winston, 1978.

Shapiro, Leonard. *Big Man on Campus: John Thompson and the Georgetown Hoyas.* New York: Henry Holt, 1991.

Shaw, Gary. *Meat on the Hoof.* New York: St. Martin's Press, 1971.

Telander, Rick. *The Hundred Yard Lie: The Corruption of College Football and What We Can Do to Stop It.* New York: Simon and Schuster, 1989.

Thompson, Charles, and Allan Sonnenschein. *Down and Dirty: The Life and Crimes of Oklahoma Football.* New York: Carroll and Graf, 1990.

Whitford, David. *A Payroll to Meet: A Story of Greed, Corruption, and Football at SMU.* New York: Macmillan, 1989.

Yaeger, Don. *Undue Process: The NCAA's Injustice for All.* Champaign, Ill.: Sagamore, 1991.

Scholarly Analysis of Intercollegiate Athletics

Andre, Judith, and David N. James, eds. *Rethinking College Athletics.* Philadelphia: Temple University Press, 1991.

Atwell, Robert, Bruce Grimes, and Donna Lopiano. *The Money Game: Financing Collegiate Athletics.* Washington, D.C.: American Council on Education, 1980.

Baker, William J., and John M. Carroll, eds. *Sports in Modern America.* Saint Louis: River City Publishers, 1983.

Berryman, Jack, and Stephen H. Hardy. "The College Sports Scene." In *Sports in Modern America,* ed. William J. Baker and John M. Carroll, pp. 63-76. Saint Louis: River City Publishers, 1983.

Brown, Gene, ed. *Sports and Society.* New York: Arno Press, 1980.

Cady, Edwin. *The Big Game: College Sports and American Life.* Knoxville: University of Tennessee Press, 1978.

Chu, Donald. *The Character of American Higher Education and Intercollegiate Sport.* Albany: State University of New York Press, 1989.

Chu, Donald, Jeffrey Segrave, and Beverly Becker, eds. *Sport and Higher Education.* Champaign, Ill.: Human Kinetics, 1985.

Cullen, Francis, Edward Latessa, and Joseph Byrne. "Scandal and Reform in Collegiate Athletics." *Journal of Higher Education* 61, no. 1 (1990): 50–64.

Fleisher, Arthur A. III, Brian L. Goff, and Robert D. Tollison. *The National Collegiate Athletic Association: A Study in Cartel Behavior.* Chicago: University of Chicago Press, 1992.

Frey, James, ed. *The Governance of Intercollegiate Athletics.* West Point, N.Y.: Leisure Press, 1982.

Gipe, George. *The Great American Sports Book.* Garden City, N.Y.: Doubleday, 1978.

Goldberg, David L. "What Price Victory? What Price Honor? Pennsylvania and the Formation of the Ivy League, 1950-1952." *Pennsylvania Magazine of History and Biography,* Apr. 1988, 227–48.

Guttmann, Allen. *From Ritual to Record: The Nature of Modern Sports.* New York: Columbia University Press, 1978.

———. *A Whole New Ball Game: An Interpretation of American Sports.* Chapel Hill: University of North Carolina Press, 1988.

Hart-Nibbrig, Nand, and Clement Cottingham. *The Political Economy of College Sports.* Lexington, Mass.: D. C. Heath, Lexington Books, 1986.

Lapchick, Richard E., and John B. Slaughter. *The Rules of the Game: Ethics in College Sport.* New York: Macmillan for American Council on Education, 1989.

Lawrence, Paul R. *Unsportsmanlike Conduct: The National Collegiate Athletic Association and the Business of College Football.* New York: Praeger, 1987.

Marmion, Paul, guest ed., and Marcy Massengale, ed. Special Issue: *On Collegiate Athletics. Educational Record* 60, no. 4 (1979).

Miller, Patrick. "Athletes in Academe: College Sports and American Culture, 1850–1920." Ph.D. diss., University of California, Berkeley, 1987.

Novak, Michael. *The Joy of Sports.* New York: Basic Books, 1976.

Padilla, Arthur, and Janice Boucher. "On the Economics of Intercollegiate Athletics Programs." *Journal of Sport and Social Issues* 11, nos. 1/2 (1987/1988): 61–73.

Pennington, Richard. *Breaking the Ice: The Racial Integration of Southwest Conference Football.* Jefferson, N.C.: McFarland, 1987.

Riesman, David, and Reuel Denney. "Football in America: A Case Study in Culture Diffusion." *American Quarterly* 3, no. 4 (1951): 309–25.

Roberts, Diane K. "The Jan Kemp Controversy: An Index to Media Coverage." Athens: University of Georgia Archives, Sept. 1987.

Roberts, Randy, and James Olson. *Winning Is the Only Thing: Sports in America since 1945.* Baltimore: Johns Hopkins University Press, 1989.

Rooney, John F., Jr. *The Recruiting Game: Toward a New System of Intercollegiate Sport.* 2d ed. Lincoln: University of Nebraska Press, 1987.

Rudolph, Frederick. "The Rise of Football." In *The American College and University: A History,* pp. 373–93. New York: Knopf, 1962.

Scott, Jack, ed. *The Athletic Revolution.* New York: Free Press, 1971.

Smith, Ronald. *Sports and Freedom: The Rise of Big-Time College Athletics.* New York: Oxford University Press, 1988.

Sperber, Murray. *College Sports, Inc.* New York: Henry Holt, 1990.

Thelin, John R. "Athletics in Higher Education." In *The Encyclopedia of Educational Research,* 6th ed., ed. Marvin C. Alkin, pp. 96–99. New York: Macmillan for the American Educational Research Association, 1992.

Thelin, John R., and Lawrence L. Wiseman. *The Old College Try.* ASHE-ERIC Report no. 4. Washington, D.C.: George Washington University and Association for the Study of Higher Education, 1989.

———. "Fiscal Fitness? The Peculiar Economics of Intercollegiate Athletics." *Capital Ideas* 4, no. 4 (Feb. 1990): 1–12.

———. "The Future of Big-Time Intercollegiate Athletics." *Planning in Higher Education* 19 (Winter 1990–91): 18–27.

———. "The Numbers Game: The Statistical Heritage in Intercollegiate Athletics." In *Monitoring the Intercollegiate Athletics Enterprise,* ed. Bruce I. Mallette and Richard D. Howard. New Directions in Institutional Research, no. 74, pp. 5–12. San Francisco: Jossey-Bass, 1992.

Tobin, John Gerald. "The Pacific Coast Conference Football Scandal and the Los Angeles Press." Master's thesis, University of California, Los Angeles, 1959.

Watterson, John S. "Inventing Modern Football." *American Heritage*, Sept.–Oct. 1988, pp. 103–13.

Wong, Glenn. *Essentials of Amateur Sports Law*. Dover, Mass.: Auburn House, 1988.

Histories of College Sports Teams and Coaches

Berkow, Ira. "A Conversation with the Ghost." In *The New York Times Book of Sports Legends*, ed. Joseph J. Vecchione, pp. 86–87. New York: Random House, Times Books, 1991.

Bertagna, Joe. *Crimson in Triumph: A Pictorial History of Harvard Athletics, 1852–1985*. Lexington, Mass.: Stephen Greene Press, 1986.

Brown, John Y. *The Legend of the Praying Colonels*. Louisville: J. Marvin Gray, 1974.

Bryant, Paul, and John Underwood. *Bear: The Hard Life and Good Times of Alabama's Coach Bryant*. Boston: Little, Brown, 1974.

Buckner, Robert. *Knute Rockne, All American*. Screenplay. Los Angeles: Metro-Goldwyn-Mayer, 1940.

Bynum, Mike, with Jerry Brondfield. *We Believe: Bear Bryant's Boys Talk*. College Station, Tex.: We Believe Trust Fund, 1980.

Chandler, Dan, and Vernon Hatton. *Rupp from Both Ends of the Bench*. Lexington, Ky.: n.p., 1972.

Clary, Jack. *Great College Football Coaches*. New York: Gallery Books, 1990.

The College Game. Indianapolis: Bobbs-Merrill, 1974.

Cox, James A. "Was 'the Gipper' for Real? You Can Bet He Was!" *Smithsonian Magazine*, Dec. 1985, pp. 130–50.

Cross, George Lynn. *Presidents Can't Punt: The OU Football Tradition*. Norman: University of Oklahoma Press, 1977.

Danzig, Allison. *The History of American Football: Its Great Teams, Players, and Coaches*. Englewood Cliffs, N.J.: Prentice-Hall, 1956.

Davies, John. *The Legend of Hobey Baker*. Boston: Little, Brown, 1966.

Durso, Joseph. "Bear Bryant, 1913–1983." In *The New York Times Book of Sports Legends*, ed. Joseph J. Vecchione, pp. 8–11. New York: Random House, Times Books, 1991.

Eskenazi, Gerald. "Red Grange, 1903–1991." In *The New York Times Book of Sports Legends*, ed. Joseph J. Vecchione, pp. 83–86. New York: Random House, Times Books, 1991.

———. "Rupp and New York." In *The New York Times Book of Sports Legends*, ed. Joseph J. Vecchione, pp. 283–84. New York: Random House, Times Books, 1991.

Falla, Jack. *NCAA: The Voice of College Sports: A Diamond Anniversary History, 1906–1981*. Mission, Kans.: National Collegiate Athletic Association, 1981.

Fox, Larry. *Illustrated History of Basketball*. New York: Grossett and Dunlap, 1974.

Herskowitz, Mickey. *The Legend of Bear Bryant*. New York: McGraw-Hill, 1987.

Hyman, Mervin D., and Gordon S. White, Jr. *Big Ten Football: Its Life and Times, Great Coaches, Players, and Games*. New York: Macmillan, 1977.

Isaacs, Neil. *All The Moves: A History of College Basketball*. Philadelphia: Lippincott, 1975.

Kelley, Robert F. "Knute Rockne, 1889–1931." In *The New York Times Book of Sports Legends*, ed. Joseph J. Vecchione, pp. 272–77. New York: Random House, Times Books, 1991.

Koehler, Michael. *America's Greatest Coaches*. Champaign, Ill.: Leisure Press, 1990.

Kornheiser, Tony. "The Baron of the Bluegrass." In *The New York Times Book of Sports Legends*, ed. Joseph J. Vecchione, pp. 285–87. New York: Random House, Times Books, 1991.

Larson, Melissa. *The Pictorial History of College Football*. New York: Gallery Books, 1989.

McCallum, John D. *Big Ten Football since 1895*. Radnor, Pa.: Chilton, 1976.

———. *Ivy League Football since 1872: The Games, Rituals, Storied Players and Coaches, Team and Conference Records*. New York: Stein and Day, 1977.

Moss, Al. *PAC-10 Football*. Greenwich, Conn.: Crescent Books, 1987.

Nelli, Bert. *The Winning Tradition: A History of Kentucky Wildcat Basketball*. Lexington: University Press of Kentucky, 1984.

Quakenbush, Robert, and Mike Bynum. *Knute Rockne: His Life and Legend*. Chicago: October Football Corp., 1988. Based on the unfinished autobiography of Knute Rockne.

Rice, Russell. *The Wildcats: Kentucky Football*. Huntsville, Ala.: Strode Publishers, 1975.

———. *The Wildcat Legacy*. Virginia Beach: JCP Corp. of Virginia, 1982.

———. *Kentucky Basketball's Big Blue Machine*. Huntsville, Ala.: Strode Publishers, 1987.

Rockne, Dick. *Bow Down to Washington: A Story of Husky Football*. Huntsville, Ala.: Strode Publishers, 1975.

Rohrich Corporation. *The Blue Book of College, University, and Junior and Community College Athletics*. Akron: Rohrich Corp., 1990.

Royal, Darrell, with Blackie Sherrod. *Darrell Royal Talks Football*. Englewood Cliffs, N.J.: Prentice-Hall, 1963.

Rupp, Adolph. *Adolph Rupp's Basketball Guidebook*. New York: McGraw-Hill, 1967.

Schoor, Gene. *One Hundred Years of Notre Dame Football*. New York: Morrow, 1987.

Sherwood, James. *Nebraska Football*. Lincoln: University of Nebraska Press, 1987.

Springer, Steve, and Michael Arkush. *Sixty Years of USC-UCLA Football*. Stamford, Conn.: Longmeadow Press, 1991.

Steele, Michael. *Knute Rockne: A Bio-bibliography*. Westport, Conn.: Greenwood Press, 1983.

Stern, Robert. *They Were Number One: A History of the NCAA Basketball Tournament*. New York: Leisure Press, 1983.

Sugar, Bert, ed. *The SEC: A Pictorial History of the Southeastern Conference*. Indianapolis: Bobbs-Merrill, 1979.

Sulek, Robert. *Hoosier Honor*. New York: Praeger, 1990.

Switzer, Barry, with Bud Shrake. *Bootlegger's Boy*. New York: Jove Books, 1990.

Thomsen, Ian. "The Grandfather Clause: Knute Rockne III Grapples with History." *Sports Illustrated* [n.d.], 1988, p. 10.

Van Leuven, Hendrick. *Touchdown UCLA: The Complete Account of Bruin Football*. Tomball, Tex.: Strode Publishers, 1982.

Vecchione, Joseph J. "Adolph Rupp, 1901–1977." In *The New York Times Book of Sports Legends*, pp. 280–83. New York: Random House, Times Books, 1991.

———. ed. *The New York Times Book of Sports Legends*. New York: Random House, Times Books, 1991.

Whittingham, Richard. *Saturday Afternoon: College Football and the Men Who Made the Day*. New York: Workman, 1985.